ame Dependent territories of Commonwealth states (in brackets) SCALE 1 : 88,000,000

Hello and welcome to *Let's go 6*!

Let's go 6 besteht aus 7 Units, vier kürzeren und drei längeren. Die Units 1, 3, 5 und 7 sind „Kurzunits“. Die Units 2, 4 und 6 sind „Langunits“.

Beide Unittypen sind ähnlich aufgebaut. Die Abschnitte **Language** enthalten immer Lesetexte und interessante Informationen zu den Themen der Units. Dann folgt jeweils ein **Workshop**. Hier wird vieles wiederholt, was du bereits gelernt hast. Unter **Words** findest du die neuen Wörter der Units. **Let's check** fasst noch einmal das Wichtigste zusammen.

In den Kurzunits gibt es noch **Mediation**-Seiten zum Übersetzen in Situationen, wie sie im Alltag vorkommen können. Nach den Units 2, 4 und 6 findest du jeweils vier Seiten **Exam practice**. Diese helfen dir bei der selbstständigen Vorbereitung auf die Abschlussprüfung.

Auf den **Extra**-Seiten findest du vier Seiten mit zusätzlichen Lesetexten und Übungen zur Vorbereitung auf die **mündliche Prüfung**.

Wörter, die du nicht mehr weißt, kannst du in der alphabetischen Wortliste ab S. 84 nachschlagen. Am Ende des Buches findest du eine Liste der unregelmäßigen Verben, die Zahlen, die englischen Laute und wichtige Grammatikbegriffe.

TIPP Die Tipp-Boxen enthalten Tipps und Tricks, die das Lernen leichter machen.

Diese Zeichen helfen dir, dich im Buch zurechtzufinden:

Diese Teile gibt es auch auf CD.

Speaking: Übungen zum Sprechen und Zusammenarbeiten

KINGFISHER

Stars

a Avril Lavigne knows what she wants. When she wrote her third album, The Best Damn Thing, she wanted to make it fun. On her tours she noticed that she preferred to play faster songs. So Avril's third album sounded very powerful, catchy and energetic.
After she had finished the album, she said: "I didn't know that making a record could be so much fun."
In 2007 Avril played in a UNITE AGAINST AIDS Concert. In the same year the Canadian singer was given two MTV Europe Music Awards.

b Orlando Bloom realized as a child that the characters on TV and in the movies weren't real and that he wanted to be an actor.
In 1993 he started to play in TV series. Orlando's first big movie was The Lord of the Rings trilogy where he played the elf Legolas Greenleaf. For the movie he had to learn archery, horse riding and to fight with two swords.
Ever since Orlando has become a star, his fans have discovered that the real Orlando is quite different from the one in the movies. Unlike the quiet Legolas he is full of energy and enthusiasm and is charming to everyone.

1 Stars

Which sentence tells you that …

1. Avril likes fast songs.
2. she enjoyed making her third album.
3. Orlando wanted to be an actor early.
4. he and Legolas are very different.
5. Robbie had problems.
6. he is very popular.
7. Venus wanted to end her career.
8. Serena has her own company.

2 Speaking: Finding out more

a) *Find out more about the stars from magazines or the Internet.*

b) *Ask your partner for information.*

A: How old is Avril Lavigne?
B: She's … .
A: And where is she from?
B: She's from … .
A: What about her family?
B: … .

c Robbie Williams' mother saw an advertisement for young singers in a newspaper: Robbie applied and became a member of the band Take That in 1990. Five years later he decided to leave the band. He felt frustrated, suffered from depression and took drugs.
But he still started a solo career and made his first album. Since then, he has sold more than 55 million records worldwide. For his 2006 World Tour 1.6 million tickets were sold in one day. Robbie also works as a UNICEF Ambassador. His organisation Soccer Aid raised over £2.5 million for UNICEF.

d Serena and Venus Williams are the two youngest of five daughters. They started to play tennis and to win tournaments when they were very young. But their father wanted them to finish school first.
The Williams sisters have been professional tennis players since the late 1990s. Sometimes they play against each other, but they also won the Wimbledon doubles title together. Serena has won all four Grand Slam tournaments and Venus won her fourth Wimbledon title in 2007.
Both have been injured, and Venus even thought about giving up tennis. The Williams sisters studied fashion design in Florida. Serena has started her own clothing label.

3 Would you like to be a star?

Would you like to be a star? Why or why not?
Make a list of the pros and cons and talk about them in class.

Think about these ideas.

travelling family money
time away from home media
free time helping others …

4 Listening: Interviews

Some actors were interviewed by the BBC. What are they talking about? Take notes.

Name	What they talk about
Will Smith	…
Renée Zellweger	…
Rowan Atkinson	…
Orlando Bloom	…

Simple past *(einfache Vergangenheit)*

Wenn du über eine abgeschlossene Handlung sprichst, verwendest du das simple past. *Das* simple past *wird durch das Anhängen von* -ed *an den Infinitiv gebildet.*
Achtung, viele Verben sind unregelmäßig, zum Beispiel: go/went, come/came.
Fragen und Verneinungen bildest du mit did *und dem Infinitiv.*
Signalwörter für das simple past *sind:* yesterday, last week, two months ago.

He **left** the band in 1995. But he **didn't stop** singing.
*Er **verließ** die Band 1995. Aber er **hörte nicht auf** zu singen.*

Did Serena and Venus **win** many tournaments last year?
***Haben** Serena und Venus letztes Jahr viele Turniere **gewonnen**?*

1 What happened? What did they do?

Put the verbs in the simple past and make sentences.

1. to play – prefer – Avril – faster songs on her tours.
   Avril preferred to play faster songs on her tours.
2. new powerful songs – she – write.
3. Orlando – to play in TV series – at the age of 16 – start.
4. to learn archery and horse riding – have – he.
5. become – a member of Take That in 1990 – Robbie Williams.
6. frustrated and – drugs – feel – he – take – not give up – but he.
7. be – very young – to win tournaments when they – begin – Serena and Venus.

2 Last weekend

Finish these questions in the simple past.

1. What …?	I went to a concert last Saturday.	What did you do last Saturday?
2. Where …?	The concert was in in the City Hall.	
3. Did …?	Yes, my friend went to the concert, too.	
4. Who …?	My friend bought the tickets.	
5. When…?	It started at 8 o'clock.	
6. Did …?	No, we didn't have very good seats.	
7. How …?	Oh, it was great!	

TIPP Du verwendest das past tense **+ ing**, wenn eine Handlung länger andauert.

3 What were you doing?

Make sentences.

repair a chair		telephone ring
read book		friend come
clean the house	when	child start to cry
watch TV		light go out
…		…

I was reading a book when the lights went out. *Go on, please.*

Present perfect *(Perfekt)*

Das present perfect *verwendest du, wenn etwas erst geschehen ist, oder wenn du etwas oft oder nie getan hast. Du verwendest es auch, wenn du die Folgen oder das Ergebnis heute noch siehst. Das* present perfect *wird mit* have *(in der dritten Person mit* has*) und dem* past participle *gebildet.*
Signalwörter für das present perfect *sind:* ever, since, for, already, never, yet.

Since then his fans **have discovered** that the real Orlando is quite different.
*Seitdem **haben** seine Fans **entdeckt**, dass der echte Orlando ganz anders* ist.

Has he **sold** many records?
***Hat** er viele Alben **verkauft**?*

4 Since then

Complete the sentences in the present perfect.

be (3 x) start sell become win
perform play

1. Robbie Williams … a star since the age of 16.
   Robbie Williams has been a star since the age of 16.
2. He … on stages all over the world.
   Go on, please.
3. Robbie … a UNICEF Ambassador for many years.
4. He … more than 55 million records worldwide.
5. Avril Lavigne … many awards.
6. She … very popular.
7. Since the Lord of the Rings trilogy Orlando Bloom … a star.
8. Serena Williams … her own company.
9. Serena and Venus … tournaments in many countries.

5 Simple past or present perfect?

Complete the sentences. Use the present perfect or the simple past.

1. He (live) in England all his life.
   He has lived in England all his life.
2. She (write) her own book a few years ago.
   Go on, please.
3. They (earn) a lot of money last year.
4. We (appear) in a film a month ago.
5. He (play) football since he was a small boy.
6. They (have) their own website for a long time.
7. He (hurt) his foot last month.
8. Yesterday she (go) to the hairdresser.
9. We (not be) to Wales since 2000.

1 Pop news

And the winner is …
Avril Lavigne and Linkin Park among those to take home MTV Awards

Monday, November 5, 2007
It was a great night at the MTV Europe Music Awards last night. Hundreds of guests from across the world came to the Olympiahalle in Munich, where the ceremony was held. About 1.5 billion people worldwide watched the show on TV.
The American rapper Snoop Dogg appeared in several costumes during the night, including traditional German lederhosen, a long fur coat and even a kilt. The Awards were dominated by Canadian pop singer Avril Lavigne. She beat the most-nominated Justin Timberlake. Lavigne was chosen Best Solo Artist, and also won the award for Most Addictive Track for her hit song Girlfriend. Nelly Furtado won Album of the Year for Loose, and Linkin Park were named Band of 2007. Tokio Hotel received the award for Best International Act. After the ceremony, featuring acts such as Mika and the Foo Fighters, MTV also gave a huge party.

1. Wo wurden die MTV Awards verliehen?
2. Stimmt es, dass der Moderator Lederhosen trug?
3. Wie viele Preise hat Avril Lavigne erhalten? Wofür?
4. Hat Justin Timberlake einen Preis bekommen?
5. Hat eine deutsche Band etwas gewonnen?
6. Wer hat sonst noch teilgenommen?
7. War nach der Verleihung eine Party?

2 Ein Filmabend

Du möchtest mit deinem Freund aus England einen DVD-Abend machen. Du schlägst ihm diesen Film vor. Erkläre ihm, worum es in dem Film geht. Übersetze nicht den ganzen Text. Fasse den Inhalt nur kurz zusammen.

GOOD BYE, LENIN!

Der Film handelt von der ehemaligen DDR zur Zeit des Mauerfalls. Im Mittelpunkt stehen der 21-jährige Alex und seine Mutter. Sie, eine überzeugte DDR-Bürgerin, hat kurz vor dem Mauerfall einen Herzinfarkt und fällt in ein Koma. In dem 8-monatigen Koma verpasst sie die Vereinigung von West- und Ostdeutschland und den Sieg des Kapitalismus. Als sie wieder erwacht, ist sie in einem neuen Land, denn die DDR gibt es nicht mehr. Dies aber darf sie nicht erfahren. Ihr Arzt gibt Alex den Rat, jede Aufregung von ihr fern zu halten, da ihr Herz sehr schwach ist. Sie würde den Schock nicht überleben. Weil sie ihr Bett noch nicht verlassen kann, hat Alex eine Idee: Er lässt die alte DDR in der 79 qm Wohnung der Mutter wieder aufleben. Er fälscht die Fernsehprogramme und die Aufkleber auf den Konserven, lässt Freunde noch als alte DDR-Typen zum Geburtstag der Mutter kommen und hindert sie, als sie wieder gesund ist, daran das Haus zu verlassen.
Aber dann möchte die Mutter doch das kleine Wochenendhaus auf dem Lande besuchen und die ganze Lüge fliegt auf.

among – *unter;* ceremony – *Feier;* billion – *Milliarde;* rapper – *Rapper;* costume – *Kostüm;* coat – *Mantel;* kilt – *Schottenrock;* dominate – *dominieren;* beat – *schlagen;* nominate – *nominieren;* addictive – *süchtig machend;* track – *Titel;* loose – *locker;* name – *nennen;* act – *Auftritt, Band;* featuring – *mit*

Unit 1

Language

8	**damn**	verdammt
	make fun	Spaß machen
	tour	Tournee
	catchy	eingängig, zündend
	energetic	voller Energie
	after	nachdem
	make a record	eine Aufnahme machen
	unite	sich zusammentun, vereinigen
	award	Preis, Auszeichnung
	realize	erkennen, feststellen
	character	Figur
	on TV	im Fernsehen
	TV series	Fernsehserie
	lord	Herr, Lord
	trilogy	Trilogie
	elf	Elfin, Elf; *hier:* Elbin, Elb
	archery	Bogenschießen
	horse riding	Reiten
	sword	Schwert
	ever since	seitdem, seit
	unlike	anders als, im Gegensatz zu
	enthusiasm	Enthusiasmus, Begeisterung
	charming	charmant
	find out	herausfinden
9	**member**	Mitglied
	frustrated	frustriert
	suffer	leiden
	depression	Depression
	solo	Solo-, solo
	worldwide	weltweit
	ambassador	Botschafter
	raise	*hier:* sammeln
	double	Doppel-, doppelt
	both	beide
	fashion design	Modedesign
	label	Marke, Label

Workshop

10	**songwriter**	Texterin und Komponistin, Texter und Komponist
11	**all over the world**	auf der ganzen Welt

Checklist

Ich kann	
… sagen, dass etwas Spaß macht.	Making music is fun.
… sagen, dass ich etwas oder jemanden lieber mag.	I prefer Linkin Park.
… sagen, was ich zu einem bestimmten Zeitpunkt in der Vergangenheit gemacht habe.	Yesterday I went to the movies. The film started at 8 o'clock.
… Fragen über die Vergangenheit stellen.	What did you do last night?
… ausdrücken, dass etwas in der Vergangenheit angefangen hat und noch andauert.	I have learned English for five years.
… sagen, dass etwas noch nicht zu Ende war, als etwas Neues anfing.	While I was watching TV, the telephone rang.
… Fragen über eine andauernde Sache in der Vergangenheit stellen.	What were you doing when the telephone rang?

Alone at sea

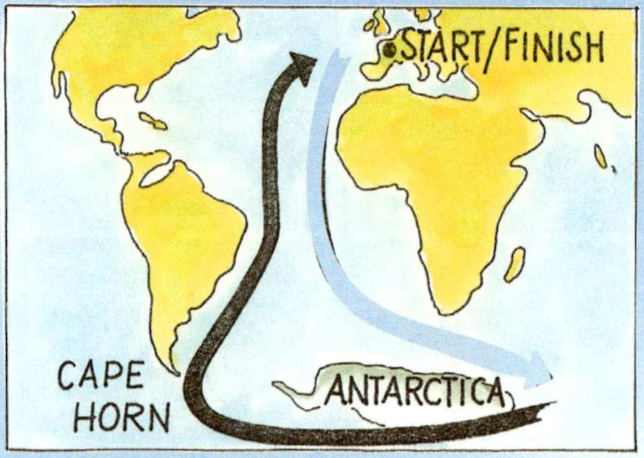

a It was a hero's welcome. Over 200,000 people and 8,000 e-mails were waiting for Ellen MacArthur when she arrived on the French coast on a cold night in the middle of February. What had the 24-year-old Englishwoman done to get so much attention?
Ellen had just become the youngest and fastest woman to sail non-stop and solo around the world. The Vendée Globe, the hardest yacht race in the world, had started in November and had lasted three months. In the end Ellen finished second.
"I'm so happy," she said, "I was not out there alone. I shared the race and the journey."
In one sense Ellen was alone. Alone for 26,000 miles and 94 days. Nobody else was on board the 60-foot yacht to help her when, on day 26 of the race, one of the sails ripped and Ellen had to work six hours to repair it by hand. And what about the time when she woke up one morning to see an iceberg the size of a block of flats 15 metres away? Then there was day 79, when the wind instruments broke and she had to climb to the top of the 25-foot mast to repair them. How did she manage all these things with no help?

1 Ellen MacArthur

1. Why were so many people waiting for Ellen MacArthur when she finished the Vendée Globe yacht race?
2. Why is the Vendée Globe such a special race? Give three reasons.
3. What kind of problems did Ellen have during the race?
4. Why did Ellen do so well in the race?

2 Vocabulary

Which word in the text means …

1. a person who has done something very special?
2. a long trip?
3. the opposite of "send" (an e-mail)?
4. someone is good at something?

3 Word families

Complete the table.

noun	adjective
1.	windy
2. strength	
3.	energetic
4. person	

b In another sense Ellen was never alone. Her boat – the Kingfisher – was full of high-tech equipment: onboard computers, an autopilot, Internet, radar, satellite phones, video and DVD players. Ellen was able to receive satellite images of the weather, locate the other boats in the race, read wind speed, measure temperatures, send e-mails and make videos of herself. Of course it takes more than the right equipment to sail around the world. After all, the other boats had the same equipment but only half of them finished the race. Ellen had great technology but she also had great sailing skills. She could "read" the weather. She could repair sails. She could fix wind instruments.

But above all Ellen had courage and strength. She was the smallest and the youngest person in the race; she was also the strongest.

Fact box: Ellen MacArthur's yacht

NAME:	KINGFISHER
BUILT:	AUCKLAND, NEW ZEALAND
LAUNCHED ON:	18 FEBRUARY 2000
LENGTH:	18.2M
WIDTH:	5.3M
WEIGHT:	7,950KG
TECHNICAL DATA:	TWO NAVIGATION COMPUTERS, TWO WEB CAMS, GPS, RADAR, VHF RADIO, SATELLITE COMMUNICATIONS

4 Listening: Ellen's boat

Listen to the text and answer the questions.

1. Who was the Kingfisher built for?
2. Why are bulkheads important?
3. While on the Kingfisher how does Ellen communicate with the outside world?
4. How long does Ellen sleep at one time while on the Kingfisher?
5. Where on the boat do you think Ellen spends most of her time? Why?

5 Your opinion

Imagine you were alone on a boat for three months.

1. What three things would you take with you (no equipment and food)?
2. What would you miss?
3. What kind of problems could a person have alone on a boat for three months?
4. Which pieces of technical equipment do you find most important? Why?

6 Computer words

a) *Find the right words and match them.*

1. [kəm'pju:tə] – That's computer.
2. [si:di:'rom] – *Go on, please.*
3. ['flætskri:n]
4. ['kɪbɔ:d]
5. ['mænjuəl]
6. [maʊs]
7. ['printə]
8. ['skænə]
9. ['spi:kə]

c

a

h

i

b) *Find a partner. Make a list of other English words that you use when you talk about work or play with your computer.*

g
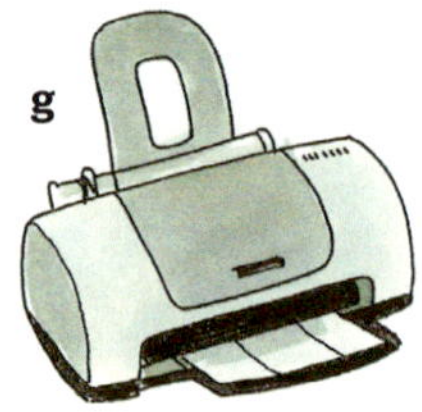
e

b

d

f

7 Topic-based task: Communication

a) *Get into small groups and prepare a short presentation for the rest of the class.*

- How did your grandparents communicate with their family and friends when they were young?
- What do they think of modern communication today (e-mails, text messages, mobile phones)?
- What do you use?

1. Sharing the work:
   If you are working in a team, make sure each person is responsible for one part of the project. What do you want to find out?
2. Finding the information:
   Remember that there is information everywhere. You can look on the Internet, you can go to a library or you can ask your family and friends.
3. Organising the information:
   Decide which information is important and which is not so important. Perhaps now is the time to go back and get some more information on the important parts of your project.
4. Presenting the information:
   Make a handout, a poster or a collage. Perhaps you can make part of your presentation a puzzle, quiz or game.

b) *Plan your project in four steps.*

8 A formal letter

In a formal letter you must be very clear about what you want. It is also important to be very polite.

a) *Read the letter and find the parts A–J.*

A a signature followed by a name
B the date
C a polite last sentence
D what you want the company to do
E your address
F things you are sending with the letter
G your reason for writing
H name/address of the firm you are writing to
I the greeting
J a formal ending

Lindenallee 16
12345 Norderstedt
Germany

Pterodactyl Fly-by-nite
Dinosaur Software
SWAMPLAND CA 92130
USA

October 12, 2009

Re: Order no. 34269870 of 28th August

Dear Sir or Madam,
I am writing to inquire about the Multi-Media Dinosaur Encyclopedia CD (English version), which I ordered from your firm on 28th August.
I had hoped to receive the CD last month and when I called your office yesterday, I was told that it had been sent in September. I am enclosing a copy of my order form.
I would be very grateful if you could deal with the matter immediately as I need the CD for a project at school.
I do hope that you will be able to help me and I look forward to hearing from you soon.

Yours faithfully,

Martin Maurer

Martin Maurer

Enclosed: Photocopy of order form

b) Imagine you have ordered a computer game from Pterodactyl Fly-by-nite. The game is a present for a friend, but your friend's birthday is next week and the game still has not arrived.
Write a letter to the firm.

Conjunctions *(Konjunktionen)*

Konjunktionen – oder Bindewörter – verbinden Satzteile und leiten Haupt- und Nebensätze ein.

He bought a computer **but** he does not have e-mail yet.
*Er hat einen Computer gekauft, **aber** er hat noch kein E-Mail.*

Ellen was never alone **although** nobody else was on board the Kingfisher.
*Ellen war nie allein, **obwohl** sonst niemand an Bord der Kingfisher war.*

1 Modern life

Complete the sentences. Use the conjunctions in the boxes.

1. Every company is on the Internet today … you can get information there.
2. You can start work later … you want.
3. Let's go home … it gets too full.
4. We decided to buy a flat screen television … it was expensive.
5. We left … we had paid.
6. I can't dance … I like to watch other people dance.

after (nachdem)
although (obwohl)
before (bevor)
because (weil)
but (aber)
if (wenn)

2 Get it together

Put the parts of the sentences together.

a) Have you been happy I've started jogging She went by train We'll wait	so that until because since	you give us a signal. she could do some work. you found a new job? I want to get fit.
b) You bought a new camera I would like to go away this weekend I can't go to my office by bus or train You can wash the dishes	while although but so	my friend is having a party here. I had to buy a car. you are waiting! you didn't have any money.

3 Speaking: What are you good at?

TIPP *Du verwendest Verben + **ing**, um etwas über eine Tätigkeit oder einen Vorgang zu sagen.*

Make dialogues with a partner.

A: What are you good at?
B: I'm good at repairing computers. And you?
A: I like repairing bikes.

be good at …
like …
hate …
be interested in …
enjoy …

draw
repair
play
wear
…

Past perfect *(Vorvergangenheit)*

Das past perfect *verwendest du, wenn Handlungen oder Ereignisse nacheinander in der Vergangenheit stattfinden. Für das Ereignis, das weiter in der Vergangenheit zurück liegt, verwendest du das* past perfect.
Du bildest das past perfect *mit* had + *dritte Form des Verbs.*
Signalwörter für das past perfect *sind:* after, before, when, because, although.

When Ellen returned to France she **had been** on the Kingfisher for 94 days.
*Als Ellen nach Frankreich zurückkam, **war** sie 94 Tage lang auf der Kingfisher **gewesen**.*

Before Ellen finished the race she **had** already **become** a star.
*Bevor Ellen das Rennen beendete, **war** sie schon ein Star **geworden**.*

Du kannst dir den zeitlichen Ablauf ungefähr so vorstellen:

Ellen became famous — Ellen finished the race — now

4 Verbs and meanings

Match the sentences (1–6) with their 'meanings' (a–b).

1. When I looked out of the window it was snowing.
2. When I looked out of the window I could see it had snowed.

a) Snow was on the ground but it was not snowing.
b) Snow was falling.

3. When they saw him he was drinking.
4. When they saw him he had drunk some lemonade.

c) He had a full glass in his hand.
d) There was an empty glass on the table.

5. When we arrived they were fighting.
6. When we arrived they had had a fight.

e) They were not talking to each other.
f) They were shouting at each other.

5 Special days

Here are some things that happened to Ellen on her trip.
Fill in the missing verbs. Use the past perfect or the simple past.

1. On day 16, after I (cross) the equator, I (open) a bottle of champagne.
2. After 20 days at sea I (complete) 20% of the race.
3. On day 37 I (go) into third place after I (not, read) my notes correctly.
4. On day 56 I (be) surprised. I (never, see) so many icebergs before.
5. On day 84, after I (make) myself some tea, I (hear) a loud noise.
6. I (look) back and (see) that I (hit) something.

Could you live in another country?

Would you be happy in another country? Answer these questions and find out.

1. When you are on holiday …
   a) you find out as much as you can about the country.
   b) you have fun with friends or your family.
   c) you can't wait to go home again.

2. You meet immigrants from Vietnam and …
   a) you ask them if they miss Vietnam.
   b) you ask them everything about how they came here.
   c) you don't know what to ask them.

3. In your free time you often …
   a) stay at home and watch TV.
   b) meet new friends.
   c) find out about other places and people.

4. The food you like best is …
   a) everything you already know.
   b) everything your parents cook.
   c) everything that's new and exciting.

5. Your favourite place to live is …
   a) where your friends and family are.
   b) where you live now.
   c) in a country far, far away.

6. You have gone to live in another country. Now you …
   a) phone home from time to time.
   b) feel terrible and lonely.
   c) find new friends, learn the language, join a club and have a great time.

You can find the answers on page 131.

TIPP

Fehlerwerkstatt: Unterschiedliche Verbformen

Das Englische verwendet meist ganz andere Verbformen als das Deutsche. Oft steckt im Englischen das, was jemand sagen möchte, bereits in der Verbform. Nimm zum Beispiel das *present progressive*. Im Deutschen brauchen wir ein extra Wort, um zu sagen, dass etwas gerade passiert oder dass jemand etwas gerade tut:

***She's playing** the trombone.* – Sie spielt **gerade** Posaune.

Bei vielen anderen Zeiten ist es ähnlich. Übersetze Zeitformen also nie wörtlich, sondern überlege immer zuerst, was du ausdrücken möchtest! Wie würdest du die folgenden Sätze übersetzen? Die Verbformen in der Box helfen dir dabei.

Ich spiele jeden Tag Computerspiele.
Ich habe bis gerade eben ein Computerspiel gespielt.
Ich habe gestern ein neues Computerspiel gespielt.

played
play
have just played

Unit 2

Language

14	**attention**	Aufmerksamkeit
	non-stop	non-stop
	yacht	Jacht
	race	Rennen, Regatta
	in one sense	in einer Hinsicht
	sail	Segel
	rip	reißen
	iceberg	Eisberg
	mast	Mast
	manage	etwas schaffen, bewältigen
15	**high-tech**	Hightech-
	onboard	Bord-
	autopilot	Autopilot
	radar	Radar
	satellite phone	Satellitentelefon
	image	Bild
	locate	orten, ausfindig machen
	measure	messen
	after all	schließlich
	fix	*hier:* reparieren
	above all	vor allem
	courage	Mut
	strength	Kraft, Stärke
	person	Person
	launch	vom Stapel lassen
	width	Breite
	technical data	technische Daten
	bulkhead	Trennwand, Schott
	communicate	kommunizieren
16	**topic-based**	themenbezogen
	text message	SMS
	everywhere	überall
	present	präsentieren
	handout	Arbeitsblatt
17	**formal**	förmlich
	polite	höflich
	signature	Unterschrift
	firm	Firma
	greeting	Gruß, Grußformel
	Dear Sir or Madam	Sehr geehrte Damen und Herren
	inquire	sich erkundigen
	encyclopedia	Enzyklopädie
	version	Version
	order	bestellen
	enclose	beifügen
	copy	Kopie
	order form	Bestellformular
	grateful	dankbar
	deal with	sich befassen mit
	matter	Angelegenheit
	immediately	sofort
	Yours faithfully	Mit freundlichen Grüßen

Workshop

19	**equator**	Äquator
	champagne	Champagner

Checklist

Ich kann	
... sagen, dass etwas in der Vergangenheit gerade geschah.	Lots of e-mails were waiting when she arrived.
... Zeiträume in der Vergangenheit beschreiben.	The race had started in November and lasted three months.
... mich über verschiedene Ereignisse unterhalten.	And what about the time when the boat almost sank?
... die technische Ausstattung von Schiffen beschreiben.	The boat was full of high-tech equipment: an autopilot, radar, satellite phones.
... sagen, was am wichtigsten von allem war.	But above all, Ellen had courage and strength.
... dafür sorgen, dass Aufgaben fair verteilt sind.	Make sure each person is responsible for one part of the project.
... Höflichkeitsformen in Briefen verwenden.	I do hope you will be able to help me.
	I look forward to hearing from you.

These pages are like a real exam. Use your dictionary if you need it.

She didn't give up!

a It all started when she was eight years old. Ellen MacArthur was on holiday on the English east coast. Her aunt took her sailing for the first time. "I loved it," Ellen said. "I just fell more and more in love with sailing."

At school Ellen MacArthur began to save her money. Instead of using it to pay for her lunch, she put the money into her 'yacht box'. After three years her dream came true. Ellen was able to buy her first boat: it was only eight feet long.

At the age of 18 Ellen became the youngest person to pass the Yachtmaster Offshore Qualification. She sailed around the whole of Britain alone and was named British Yachtsman of the Year. Ellen began to look for sponsors. She wrote about 2,500 letters but received only two answers.

b But Ellen didn't give up. She took a one-way ticket to Brest in France. There she learned French and began repairing an old yacht that she had bought.

To save money she camped under the boat. Then she took part in a transatlantic race and sailed the 2,700 miles in record time: 33 days.

Soon some big companies began to take notice of Ellen. One of them, Kingfisher, offered £2 million to sponsor her in the Vendée Globe, a famous single-handed yacht race. Ellen accepted and started preparing for the biggest and hardest adventure in her life. She trained with a chronobiologist – an expert in the body clock – so that she could learn to sleep for fifteen minutes at a time. Then she went to New Zealand to pick up the boat and sail her back to France. The rest is history.

Why did Ellen take part in the most difficult yacht race in the world? "I love being tested to my limits," she explained. "I love racing through the water at 30 knots. It's like being on an out-of-control Tube train in the dark."

1 Global understanding

All these sentences are wrong. Correct them.

1. When Ellen was at school her parents bought a boat for her.
2. Ellen called 2,500 sponsors.
3. When Ellen went to Brest in France she had a lot of money.
4. Kingfisher wanted to give Ellen money to take part in a transatlantic race.
5. Ellen needs only 15 minutes of sleep every day.
6. Ellen often rides the Tube in the dark.

2 Questions on Ellen

a) *Answer the questions in complete sentences.*

1. What did Ellen do with her lunch money when she was at school? Why?
2. Why did she write 2,500 letters?
3. Why did Ellen camp under her boat when she was living in France?
4. Before doing the Vendée Globe race Ellen worked together with a chronobiologist. Why?
5. Why did Ellen take part in the Vendée Globe?

b) Ellen likes "racing through the water at 30 knots". *What do you like doing?*

3 Text production: An open-ended story

Finish the story in your exercise book.
Find a good title and write at least 100 words.

One morning Ellen woke up and saw someone standing on deck. He was taking photos. Ellen could not believe her eyes. How could someone get onto the Kingfisher in the middle of the ocean?
"Hey!" Ellen shouted. "What are you doing?"

4 The Kingfisher story

Complete the text. Use the verbs in the correct forms.

1. The Kingfisher story (begin) in New Zealand in 1998.
2. It (be) then that a team of international experts (start) building a yacht for Ellen MacArthur.
3. The Kingfisher (design / *use the passive*) by Rob Humphreys, who (want, make) a "faster and better yacht than ever before".
4. Finally, on 18 February, 2000, the Kingfisher (launch / *use the passive*). Ellen (fall) in love with her new yacht at first sight. She (climb) the mast and (shower) the crowd with champagne. "I (wait) since 1997 for this," she said. "This is a moment I (not, forget / *use the will-future*)."

5 Mediation: Ellen's blog

In the middle of the Atlantic Ocean Ellen answers her fans' questions in her blog.
Translate the following text into German.

Kate Hillborne: Q: Do you get bored a lot?
A: I must say that in the last two months there's not been one second when I've been bored. You spend all your time looking at the weather and making sure the boat is sailing as fast as possible. That's quite hard work.

Andrew John: Q: Can you really sleep without worrying about what's happening outside?
A: No, not really. When you sleep, it's a kind of semi-sleep. I have a computer programme which watches exactly what's happening to the boat. Usually I wake up quickly when the wind changes.

Raymond Zaloof: Q: You've been away from home since November 9. If there was one thing you could have now, what would it be?
A: It would be something I would wish for: that all the people out here get back safely.

6 Yacht races

What did Ellen say?
Choose the right adjective.

1. "All yacht races are really (exciting/excited) from beginning to end.
2. You probably can't imagine it but you are never (boring/bored) on a boat.
3. Of course there are always (scared/scary) moments.
4. Sometimes you have to climb to the top of the mast and repair something. That can be very (tiring/tired), too.
5. You're alone on the boat but you're never lonely. There's so much to do. And you always get nice messages from people who are (interesting/interested) in sailing."

7 Difficult days

Complete Ellen's diary with the present simple or the present progressive.

1. *Day 13: I (feel) well but my hands hurt. The hot weather (not, help).*
2. *Day 29: The sea temperature (go down).*
   I (put) on a lot of clothes now.
3. *Day 32: Waves (come) from everywhere.*
   We (get) faster and faster.
4. *Day 39: My whole body (hurt). I (lose) miles because a sail has ripped.*
5. *Day 53: I (look) at the computer often. I can't see if the weather (change).*
6. *Day 79: My wind instruments (not, work).*
   The boat (get) slower and slower.

8 Opposites

Find the opposites. How do you pronounce the words?
1. save (money) 2. buy 3. biggest 4. wrong 5. aunt 6. love

9 Listen and say: 'a'

'A' is pronounced in different ways.
Say these words, and say which 'a' it is.

[ɑ:] [æ] [ɒ] [ɔ:] [eɪ]

understand female yacht glasses dark water back came

10 Just in time!

It is a foggy day near the coast. The captain of a motor boat can't see anything because the fog is too thick. Suddenly the motor boat hits a sailing boat.

Look at the pictures and tell the story. You can start like this.

Both boats begin to sink. The captain of the motor boat …

11 Listening: At the airport

a) *Listen to the six dialogues and put the headings in the correct order* (1–6).

- Checking-in
- Finishing a meal
- Getting the luggage
- Getting off the plane
- Getting on the plane
- Going through the security check

b) *Match a word on the left with a word on the right to make seven expressions.*

1. arrival	lounge
2. baggage	card
3. boarding	check
4. check-in	control
5. departure	reclaim
6. security	hall
7. passport	desk

India

Find New Delhi on the map, then read the story about auto-rickshaw driver Anand Singh and his life on the streets of New Delhi.

New Delhi street life

When I came to New Delhi eight years ago, I worked as a 'scrap-picker'. I was nine years old then. Lots of children like me have left their home to find work and live on the streets of New Delhi. Everyone says that the opportunities are better here.
I never went to school, my parents didn't have enough money to pay for a uniform. I can't read or write, but I have learned to speak some English.
Now, eight years later, I make good money in New Delhi as an auto-rickshaw driver. An auto-rickshaw is a kind of motorbike with three wheels. I don't have a driving license of course, but over 300,000 other rickshaw drivers don't either. The government always says it is going to do something about drivers without licenses, but nothing really happens, so we don't worry too much.

The roads in New Delhi are big, but the traffic is chaotic and drivers have to be aggressive or they won't get anywhere.

Drivers will slow down to avoid sacred cows. Being a taxi driver in New Delhi isn't an easy life. I start work very early in the morning and don't finish until late at night. My best customers are tourists. Although I always give them a fixed price before I take them anywhere, they usually give me a good tip. Tourists also love to take photos of me and my rickshaw which they think is funny.

1 Being a rickshaw driver

1. Why do people go to New Delhi?
2. What do you know about Anand's education?
3. What is special about cows in India?
4. How long does Anand work each day?
5. Why does he like the tourists in New Delhi?
6. What jobs do many people do to make money?

2 Bollywood

a) *Read the text* "Hollywood in India".

b) *Write down all the words that you do not know. Guess what the words mean. Then look them up in your dictionary. Say the new words.*

c) *Now read the text to your partner. Read slowly and make it sound interesting.*

Hollywood in India

Sex and dangerous stunts sell films in the USA, but in the world of Indian cinema it is singing that makes films popular. Singing good guys, singing bad guys and singing lovers are the most important ingredients of an Indian film. Add some dancing and you get Bollywood, Bombay's Hollywood. Bombay is now called Mumbai, but the name Bollywood has not changed.

India has got the biggest film industry in the world. It produces more films than any other country and sells them to more than 50 countries around the world. Britain is one of India's largest customers.
"It's wonderful that we can buy Hindi films here. They are a link to home," said Sunil Aravind who left Calcutta in 1952 to come to London. "Even my kids, who were born here in England, love them!"

Hindi films offer Indian families good "clean" entertainment. Good always wins over bad, love wins over hate and the good guys live happily ever after. The women are always beautiful and the men are attractive, but sex has no place in most Indian films. The Indian film industry certainly has something to sing about. Each year it produces around 800 films and makes 200 million US dollars!

3 Project: India

Work in groups and find out more about India. Compare what you've learned about India to what you know about Germany.

size population religions
languages education industries
weather interesting sights to visit
plants and animal life clothes
films and TV

4 Listening: City explorer

Listen to the radio report about Old and New Delhi and answer the questions.

1. How is New Delhi different from Old Delhi?
2. What do you find more interesting, New Delhi or Old Delhi ? Say why.

Future with going to *(Zukunft)*

Man benutzt going to, *wenn man über Entscheidungen oder Pläne spricht, die man für die Zukunft gemacht hat, oder wenn man andere Leute nach ihren Plänen und Entscheidungen für die Zukunft fragt.*
Signalwörter sind: tonight, tomorrow, next week, next year.

She **isn't going to go** to her Hindi class tomorrow.
Sie ***hat nicht vor****, morgen zu ihrem Hindikurs* ***zu gehen****.*

Are you **going to watch** the Indian film on TV tonight?
Hast du vor*, heute abend den indischen Film im Fernsehen* ***zu sehen****?*

1 Holiday plans

Complete the dialogue. Use the future with 'going to'. Sometimes you have to make questions or use 'not'.

fly ride buy go (2 x) do get in visit be stay (2 x)

David: Where … you … on holiday this year?
Kim: I … to India with my family.
David: Wow! That sounds like it … exciting.
Kim: We … in Delhi for two weeks. Of course we … in one of those expensive hotels, but Dad found a good hotel in Old Delhi.
David: I've read about Old Delhi.
… you … the Red Fort and the big mosque?
Kim: Of course. And Mum loves Indian food so she … lots of Indian spices there.
David: … you … in one of those rickshaws when you are there?
Kim: I really want to, but Dad says he … a rickshaw because they look so dangerous. But my mum and my sister say that they … everywhere, so maybe he will come with us. And you, what are you … this holiday?

2 Relative clauses

Connect the two sentences with a relative pronoun.

TIPP In Relativsätzen benutzt du *who* und *whose* für Menschen und *which* für Dinge.

1. Mahatma Gandhi was a very famous man. He helped India to become independent from Britain.
2. His protests against the British were an inspiration to many people. Gandhi's protests were never violent.
3. Gandhi was often put into prison by the British. He never gave up his protests.
4. Mahatma Gandhi was killed in 1948. Gandhi's life was made into a film.
5. The Mani Bhavan is where Gandhi stayed when he was in Mumbai. The Mani Bhavan is now the Mahatma Gandhi museum.
6. Martin Luther King learned a lot from Gandhi. King fought for blacks' rights in the USA.

Will future *(Zukunft)*

Man benutzt will, *wenn man über Ereignisse in der Zukunft spricht, Vorhersagen und Vermutungen über die Zukunft macht oder Menschen spontan Hilfe anbietet. Signalwörter sind:* perhaps, probably, maybe, hope, think.

I hope the man **won't kill** the tiger.
*Ich hoffe, der Mann **wird** den Tiger **nicht töten**.*

Will we **see** any wild animals in the park?
***Werden** wir irgendwelche wilden Tiere im Park **sehen**?*

I'll help you find some pictures of India.
***Ich werde** dir **helfen** einige Indienbilder zu finden.*

3 Working in India

Ben wants to work in India next year. What will he do? What won't he do?
Write down what you think.

I don't think he'll .... He won't .... Maybe he'll .... He hopes he'll ....

1. I don't think he'll work as an auto-rickshaw driver, but maybe he'll work as a .... .

4 Will or going to?

Translate these sentences. Use the right future tense.

1. Wir haben vor, nächste Woche nach London zu fahren.
2. Wir werden den Zug um 7 Uhr nehmen.
3. Wir planen das Wembley Stadion zu besichtigen.
4. Die Reise nach London wird eine Stunde dauern.
5. Wir haben vor, eine Nacht im Hotel zu verbringen.

1 Cheap children

This is Sindhu. She's twelve years old and she comes from Tamil Nadu in India. In the photo Sindhu is working in a factory. She's making matches. Sindhu is just one of millions of children in India who have to work. She has three younger brothers and a sister. "Last year my father had a bad accident. Now he can't work. So I have to earn some money. I come here every day with my mother," she explains. The children must work in a room without windows for 13 hours every day. Sindhu earns 30 rupees a day. That's about 50 Cents.
With the money she must buy food for all the family. "My fingers hurt and I feel very tired but we need the money," she tells us as she puts the sticks into hot sulphur.
The smell of sulphur in the air is very strong. Suddenly the owner of the match factory comes in and tells us to leave. He doesn't want people to know that children work in his factory. India is just one of many countries in the world where children under 14 have to work. This is wrong.
They should be in school. But children are cheap, much cheaper than their parents.

You show your friend the photo of Sindhu. *Answer his or her questions.*

1. Wo ist sie?
2. Was macht sie?
3. Wieviel verdient sie?
4. Warum geht sie nicht in die Schule?
5. Passiert so etwas nur in Indien?
6. Wie sind die Arbeitsbedingungen?

2 An Indian friend

Your friend, Kevin, is doing a project on India. You have an Indian friend, Hamida Aziz, who he wants to meet. Kevin does not speak English well, so you translate his questions into English. *Give a summary of Hamida's English answers in German.*

Kevin: Guten Morgen, Frau Aziz. Ich würde gerne etwas von Ihrem Heimatland Indien erfahren. Wie lange sind Sie eigentlich schon in Deutschland?
Hamida: Hello. I've been working at a German export company for more than two months now.
Kevin: Aus welcher Stadt kommen Sie?
Hamida: I'm from New Delhi. You know that's the capital of India with about 12,000,000 people. That's quite a lot compared with Germany, I think.
Kevin: Sprechen alle Inder Englisch?
Hamida: No, there are two official languages: Hindi and English. And there are many, many dialects.
Kevin: Wir haben gelesen, dass es in Indien ein zweites Silicon Valley gibt.
Hamida: True, Bangalore has become an important centre for high-tech firms. It's in the south of India. There are good institutes where young Indians are trained to become computer experts.
Kevin: Danke für das Gespräch.
Hamida: You're welcome. I really enjoyed talking to you.

match – *Streichholz;* rupee – *Rupie;* stick – *Stab;* sulphur – *Schwefel;* summary – *Zusammenfassung;* export – *Export;* dialect – *Dialekt;* centre – *Zentrum,* institute – *Schule*

Unit 3

Language

26	**auto-rickshaw**	Auto-Rickscha
	scrap-picker	jemand, der Müll sammelt und wieder verkauft
	opportunity	Chance, Möglichkeit
	not ... either	auch nicht
	without	ohne
	worry	sich Sorgen machen
	chaotic	chaotisch
	aggressive	aggressiv
	anywhere	irgendwo
	slow down	abbremsen, langsamer fahren
	avoid	vermeiden
	sacred	heilig
	tip	Trinkgeld
27	**sex**	Sex
	stunt	Stunt, Trick
	lovers	Liebende, Liebespaar(e)
	ingredient	Bestandteil
	wonderful	wunderbar
	link	Verbindung
	entertainment	Unterhaltung
	hate	Hass
	ever after	bis an ihr Lebensende
	attractive	attraktiv, gut aussehend
	certainly	bestimmt, gewiss
	size	Größe
	population	Bevölkerung

Workshop

28	**spice**	Gewürz
29	**independent**	unabhängig
	protest	Protest

Checklist

Ich kann	
... sagen, was ich mit anderen gemeinsam habe.	Lots of children like me have left their homes to find work.
... sagen, dass sich etwas gelohnt hat.	Now, eight years later, I make good money.
... ein nicht alltägliches Fahrzeug beschreiben.	An auto-rickshaw is a kind of motorbike with three wheels.
... sagen, was nötig ist, um ein Ziel zu erreichen.	Sometimes you have to be aggressive or you won't get anywhere.
... sagen, was gewöhnlich der Fall ist.	They usually give me a good tip.
... besonders wichtige Eigenschaften hervorheben.	It is the stars that make films popular.
... sagen, was sonst noch wichtig ist.	Add some action and you get a great movie!
... wichtige Merkmale von etwas zusammenfassen.	Good always wins over bad, and love wins over hate.
... sagen was ich vorhabe.	I'm going to have a party next Saturday.
... Vermutungen und Voraussagen über die Zukunft äußern.	I hope all my friends will come.

Women around the world

Women around the world have different opportunities. *Read the four texts to find out about the lives of women around the world.*

Helen Clark, New Zealand

a At a meeting called 'What do women want?' Margaret Sievwright explained, "We want men to stand out of our sunshine, that's all." That meeting was held at the beginning of the 1900s. New Zealand had already taken a big step forward in 1893 when it gave women the vote. It was the first country in the world to do so. Since then women have become more and more involved in politics. Helen Clark is one of these women. Helen studied politics at Auckland University. In 1981 she was elected to parliament and in 1989 she became deputy prime minister. Four years later she was the leader of the opposition and on 27th November 1999 she became New Zealand's second female prime minister.

b When Fidel Castro became president in 1959 he started an organisation especially for women. This organisation's first job was to teach women how to read and write and give them an education. Today over 50% of the doctors in the country are women. At one time 75% of the young people studying at science and technology universities were women. The government had to change the university entrance, so that more male students could go to university. However, today over 60% of the students at science and technology universities still are women. In this country women have more rights than many women in fully developed countries. There is even a law which says that men and women must share childcare and housework equally.

A student in Cuba

1 What's wrong?

All the sentences are false. Find the mistakes and correct the sentences.

1. Maasi women must buy their husbands with huts.
2. Helen Clark studied computer science in India.
3. In Cuba women must do all the housework.
4. Cowgirls are better rodeo riders than cowboys.

2 Your opinion

Answer the questions.

1. Do you think women should ride in rodeos?
2. What would you do if your parents wanted to choose your future husband or wife for you?

c Rodeos are the only places where you can see real cowboys these days, but even that is changing. Now, when you visit a rodeo in the US you will see more and more real cowgirls. Over the past years, many cowgirls have been as successful as men in the sport. Jan Youren, now 'grandma of rodeo', took part in her first rodeo in 1955. Since then she has been the female world champion five times and is still riding rough in the saddle. Rodeo riders only have to stay on a bull or horse for six seconds, but those very difficult six seconds can feel like a long time and both cowboys and cowgirls are often hurt. Of course there is still one big difference between men and women rodeo riders: the men can get around twice as much money as the women.

A cowgirl in the USA

A young woman in Kenya

d Maasi girls between the ages of 13 and 15 are usually married to an older man who often already has several wives. Men must buy their wives with cattle and can have as many wives as they can afford.
Once married, a woman will move into her husband's 'enkang'. The enkang is a collection of huts with a round fence made of bushes. Wives are responsible for building their huts themselves. These huts are very small. While the men look after their cattle, the women look after the home. They take care of the children, collect water and wood for the fire, cook, clean and prepare animal skins.

3 Speaking: How is it in Germany?

Make a table like this and complete it.

Facts	Country	Compared to your country
Woman prime minister	New Zealand	Angela Merkel became the first female chancellor of Germany in 2005.
50 % of the doctors are female	...	...
Women ride in rodeos	...	...
Enkangs	...	...

4 Mediation: One text

Choose one text and tell your partner in German what it's about. Then ask him or her some facts.

A: A woman is prime minister there.
B: That's in New Zealand.
A: How is it in Germany?
B: Angela ... .

5 Women at work

a) *Describe what you see in the cartoon.*
b) *What is the cartoon's message?*
c) *Answer these questions about women.*

1. Do women have the same career opportunities as men? What do you think? Give examples for your answer.
2. Should women with a family go out to work? Give reasons for your answer.
3. Would you like to have a woman as your boss? Say why or why not.

6 Listening: Hillary Rodham Clinton

a) *Look up the new words in the box and check for any new words in the questions. Now listen to the radio program 'Women in Power'. Then answer the questions about Hillary Clinton.*

senator confident active
Girl Guide migrant worker lawyer
stare support bestseller

1. What was Hillary Clinton like as a child?
2. What did she become interested in at Yale Law School?
3. Where did she introduce herself to Bill Clinton?
4. How did Hillary Clinton help her husband with his career?
5. Name three things which she did while her husband was governor of Arkansas and then president.
6. How do you know that Hillary Clinton's political career is moving up?
7. What has she shown people in the US?

b) *Describe Hillary Clinton's character in three or four sentences.*
You can start like this: Hillary Clinton is a very confident and … .

Rights at work

Today people have many rights at work. But it used to be different 200 years ago.

Emily lives in Bristol. She left school when she was 16. She works for a large fashion store.

"I work 40 hours a week. If I work longer, the store pays extra. I get £ 6.50 an hour. It's not much, but it's more than the minimum wage. The working conditions are quite good. I have four weeks' paid holiday a year. My lunch break is one hour. I can buy clothes cheaply from the store".

200 years ago a young girl called Emily had a different life.

When she was nine years old, she started to work in a factory. Her day started at 7 o'clock in the morning and finished at 6 o'clock in the evening. She worked six days a week and her job was low-paid. She didn't earn much money. The conditions were terrible. The machines were loud and the factory was very hot. The work was dangerous, so many people had accidents. She was often ill. She had one week's holiday per year, but it wasn't paid.

7 Emily

a) *Look at the text and make two lists.*

	Emily now	Emily 200 years ago
left school	when she was 16	?
job	works for …	?
hours a week	?	?
working conditions	?	?
holidays	?	?

b) *Ask your family and friends about their working conditions. Tell the class.*

8 Children's rights

1819	Children under 8 must not work in factories.
1880	Children from 5 to 10 must go to school.
1901	Children under 12 must not work.
1918	Children must go to school until they are 14.
1947	Children must stay at school until they are 15.
1997	All children must stay at school until they are 16.
2025	…

When will children leave school and start work in 2025? What do you think?

Reported speech *(Indirekte Rede)*

In der indirekten Rede werden die Verben wie folgt verändert, wenn der Einleitungssatz im simple past *steht:*

Simple present	→	Simple past
Simple past and present perfect	→	Past perfect
Will future	→	Conditional

Auch einige Pronomen müssen verändert werden. Zum Beispiel:

"I want to spend **my** holidays in Scotland."
She said that she wanted to spend **her** holidays in Scotland.

Signalwörter sind: said that, explained that, reported that, told somebody that.

"Men and women **have** the same rights."
She said that men and women **had** the same rights.
Sie sagte, dass Männer und Frauen die gleichen Rechte ***haben****.*

"The organisation **taught** women to read and write."
She explained that the organisation **had taught** women to read and write.
Sie erklärte, dass die Organisation Frauen Lesen und Schreiben ***beigebracht hat****.*

"Women **will** always **fight** for their rights."
She told me that women **would** always **fight** for their rights.
Sie sagte mir, dass Frauen immer für ihre Rechte ***kämpfen werden****.*

1 Talking about women

Women from different countries were interviewed about women in their culture.
Write down what each woman said. Use reported speech and different signal words.

1. Botswana:
   Many women work for the government.
2. New Zealand:
   Women really enjoy playing hockey and rugby here.
3. India:
   Young women don't wear traditional clothes. They prefer jeans and T-shirts.
4. Cuba:
   More women go to technology universities than men.
5. USA:
   There are a lot of good women rodeo riders here.
6. Kenya:
   Maasi women have to build their homes themselves.
7. Germany:
   Today there are many more women in politics.
8. USA:
   Many men still think of actresses as just sex symbols.
9. China:
   A lot of parents prefer sons to daughters.
10. England:
    Many women work and look after their family.
11. Kenya:
    The women's job is to look after their homes.
12. India:
    Indian women don't have the same job opportunities as men.

2 A school in Kenya

a) Sandra Wilson, a teacher from England, visited Machakos Girls School in Kenya. This is what she said about a typical day at the school. *Copy the text and underline all the verbs.*

Wilson: Every morning the girls collected water. Then they ate breakfast. After breakfast they went to their lessons. The teachers taught all their subjects in English, except for Swahili, of course. In the afternoon the girls played netball or volleyball. At 6 pm they had dinner. Then they did their homework.

b) You have to write a report for school about schools in Kenya. *Put Wilson's sentences into reported speech. Use different words for 'said' in your sentences.*

3 What New Zealand's men think of women prime ministers

A local newspaper reporter interviewed some men in New Zealand about what they thought of women prime ministers.

Write the report for the newspaper. Use reported speech. Make sure you choose the correct verb forms.

You can start like this:

Ted Blake, an engineer, said that although this was New Zealand's second woman prime minister, it still …

> This is our second woman prime minister, but it still seems strange to me.

Ted Blake – engineer

> I am sure she will do her best for the country.

Terry Walters – mechanic

> It's crazy to have a woman as prime minister. I have never voted for a woman and I never will.

Vic Brown – unemployed

> I like the idea of a woman prime minister. We have already had one and there will be more in the future.

Dave Parker – bus driver

> Lots of men voted for her. That means they wanted her.

Will Herrick – waiter

> I don't think that a woman will do more damage to the country than a man.

Bruce James – teacher

Teenagers' rights in Great Britain

You already know how old German teenagers must be for some things. How much do you know about teenagers' rights in Great Britain? Answer these questions.

1. When can you buy a pet?
   a) 12 b) 8 c) 13
2. When can you buy and own a gun?
   a) 16 b) 17 c) 18
3. When can you get a tattoo?
   a) 18 b) 17 c) 14
4. When can you marry?
   a) 16 b) 17 c) 18
5. When can you leave your parents' home and live alone?
   a) 16 b) 17 c) 18
6. When can you be sent to prison?
   a) 13 b) 17 c) 18
7. When can you buy cigarettes?
   a) 15 b) 16 c) 17
8. When can you go into a bar alone if you don't drink alcohol?
   a) 12 b) 14 c) 15
9. When can you have a job after school?
   a) 13 b) 14 c) 15
10. When can you have a real job?
    a) 14 b) 16 c) 17
11. When can you drive a car?
    a) 16 b) 17 c) 18
12. When can you buy fireworks?
    a) 16 b) 17 c) 18

You can find the answers on page 131.

TIPP

Fehlerwerkstatt: False friends

Es gibt viele englische Wörter, die dem Deutschen sehr ähnlich sind, aber eine ganz andere Bedeutung haben. Bei diesen ‚falschen Freunden' (*false friends*) musst du aufpassen:

- **become** *heißt zum Beispiel nicht ‚bekommen', sondern ‚werden'.*

  Ich bekam einen Hund zu Weihnachten. – *I got a dog for Christmas.*
  FALSCH: I became a dog for Christmas. (Ich wurde an Weihnachten ein Hund.)

- **handy** heißt nicht ‚Handy', sondern ‚praktisch' oder ‚geschickt'.
  Im Englischen heißt ‚Handy' *mobile* (BE) oder *cell phone* (AE).

  Ich habe ein neues Handy. – *I've got a new mobile.*

- **programme** (*AE: program*) heißt nicht ‚Programm', sondern ‚Sendung'.
  Das englische Wort für ‚Programm' ist ‚channel'.

  Der Film kam im 1. Programm. – *The film was on channel 1.*

Unit 4

Language

32	**forward**	vorwärts
	vote	Wahlrecht
	involve	jemanden an etwas beteiligen
	politics	Politik
	elect	wählen
	parliament	Parlament
	deputy prime minister	stellvertretende Premierministerin, stellvertretender Premierminister
	opposition	Opposition
	science	Wissenschaft
	university entrance	Hochschulzulassung
	develop	entwickeln
	share	teilen
	childcare	Kinderbetreuung
	housework	Hausarbeit
	equal	gleich
	false	falsch
	rodeo	Rodeo
33	**cowgirl**	weiblicher Cowboy
	past	vergangen
	successful	erfolgreich
	champion	Meister, Meisterin, Champion
	rough	rau, hart
	saddle	Sattel
	rider	Reiter, Reiterin
	bull	Stier, Bulle
	marry	heiraten
	hut	Hütte
	round	rund
	themselves	sich, selbst
	skin	Haut, Fell
	chancellor	Kanzler, Kanzlerin
34	**program (AE)**	Sendung
	senator	Senator, Senatorin
	confident	zuversichtlich, selbstsicher
	active	aktiv
	Girl Guide	Pfadfinderin
	migrant worker	Wanderarbeiter
	support	unterstützen
	bestseller	Bestseller
	introduce someone	jemanden vorstellen
	name	nennen, ernennen
	governor	Gouverneur, Gouverneurin
	political	politisch
	move up	aufsteigen
35	**used to be**	war früher
	extra	Extra-, extra
	minimum wage	Mindestlohn
	working conditions	Arbeitsbedingungen
	low-paid	schlecht bezahlt
	machine	Maschine
	symbol	Symbol

Workshop

37	**except for**	außer
	netball	Korbball
	vote	wählen, abstimmen

Checklist

Ich kann	
... sagen, welche Ziele für jemanden am wichtigsten sind.	We want you to stand out of our sunshine, that's all.
... sagen, was sich im Lauf der Jahre ereignet hat.	Since then women have become more and more involved in politics.
... sagen, was das Besondere an etwas ist.	Rodeos are the only places where you can see real cowboys.
... gleichzeitig stattfindende Ereignisse beschreiben.	While the men look after their saddles, the women look after their homes.
... Arbeitsbedingungen beschreiben.	I work 40 hours a week. If I work longer, the store pays extra.
... über Rechte und Pflichten von Jugendlichen sprechen.	All children must stay at school until they are 16.

These pages are like a real exam. Use your dictionary if you need it.

A true rags-to-riches story

a Mention the name Caryn Johnson and probably nobody will know who you are talking about. Change that name to Whoopi Goldberg and everyone immediately thinks of that tough talking, black American actress with dreadlocks. But once upon a time Whoopi Goldberg was Caryn Johnson. She was no different than many other young black Americans who were fighting to build a future for themselves.

b Caryn was born in New York City. Her father left the family when she was very young and she grew up with her mother and brother in Manhattan. She started her acting career when she was eight. Then she dropped out of school in ninth grade and started taking drugs. When she realised that she had a serious heroin problem, she knew she had to stop. And she did. She got help at a drug center in New York and came out clean. She married her drug counsellor and they had a daughter called Alexandra. But the marriage did not work and they soon got divorced.

c Caryn moved to California with her daughter. She got some acting jobs there but also had to support herself and her daughter by working as a bricklayer and a funeral parlor make-up artist. She decided that dead people were less fussy than live ones.

1 Global understanding

Decide whether these sentences are true or false. Then correct the false ones.

1. When Whoopi was young she had a drug problem.
2. Whoopi had a happy first marriage.
3. She made the film headlines with her 'Spook Show'.
4. Before Whoopi, no woman or black American had hosted the Oscars.
5. Whoopi spends all her time acting.

2 Questions about Whoopi

1. What happened after Whoopi dropped out of school?
2. How did she earn money in California? Give two facts.
3. Why did she decide not to call herself Whoopi Cushion?
4. How do you know that Whoopi's Spook Show was a success? Give two reasons.
5. How did Steven Spielberg help Whoopi's film career?
6. Who was Oda Mae Brown?
7. Whoopi is rich today but she still cares about other people. How do you know this? Give three reasons.

This was also when Caryn decided to change her name. At first she wanted to call herself Whoopi Cushion, but her mother told her that nobody would respect a name like that. So Caryn changed the Cushion to Goldberg and from then on became Whoopi Goldberg.
Whoopi moved again. This time she went to San Francisco. Here she developed a one-woman show called the 'Spook Show'. The show was so successful that she took it on tour in Europe. Later, in 1985, it won her the Grammy for the best comedy recording of the year. Whoopi finally made the film headlines when Steven Spielberg gave her the main part in The Color Purple and she won an Oscar nomination and the Golden Globe.

d Since then Whoopi has appeared in many films and on TV, including Star Trek. The film Ghost, where she plays the chaotic fortune teller Oda Mae Brown, won her the Oscar for best supporting actress. The blockbuster film Sister Act made her even more famous and brought her millions of dollars. Whoopi has now won many awards, and she was the first woman and black American to host the Oscars. Whoopi's life is a true rags-to-riches story of a black American woman. But she has not forgotten her past. She also works in campaigns to stop AIDS and drug addiction and to help the homeless.

3 Sister Act

Translate the following text.

FILM REVIEW: SISTER ACT

Finally a film where Whoopi Goldberg can show her real talent for comedy! Whoopi plays a fantastic Dolores Van Cartier, a singer in her boyfriend's casino. But her boyfriend is a gangster and one day she sees him kill his driver. From then on Dolores's life is in danger. She runs to the police and to protect her they put her in a convent.

At first Dolores is not very happy about living in a convent but she starts to influence the sisters with her modern ideas. She is responsible for the choir and teaches the sisters all about jazz. The Mother Superior does not think it is a good idea to have Dolores in the convent, but the sisters begin to like Dolores a lot. She brings adventure and change into their boring lives.

The funny actors and the crazy situations will make you laugh. The singing is so good that you will want to sing along. Everyone will enjoy this film, especially Whoopi Goldberg fans!

4 Open-ended story

Finish this story. Find a good title and write at least 120 words.

Mark was alone in the house.
It was Friday evening and he was sitting in his bedroom.
Suddenly he heard something outside.
He looked out of the window and saw …

5 Reported speech

Kyle Anderson, a reporter from Modern Teen Magazine, interviewed Sue Taylor, one of Whoopi Goldberg's biggest fans, for an article about stars and their fans. Sue said:

1. "I really liked Whoopi Goldberg's last film because she played a strong character."
2. "She had a hard life as a black American child."
3. "But she has worked hard and was very successful in Hollywood."
4. "I think she is a great actress and I love her films."
5. "She will always be a special woman for me."
6. "She has given young black American girls like me hope for the future."
7. "I don't want to be a film star, but I want a good career for myself."
8. "When I look at Whoopi, I know that if I work hard I will have a good career, too."

Put the sentences into reported speech. Use different words for 'said'.

6 Opposites

Find the opposites. How do you pronounce the words?

1. laugh   2. disappear   3. clean   4. less   5. win   6. survive   7. expensive
8. wet   9. save   10. switch on   11. enemy   12. colder

7 Listen and say: [dʒ] and [tʃ]

Do you say [dʒ] or [tʃ]? *Say these words and make two lists.*

children   adventure   teacher   jungle   jeans   chance
charity   garage   dangerous   geography

8 The House of Ruth

Complete the text. Use the the correct forms of the verbs.

The House of Ruth (be) a charity organisation which (start) in 1976. It is also one of the charities which Whoopi Goldberg (support). Since 1976, the House of Ruth (help) many women and children living in violent homes or on the streets. It (offer) them a safe place to stay. Some of the women (already/become) addicted to drugs, but counsellors at the House of Ruth (be able to) help them. Last year thousands of people (show) their interest in the House of Ruth and (give) money to help it.

9 Listening: Johnny Depp in his own words

Johnny Depp is one of the most famous actors in Hollywood.

a) *Listen to the text in which he describes his life and career. Take notes.*

b) *Now find the right answer.*

1. Johnny …
   a) didn't finish high school.
   b) never went to high school.
   c) finished high school.

2. He …
   a) didn't like practising the guitar.
   b) played the guitar all the time.
   c) gave the guitar to another kid.

3. His most famous movie series was called …
   a) *Lord of the Rings.*
   b) *Pirates of the Caribbean.*
   c) *Indiana Jones.*

4. Working as an actor is …
   a) sometimes difficult.
   b) always easy.
   c) never difficult.

c) *Make sentences about Johnny. Use the words from the box and your notes.*

parents	school	at 12	at 16
musician	Los Angeles	movies	

Ireland

a Ireland is divided into Northern Ireland and the Republic of Ireland. It has a population of nearly 6 million people. That is less than the population of London. The most important Irish cities are Dublin and Belfast.

The flag of the Republic of Ireland has three colours: green, white and orange. It is said that green symbolizes the colour of the countryside and the Catholic population and orange stands for the Protestants. The white stripe in the middle symbolizes peace between the two confessions.
There are good reasons for that:

- For hundreds of years Ireland was a Catholic country ruled by Britain.
- In 1922, two countries were formed: Northern Ireland stayed part of Britain and the Republic of Ireland became an independent country.
- About 60% of the people in Northern Ireland are Protestants, about 30% are Catholics.
- Many Protestants in Northern Ireland want to stay part of Britain.
- Many Catholics in Northern Ireland want to be part of the Republic of Ireland.
- There has been a lot of violence between Catholics and Protestants in the past. Between 1969 and 2001 more than 3,500 people were killed in the conflict.
- Today the fighting has stopped, but there are still two countries.

1 Facts about Ireland

Is the information right or wrong? Correct the sentences.

1. Over 6 million people live in Ireland.
2. More people live in Ireland than in London.
3. Most people in Ireland speak Gaelic.
4. There are more Protestants than Catholics in Northern Ireland.
5. The Blarney Stone has special powers.
6. Finn McCool was a Scottish giant.
7. Ireland is still an agricultural country.

2 Find the words

Read the text again and find a word that means ...

1. separated
2. almost
3. feelings or religion
4. many people
5. beautiful
6. problem
7. spend
8. someone who is big and strong

b Two official languages are spoken on the island: Gaelic and English. The large majority speaks English. However, children have to learn Gaelic at school.

> **TIPP**
> *Slán.* – Goodbye
> *Go raibh maith agat* – Thank you.
> *Conas atá tú?* – How are you?
> *Baile Átha Cliath* – Dublin
> *Éire* – Ireland

The Giant's Causeway is one of the most famous sights in Northern Ireland. It looks like a road of very big stones that goes from the land into the sea. There are 40,000 stones and they are all of a different size. A legend says the Causeway is the work of the Irish giant Finn McCool. He loved a woman giant who lived in Scotland. So he started to build a road that could bring her across the sea to Ireland, but he never finished it.

Ireland has long been an agricultural country but in the mid 1990s, much was being done to modernize the country. A lot of money was being invested in tourism and the software industry.

Blarney Castle is situated on a steep rock near Cork in the south of Ireland. It is popular with tourists who want to visit the castle and its pretty gardens or kiss the Blarney Stone. The stone was built into the walls of the castle in 1446. It is said that the stone has magical powers:
The person who kisses it will find it easy to make contact and talk to other people.

3 Dates and numbers

Look at the text again.
What do these numbers stand for?

1. 1922
2. 30
3. 60
4. 3
5. 3,500
6. 40,000
7. 1446
8. 2

4 Listening: Going to Ireland

Listen to the text and answer the questions.

1. Write down the route Klara and Martin are going to take to Ireland.
2. Why does Martin not want to go by ferry? What alternatives are there?
3. How long are they going to stay?
4. When is it cheaper to take the ferry?
5. When are Klara and Martin coming back?

Passive *(Passiv)*

Das Passiv wird mit einer Form von be *und der dritten Verbform gebildet. Mit dem Passiv drückst du aus, was mit etwas oder jemandem gemacht wird oder gemacht worden ist. Die Person, die die Handlung ausführt, wird mit* by *angehängt, wird aber auch oft weggelassen.*

Present
Ireland **is called** Éire in Gaelic.
*Irland **wird** im Gälischen Éire **genannt**.*

Past
Many people **were killed** between 1969 and 2001.
*Viele Menschen **wurden** zwischen 1969 und 2001 **getötet**.*

Present perfect
Since 2001 many books **have been written** about her.
*Seit 2001 **sind** viele Bücher über sie **geschrieben worden**.*

Future
The party **will be planned** by the class next month.
*Die Party **wird** von der Klasse nächsten Monat **geplant werden**.*

1 About Ireland

Make sentences in the passive. Write them in your exercise book.

Ireland	be taught	in the south.
Two languages	be built	by most people.
English	be divided	in 1922.
Gaelic	be formed	by an Irish giant.
Two countries	be situated	in schools.
Blarney Castle	be spoken	into Northern Ireland and the Republic of Ireland.
The Giant's Causeway	be spoken	on the island.

2 Welcome to Ireland

Complete the sentences. Put the verbs into the passive.

1. Ireland (separate) from Great Britain by the Irish Sea.
2. Every year many Irish towns (visit) by thousands of tourists.
3. Since 2000 a lot of new shops (open) in Dublin.
4. U2, Ireland's most famous rock band, (start) in 1976.
5. When we were in Galway last summer, we (tell) lots of old Irish stories.
6. Next week a group of German tourists (teach) some lessons in Gaelic.

Passive: progressive forms *(Passiv: Verlaufsformen)*

Das present progressive *beschreibt eine Handlung, die gerade abläuft und noch nicht abgeschlossen ist.*

Mit dem past progressive *beschreibst du Handlungen, die in der Vergangenheit abgelaufen sind.*

The city **is being modernized.**
*Die Stadt **wird** gerade **modernisiert**.*

A lot of money **was being invested** in tourism between 1995 and 2002.
*Viel Geld **ist** zwischen 1995 und 2002 in die Tourismusbranche **investiert worden.***

3 On the beach

Look at the picture and answer the questions.

coconuts kite surfing fish
heart football and volleyball

1. What is being sold?
2. What is being repaired?
3. What is being taught?
4. What is being cooked on the barbecue?
5. What is being drawn in the sand?
6. What games are being played?

4 A song: Peace on Earth

a) *Listen to the text about the song. Then finish these sentences.*

1. When he got the letter from U2, Stanley McCombe felt … .
2. Bono had asked him if it was OK to use Ann's … .
3. As well as writing a letter to Stanley McCombe, Bono also sent him … .
4. Stanley McCombe is going to … .

folks – *Leute;* drowning – *ertrinkend*

b) *Now listen to the song.*

Text: Hewson/Evans/Mullen/Clayton

They're reading names out
Over the radio
All the folks the rest of us
Won't get to know

Sean and Julia,
Gareth, Anny, and Breda
Their lives are bigger than
Any big idea

Jesus can you take the time
To throw a drowning man a line
Peace on Earth

1 Holiday neighbours

The Seidels from Bamberg have arrived at their holiday cottage in Ballycastle. Their neighbour Mrs O'Hare wants to talk to them, but only Oliver Seidel speaks English. *What does he say?*

Mrs O'Hare: Have you ever been to Ireland before?
Oliver: …
Frau Seidel: Nein. Aber sag ihr, dass unsere Nachbarn letztes Jahr in Nordirland waren. Sie erzählten uns, wie schön es hier ist.
Oliver: …
Mrs O'Hare: Well, it's nice to meet visitors from another country. I hope you have good weather.
Oliver: …
Frau Seidel: Wir auch! Aber wir sind sicher, es wird uns hier gut gefallen.
Oliver: …
Mrs O'Hare: Perhaps I can give you a few tips about the things you can see and do here.
Oliver: …
Frau Seidel: Danke schön. Das ist sehr nett von ihr.
Mrs O'Hare: Why don't you come to my house tonight? Then you can tell me what you're interested in.
Oliver: …
Frau Seidel: Sag ihr, wir kommen gerne. Unsere Nachbarn erzählten uns auch, wie freundlich die Iren sind.
Oliver: …
Mrs O'Hare: Well, see you tonight.
Oliver: …

2 Hurling

The Seidels have decided to go to a hurling game but first they want to know more about the popular Irish sport. *Can you answer their questions in German?*

HURLING

CONTACT
SITEMAP
SEARCH

A popular Irish sport: Hurling
The Celts brought hurling to Ireland over two thousand years ago. Hurling is like hockey and Gaelic football but it is older than these games. It is the fastest field game in the world: Only hockey on ice is faster! The field is about 137 metres long and 82 metres wide. A team has 15 players (hurlers). They play with sticks (hurleys) which are like hockey sticks, only larger. Players try to hit the ball (sliothar) into the goal, which looks like a big 'H'. Of course, a goalkeeper from the other team must try to stop them. If the ball goes into the goal, they score three points. If it goes over it but through the top part of the 'H', then they get one point. In hurling you can have the ball in one hand but you can only go four steps with it. And you mustn't pick the ball up or throw it with your hand.

1. Hurling kommt doch aus Schottland?
2. Wie viele Spieler hat ein Team?
3. Spielt man das in der Halle?
4. Wie sieht das Tor aus?
5. Wie punktet man?
6. Darf man den Ball mit der Hand werfen?

hurling – *das Hurlingspiel;* Celts – *Kelten;* wide – *breit;* goal – *Tor;* goalkeeper – *Torwart, Torfrau;* score a point – *einen Punkt machen;* pick up – *aufheben*

Unit 5

	Language	
44	**catholic**	katholisch
	protestant	evangelisch, protestantisch
	flag	Flagge, Fahne
	symbolize	symbolisieren
	stripe	Streifen
	confession	Konfession, Glaubensrichtung
	rule	beherrschen, regieren
	violence	Gewalt
	conflict	Konflikt, Auseinandersetzung
	Gaelic	gälisch
	agricultural	landwirtschaftlich
45	**majority**	Mehrheit
	giant	Riese, Riesin
	mid	in der Mitte
	modernize	modernisieren
	invest	investieren
	tourism	Tourismus
	software	Software
	situated	gelegen
	steep	steil
	kiss	küssen
	magical	magisch
	ferry	Fähre
	alternative	Alternative
	Workshop	
47	**coconut**	Kokosnuss
	kite	Drachen
	heart	Herz

Checklist

Ich kann	
... überlieferte Sagen und Gebräuche beschreiben.	It is said that green symbolizes the colour of the countryside.
... Gruppen innerhalb der Bevölkerung beschreiben.	About 60% of the people are Protestants, about 30% are Catholics.
... sagen, was die Mehrheit einer Gruppe tut.	The large majority speaks English.
... eine Natursehenswürdigkeit näher beschreiben.	It looks like a road of very big stones that goes from the land into the sea.
... beschreiben, wie sich ein Land verändert hat.	Ireland has long been an agricultural country, but in the 1990s much was being done to modernize it.
... die Lage von Sehenswürdigkeiten beschreiben.	Blarney Castle is situated on a steep rock near Cork.
... sagen, was in diesem Moment gerade passiert.	A game is being played.
... sagen, wann eine Band gegründet wurde.	U2 was started in 1976.

Our changing planet

The coast of the Maldives before (left) and now (right)

a As the oceans become warmer, the sea level rises because glaciers melt. Worldwide the sea level has risen by about 15 to 20 centimetres in the last century. This may not sound like very much, but scientists say that if global warming continues, the sea level could rise by nearly 50 centimetres in 2080. This means that the number of people whose homes are flooded each year will increase from 13 million to 94 million. Countries on the coast that are in danger of losing land include the Netherlands, Bangladesh, Pakistan and many islands in the Pacific and Indian oceans. Some islands may disappear completely. Millions of people will have to migrate as the sea takes away their homes.

1 False facts

Find the mistakes in each sentence. Then write the sentences correctly.

1. The sea level has risen by 50 centimetres in the last year.
2. If global warming continues, fewer people's homes will be flooded each year.
3. Acid rain puts minerals in the soil and helps plants and trees to grow.
4. The melting ice makes it easier for seals and whales to find fish.
5. Cold and dry weather will cause forest fires.
6. Millions of people will get new homes from the sea.
7. Floods in India left about 10 million people homeless.
8. Hurricane Katrina killed people in Asia.

b Global warming and pollution are killing wildlife and plant life. Acid rain is attacking forests and plants. Many forests are dying in different countries in the world. Acid rain takes away minerals from the soil which plants need and they cannot grow properly. As the sea becomes warmer, coral reefs and fish are disappearing. The melting ice in the Arctic is making life difficult for polar bears and they are having fewer cubs. Seals and whales are losing their food supply.
The changing climate will destroy the habitat of many animals and they will be forced to migrate, others may not survive the change like these penguins in the Antarctic.

c Natural disasters are happening more and more often around the world. This increase is no accident and is now being connected to global warming. Hurricane Katrina was one of the strongest hurricanes in the history of the United States. The tropical storm formed in August 2005 and caused devastation along the Gulf Coast. 80% of the city of New Orleans was flooded. At least 1,800 people died in the hurricane.
2007 was one of the worst years for floods in Britain. June was one of the wettest months on record. In some areas it rained as much in 24 hours as it usually does in a month. Thousands of people had to leave their homes because of floods.
In the same year a series of forest fires broke out in Greece. Over 3,000 forest fires were recorded across the country. They were the result of hot temperatures and drought.
In August 2007 terrible floods in India, Bangladesh and Nepal left about 20 million people homeless. About 60,000 homes were completely destroyed.

2 Climate changes

a) *Work with a partner.*
Find a heading for each part.

1. Part a): … *Go on, please.*

b) *Work in groups.*
Find ten weather words.
Which group is first?

3 What is good for you …

… is often good for the environment, too.

a) *Write down three things you can do to help the environment.*

b) *Write down things you have changed already.*

1. I used to go by bus but now I ride my bike to school.
2. I used to … but now I … . *Go on, please.*

4 Listening: Global warming

a) Kevin, Mary and Chad are presenting a project on global warming.
Look at the posters and look up any new words before you listen to their project.

Global warming!

Light from the sun goes through the greenhouse gases and heats the earth.
The earth gets warm and gives out heat. Some heat goes through the greenhouse gases, but some is trapped and keeps the earth warm.

Stop global warming!

We have to reduce the greenhouse gases! There are six main greenhouse gases, but carbon dioxide is the most important one. Every time we use fuels like oil and coal, we produce carbon dioxide. Many industries, power stations and vehicles use these fuels.

b) *Listen to the text and answer these questions.*

1. What would the earth be like without the greenhouse effect?
2. Which things produce the most greenhouse gases?
3. Why does Mary take a break?
4. Why is it a surprise to learn how much greenhouse gases are produced by the USA?
5. What does Kevin say about computers and lights?
6. What can people do at home to reduce greenhouse gases? Write four things.

5 A song: The rape of the world

Text: Tracy Chapman

Mother of us all
Place of our birth
How can we stand aside
And watch the rape of the world
This the beginning of the end
This the most heinous of crimes
This the deadliest of sins
The greatest violation of all time

Mother of us all
Place of our birth
We all are witness
To the rape of the world
You've seen her stripped, mined
You've heard of bombs exploded underground
You know the sun shines
Hotter than ever before

rape – *Vergewaltigung;* aside – *daneben;* heinous – *abscheulich;* deadly – *tödlich;* sin – *Sünde;* violation – *Verletzung;* witness – *Zeuge;* strip – *ausziehen;* mine – *verminen;* explode – *explodieren;* shine – *scheinen*

6 How green are you?

a) *How many of these environment questions can you answer with YES?*

How green are you?

1. Do you brush your teeth without leaving the water on?
2. Do you buy books that are made from recycled paper?
3. Do you use a backpack when you go shopping?
4. Do you take back empty bottles?
5. Do you pick up other people's litter?
6. Do you try not to use sprays?
7. Do you use rechargeable batteries for your camera, etc.?
8. Do you put on a warm jacket or pullover when it's getting a bit colder in the house?
9. Do you always take your litter home after a picnic?
10. When you have a party, do you use normal plates and glasses and not plastic ones?

b) *Now find out how 'green' you are. Count your 'yes' answers.*

1 – 3 'yes':
STOP and start thinking. It is worth doing something for the environment instead of hurting it.

4 – 6 'yes':
You are on the right track but you could still do better.

7–10 'yes':
You are used to protecting the environment. Congratulations! People should see you as a good example.

7 Topic-based task: Your environment

Work with a partner and find the answers to these questions.

1. Which plants and animals in your country have been affected by global warming? Give three examples.
2. Which environmental groups are active in your country? Name three.
3. Find out about a project your government has recently started to protect the environment.

If-clause type I and II *(If-Satz Typ I und II)*

If-*Satz Typ I wird benutzt, wenn es wahrscheinlich ist, dass das beschriebene Ereignis eintritt. Das Verb im* if-*Satz steht im* simple present, *im Hauptsatz benutzt du das* will-future.

If-*Satz Typ II wird benutzt, wenn man Vermutungen über eine Situation anstellt. Es ist gleichgültig, welcher Satzteil am Anfang steht. Das Verb im* if-*Satz steht im* past tense, *im Hauptsatz benutzt du* would.

Many animals **will lose** their habitat if global warming **goes on**.
*Viele Tiere **werden** ihren Lebensraum **verlieren**, falls die Erderwärmung **fortschreitet**.*

If we **used** less energy, we **would save** money.
*Wenn wir weniger Engerie **verbrauchten, würden** wir Geld **sparen**.*

1 In the future

Look at the pictures and say what will happen to our environment. Use type I if-clauses.

1. If the weather changes, there will be more … . *Go on, please.*

2 Talking about the environment

Some people are talking about the environment. *Find out what they think by completing the sentences. The words in the box will help you.*

1. If there were no greenhouse gases, … .
2. If people were not allowed to drive cars in towns, … .
3. …, the forests would not die.
4. …, they wouldn't use so much water.
5. If we built more solar power stations, … .

acid rain · cleaner energy · much colder · less pollution · pay more

If-clause type III *(If-Satz Typ III)*

Du benutzt den if-*Satz Typ III, wenn du Vermutungen über ein Ereignis in der Vergangenheit anstellst, das nicht eingetreten ist.*

Das Verb im if-*Satz steht im* past perfect. *Im Hauptsatz benutzt du* would have + past participle. *Es ist gleichgültig, welcher Satzteil am Anfang steht.*

If I **had met** you earlier, I **would have told** you about the demonstration.
*Wenn ich dich früher **getroffen hätte, hätte** ich dir von der Demonstration **erzählt**.*

I **wouldn't have seen** a polar bear if I **hadn't won** the trip to the Arctic.
*Ich **hätte keinen** Eisbären **gesehen**, wenn ich den Trip in die Arktis **nicht gewonnen hätte**.*

3 Protesters win

Protesters save the town's park

Last week the people in Blakewell town won the fight to save their park.

The town had decided to build a road through Blakewell's beautiful park. This made the people who live in the town very angry. Some protesters put up posters around the town to organise a meeting. The people knew that if the town built a road through the park, they would have to cut down a lot of trees. This would mean that many birds would lose their home. After the meeting, thousands of protesters held a demonstration in the park. Finally the town decided to build the road outside Blakewell.

Read the article. Then match the correct parts and put the complete sentences in the right order.

If the protesters had not put up posters,
If the town had built a road through the park,
If the people had not protested,
If the town had not decided to build a road through the park,
If the town had cut down trees in the park,

the people would not have been angry.
many birds would have lost their home.
the town would have built a road through the park.
it would have cut down a lot of trees.
people would not have come to the meeting.

What can you do for a healthier lifestyle?

Match sentences 1–6 with sentences a–f.

1. You are too thin or too heavy.
2. You get angry quickly. You find it difficult to relax.
3. You smoke, drink alcohol or take drugs.
4. You don't eat healthy foods (fresh fruit and vegetables) five times a day.
5. You don't exercise every week.
6. You don't sleep enough.

a) Write down what you eat. Eat lots of energy food like bread, pasta, potatoes, rice plus fruit and vegetables – but chocolate and cake from time to time won't hurt!

b) Compare how long you sleep with how you feel in the morning. Healthy living also means getting enough sleep.

c) Find out about different sports where you live: Sports are also great for making friends. Try not to take the bus – walk or ride your bike instead.

d) What is too thin or too heavy? If you are worried, talk to a parent or a doctor. But maybe you just need to eat more or eat fewer sweets and do more exercise.

e) Getting angry quickly often comes from a lot of pressure. Talk through your problems with someone. Try and get more fresh air and exercise. That usually helps!

f) Ask yourself: Why am I doing this? Is it because your friends do it? Don't let them decide for you. You know it's bad for you, so try and stop.

You can find the answers on page 131.

TIPP

Fehlerwerkstatt: Satzbau

Viele Fehler entstehen, wenn man deutschen Satzbau wörtlich ins Englische übersetzt. Beachte, dass der englische Satzbau oft anders funktioniert:

Wie du weißt, **wohnt mein Onkel** in London.

*As you know **my uncle lives** in London.*

→ Im Englischen steht das Subjekt (*my uncle*) vor dem Prädikat (*lives*).
Im Deutschen kann das Prädikat (*wohnt*) auch vor dem Subjekt (*mein Onkel*) stehen.

Auch bei Fragen kann der deutsche Satzbau nicht einfach übersetzt werden. Meistens wird im Englischen ein Hilfsverb (z.B. do) verwendet:

Gehst du noch zur Schule? → ~~*Go you still to school?*~~ → ***Do you** still **go** to school?*

Unit 6

Language

50	**planet**	Planet
	sea level	Meeresspiegel
	rise	ansteigen
	centimetre	Zentimeter
	may	vielleicht
	scientist	Wissenschaftler
	global warming	Erderwärmung
	flood	überschwemmen
	increase	steigen, ansteigen
	danger	Gefahr
	include	einschließen
	completely	völlig
	migrate	wegziehen, umsiedeln
51	**pollution**	Umwelt-verschmutzung
	acid rain	saurer Regen
	attack	angreifen
	minerals	Mineralien
	soil	Boden, Erdreich
	properly	richtig
	coral reef	Korallenriff
	polar bear	Eisbär
	cub	Jungtier
	seal	Seehund
	supply	Vorrat
	climate	Klima
	habitat	Lebensraum, Heimat
	survive	überleben
	change	Veränderung
	penguin	Pinguin
	increase	Anstieg
	hurricane	Orkan, Hurrikan
	tropical	tropisch
	devastation	Zerstörung
	flood	Überschwemmung, Hochwasser
	on record	bekannt, belegt
	drought	Trockenheit, Dürre
	homeless	obdachlos
	environment	Umwelt
52	**greenhouse gas**	Treibhausgas
	trap	stauen, fangen
	carbon dioxide	Kohlendioxid
	oil	Öl
	power station	Kraftwerk
53	**brush one's teeth**	sich die Zähne putzen
	recycled paper	Recyclingpapier
	spray	Spray
	rechargeable	wieder aufladbar
	plastic	Plastik
	it's worth doing	es lohnt sich zu tun
	affect	sich auswirken auf, beeinflussen
	environmental	Umwelt-, die Umwelt betreffend
	recently	vor kurzem

Workshop

54	**solar power**	Sonnenenergie
55	**protester**	Protestierende, Protestierender

Checklist

Ich kann	
... sagen, was ich früher anders gemacht habe.	I used to take the bus but now I ride my bike to school.
... beschreiben, was gleichzeitig mit etwas anderem passiert.	As the oceans become warmer, the sea levels rise.
... sagen, welche Folgen Entwicklungen haben können.	Every time we use fuels like oil and coal, we produce carbon dioxide.
... beschreiben, was vorher so noch nicht vorgekommen ist.	In some areas it rained as much in 24 hours as it usually does in a month.
... sagen, dass sich der Einsatz für etwas lohnt.	It is worth doing something for the environment.

Greenpeace: Save the planet

These pages are like a real exam. Use your dictionary if you need it.

a Mahatma Gandhi once said, "First they ignore you, then they laugh at you, then they fight you, then you win." It is no use ignoring Greenpeace. In over forty years, Greenpeace has grown from a small group of people to a huge international non-governmental organisation with offices in thirty-nine countries. People now know that its warnings are no jokes; it has fought many battles to protect the environment and it has won! Enemies of Greenpeace, including governments and big companies, have said that Greenpeace has strong and widespread international connections. Greenpeace is a non-violent organisation that wants to make our planet a better place to live on. Greenpeace's main aim is to save the environment. That means the air we breathe, the water we drink, the ground we walk on and the food we eat. Some people do not realise or do not want to know that our daily activities often pollute the earth, which then affects plants and animals and ourselves.

b How did Greenpeace start? It started with protests against nuclear bomb testing. In 1969, the USA wanted to test a nuclear bomb on a small island called Amchitka near Alaska. Many people were against this because there are a lot of birds, otters and other animals that live on the island. The island is also in an area where earthquakes happen and people were scared that the bomb might cause an earthquake.
About ten thousand people protested against the bomb with banners, but the

1 Questions on Greenpeace

Answer the questions.

1. Who are Greenpeace's enemies? And why?
2. Why did people protest against the nuclear bomb testing in 1969?
   Give two reasons.
3. In what way were the twelve people from Vancouver successful in 1971 and 1972?
4. Who is Greenpeace fighting against in the Amazon rain forest?
5. Why is the Amazon rain forest so important?
6. Why will Greenpeace never give up the fight to save the planet?

2 Vocabulary

a) *Which word in the text means …*

1. … big posters
2. … not part of the government
3. … land with water all around it
4. … doing something which is against the law
5. … keep something safe
6. … very big
7. … try something out
8. … which live

b) *Give definitions for these words from the text. Use relative clauses.*

1. an office
2. an enemy
3. a bird sanctuary
4. a banner
5. a logger

US government detonated the bomb anyway. Then in 1971, they wanted to detonate another bomb. Twelve people in Vancouver, who later called themselves Greenpeace, decided to do something against the bomb.
They took a fishing boat and went to the place where the bomb was going to be tested. Although they could not stop the bomb test, this time they got a lot of public interest. The group called Greenpeace did not give up and finally in 1972 nuclear bomb testing on the island was stopped. The island Amchitka is now a bird sanctuary.

c Since Greenpeace started it has not only stopped some nuclear testing, it has also protected the Antarctic from industrial development, stopped the sea from being used as a dustbin for nuclear waste, banned many of the world's most dangerous chemicals, saved the lives of whales and much, much more. Today one of Greenpeace's big campaigns is to protect one of the most important rain forests on our planet. Greenpeace is working together with local Indians to save the Amazon rain forest from loggers. Around 80% of the loggers are cutting down trees illegally and the forest is disappearing fast. 50% of the world's animals, which live on land, need the Amazon rain forest to survive. Greenpeace will never give up the fight for the planet because it may soon be too late to save our environment.

3 Greenpeace campaigns

Here are some big Greenpeace campaigns. *Which one is most important to you? Why? Write a short text.*

1. Stop climate change – Take part in an energy revolution to go from a world powered by nuclear and fossil fuels to one running on renewable energy.
2. Defending our oceans – Fight against the exploitation of the oceans, which nature can no longer control. Save the marine environment and the people who depend on it.
3. Saving our forests – All over the world forests are in crisis. Many of the plants and animals that live in these forests face extinction. Join us in our fight to protect these forests and the life they support.

4 Additional work

Answer each question. Write three or four sentences for each question.

1. If the government wanted to test a nuclear bomb near you, would you protest about it? Say why or why not.
2. What do you think would happen if the Amazon rain forest was destroyed?

5 Mediation: What can we do?

What can we do to save the planet? *Translate the text and find out.*

Save water!
- Don't leave taps on when you are not using the water.
- Have a shower instead of a bath.
- Only turn on a dishwasher or washing machine when they are full.

Save energy!
- Don't leave lights on around the house when you don't need them.
- Use energy-saving light bulbs. They may be more expensive, but they last eight times longer than ordinary ones, use a quarter of the energy and are just as bright.
- If you turn down the heating in your home by one degree Celsius, you will not only save energy, but you will save money, too!
- Don't put hot food in the fridge and don't leave the door open for a long time.

Help the earth!
- Plant trees in your garden or at school. They use carbon dioxide and help to clean the air.
- Don't travel by car if you don't have to. Walking and cycling are better for you anyway.
- Why not start your own green organisation at school with some friends and teachers?

6 Text production: Solar power

a) You are interested in solar power. *Write a letter to Clean Power and find out more about these things.*

- benefits
- how expensive
- work in winter
- send brochures
- thank for help

Solar power in your home

Get clean power into your home. Do something to help the planet and make your house environmentally friendly.

For more information write to:
Clean Power Ltd, 11 Rait St., London, UK

b) *Read the key words. Choose six of the words and write a story. Don't forget to give your story a title. Write at least 120 words.*

plastic bag   collect   towards   river   surprised   prize   phone   foggy   interview   pollute

7 Passive

Put the sentences into the passive.

1. Greenhouse gases cause global warming.
2. Greenpeace has planned many protests to save the environment.
3. In the future, global warming will spread diseases.
4. Acid rain is destroying forests all over the world.
5. Greenpeace stopped nuclear bomb testing on Amchitka.

8 Reported speech

A member of Greenpeace was interviewed about his organisation. *Write a report about what he said. Use reported speech and different verbs for 'said'.*

1. "Greenpeace started with protests against nuclear bomb testing."
2. "For almost 40 years we have fought many battles to protect the environment."
3. "We're a non-violent organisation. We want to make our planet a better place to live."
4. "In the future we will try to do more for the rain forests."
5. "We'll never give up our fight to save our planet because in 30 years it may be too late."

9 If-clauses

Make sentences.

If you turn down the heating,	you will get clean power.
If they had planted more trees,	they wouldn't have built the new road.
If you rode your bike more often,	you will save energy.
If more people had protested,	the air would have been cleaner.
If you choose solar power	you would be fitter.

10 Listen and say: 'ea'

The sound 'ea' is pronounced in different ways: [ɪə], [ɜ:],[e] or [i:]. *Look at the words and make four lists.*

idea rehearsal increase mean appear earn bread earth already
weather search spread heat disease realise hear

[ɪə]	[ɜ:]	[e]	[i:]
hear	rehearsal	bread	disease
appear	…	…	…

Free at last!

a On December 1, 1955, Rosa Parks, a 43-year-old black woman, had gotten on a bus in Montgomery, Alabama. Feeling tired after a long day's work, she had decided to sit down at the front of the bus which was for white people. A man told her to give it up and move to a seat for black people, but Rosa Parks refused. The bus driver called a policeman and Rosa Parks was arrested for breaking Montgomery's segregation laws.

Because they knew that they would have the support of the people of Montgomery, a group of black people in the city decided to boycott the bus company. First they gave people leaflets. On them they wrote, "Don't ride the buses to work, to town or to school on Monday, December 5." At a meeting the next day, they chose a priest called Martin Luther King as their leader. He was only 27 years old but clever, respected and too new in Montgomery to have made any enemies.

Martin Luther King was sure the bus boycott would work. He was right. Getting up early on Monday 5 December, he drove through the streets of Montgomery. He could not believe his eyes. All the buses were empty. Most people were walking to work. Some were taking taxis. Others had been offered lifts. The bus boycott lasted for 382 days. In December 1956 the buses in Montgomery became desegregated.

1 Understanding the details

Look at the texts and finish the sentences.

1. December 1, 1955 is an important day in the history of the American civil-rights movement because … .
2. In 1955 there was segregation on the buses in Montgomery. That meant black people … .
3. Although he was young and new to Montgomery, Martin Luther King … .
4. Black people in Montgomery must have felt sure that the bus boycott was important because … .
5. At the Lincoln Memorial Martin Luther King gave a famous speech in which he … .
6. In 1964 Martin Luther King became famous all over the world when he … .

b Many people have forgotten Rosa Parks. But people have not forgotten Martin Luther King. In the 1960s King became the leader of the black civil-rights movement in the US. In August 1963, he led 250,000 people in a protest march through Washington, DC.
At the Lincoln Memorial the crowds shouted, "We want the freedom in 1963 promised in 1863." King got up to make a speech that has become history:
"I have a dream," he said. "I have a dream that one day on the red hills of Georgia, the sons of former slaves and the sons of former slave owners will be able to sit down together at the same table." The people cheered as King spoke of his dream that one day all people would join hands and sing the words of the great black song, "Free at last! Free at last! Thank God Almighty, we are free at last!" King's ideas and hard work made a difference.
In the summer of 1964 the US Congress passed a law which made racial discrimination illegal in the US.
That winter King travelled to Norway. "I accept the Nobel Prize for Peace," he said, "at a moment when 22 million Negroes of the United States are engaged in a creative battle to end racial injustice."
Martin Luther King did not live long. In the spring of 1968 he travelled to Memphis.
On April 4, while standing on the balcony of the hotel where he was staying, King was shot and killed.

2 Listening: Segregation

a) *Answer these questions before you listen to the text on Martin Luther King.*

1. When do you think Martin Luther King was born?
2. Do you think he went to school? If yes, do you think he was a good student?
3. Do you think he was hurt by segregation?

b) *Listen to the first part of the text. Does it help you to answer the questions? Listen to the rest of the text and choose the correct answer.*

1. The policeman wanted to see King's father's address / licence / passport.
2. Martin's father did not like it when the policeman called him son / man / boy.
3. Martin's father said he would never fight segregation / accept segregation / understand segregation.
4. Although Martin Luther King died in 1968, his father lived until the late-1970s / the mid-1980s / the early-1990s.

Participles *(Partizipien)*

Es gibt zwei Partizipien: Das Partizip der Gegenwart und das Partizip der Vergangenheit.
Das Partizip der Gegenwart (present participle), *das auf* -ing *endet, kann auch als Adjektiv verwendet werden.*
Das Partizip der Vergangenheit (past participle), *das der dritten Form des Verbs entspricht, kann auch als Adjektiv verwendet werden.*

She got into a **waiting** bus.	*Sie stieg in den* ***wartenden*** *Bus ein.*
They threw away the **stolen** bag.	*Sie warfen die* ***gestohlene*** *Tasche weg.*

1 Adjectives

Make sentences. Write them in your exercise book.

a) *First make present participles out of these verbs. Then write them in the correct sentences.*

1. Did you see the … parrot outside the pet shop?	move
2. Martin Luther King stood up and spoke to the … crowd.	sink
3. The accident was caused by a … car.	wait
4. The tourists jumped off the … ship.	talk

b) *Now make past participles out of the following verbs. Then write them in the correct sentences.*

1. I fell on a … bottle.	steal
2. He doesn't like … exercises.	break
3. We repaired the … roof.	damage
4. They bought a … car.	write

2 The correct adjective

Choose the right words.

1. They thought the film was very exciting / excited.
   We thought it was terrifying / terrified!
2. She was surprising / surprised about the good result.
   He was shocking / shocked.
3. Did you think the subject was a bit boring / bored?
   We found it quite interested / interesting.
4. I'm disappointing / disappointed that you can't come with me.
   But it's really embarrassing / embarrassed that my mother will come.

3 Comparisons

Complete these sentences.

a) 1. Used cars are not as … as new cars.
2. Spoken exercises are not as … as written exercises.
3. Frozen food is not as … as fresh food.
4. München is not as … as New Delhi.

b) 1. Ten meters is as … as 1,000 centimeters.
2. Two kilos of hair is as … as two kilos of stones.
3. One liter of milk is as … as 2 half-liters of milk.
4. A man running 20 mph is as … as a dog running 32 kph.

4 Taboo adjectives

- Be careful when you talk about black people from the United States. Some words should not be used: colored, negro, nigger
- It is better to use these words and expressions: black, African-American, Afro-American

Go back to the text on page 62/63.

Which of the words in a) and b) are used? Why?

5 Adverbs and adjectives

Complete each sentence with an adjective or an adverb.

TIPP Adjektive beschreiben Personen oder Gegenstände, Adverbien beschreiben Tätigkeiten. Du bildest Adverbien durch Anhängen von -ly an das Adjektiv.

1. Try our new MP3 players. Hear your favourite music … ! (clearer / more clearly)
2. Download … songs more quickly! (new / newly)
3. You can compare prices on the internet … . (easy / easily)
4. This is a … camera, but it works very … . (nice / nicely, slow / slowly)
5. My phone is making a … noise. I can't hear you very … . (terrible / terribly, good / well)
6. Think … before you put any photos on your profile. (careful / carefully)
7. I'd like to take a picture of you. Please smile … . (sweeter / more sweetly)

6 Topic-based task: Black Americans

Find out more about Blacks in America by answering these questions.

1. Why did black people first come to the US?
2. Where did they come from?
3. When did black Americans start to win more rights?

1 Black universities

Your friend has found a homepage called 'Black Universities Go White' designed by Sidney Preston. Your friend wants to use the Internet to talk to him, but he doesn't speak English very well. *Translate his German questions into English. Then give a summary of Sidney's answers in German. You do not have to translate every word.*

Max: Hallo, Sidney. Wir interessieren uns für das Thema 'Black Universities Go White'.
Sidney: Well, I decided to go to Lincoln University, a traditionally black university in Missouri. But when I arrived there I got a shock.
Max: Warum warst du schockiert?
Sidney: You won't believe it, but I was the only black face in the room, the only black student!
Max: Und warum gehen heute so viele weiße Studenten an eine Universität für Schwarze?
Sidney: Well, many black universities offer a better education for about half the price of other universities.
Max: Warum gibt es eigentlich eigene Universitäten für Schwarze? Ist es nicht besser, wenn alle an ein und derselben Universität lernen können?
Sidney: Of course, it's better. But black universities go back to the time before 1965 when African-Americans were not allowed to go to most white universities.
Max: Vielen Dank für das Gespräch.
Sidney: It was nice talking to you.

2 Rosa Parks' funeral

This is a newspaper article about Rosa Parks' death. *Translate it into German.*

Rosa Parks lived in Detroit until she died at the age of ninety-two on October 24, 2005, in her apartment on the east side of the city. City officials in Montgomery and Detroit announced on October 27, 2005, that the front seats of their buses would be reserved in honor of Parks until her funeral on November 2, 2005. Parks' coffin was flown to Montgomery and taken by horses to the St. Paul African Methodist Episcopal (AME) church. Secretary of State Condoleezza Rice said that without Rosa Parks, she would probably never have become the Secretary of State.

funeral – *Beerdigung;* city officials – *kommunale Behörden;* announce – *ankündigen;* front seat – *Vordersitz;* reserve – *reservieren;* coffin – *Sarg*

Unit 7

Language

62	**at last**	endlich
	refuse	sich weigern
	segregation	Rassentrennung
	support	Unterstützung
	boycott	boykottieren
	leaflet	Flugblatt
	clever	klug
	respected	respektiert
	boycott	Boykott
	lift	Mitfahrgelegenheit
	desegregate	die Rassentrennung aufheben
	detail	Detail, Einzelheit
63	**civil-rights movement**	Bürgerrechtsbewegung
	march	Marsch
	speech	Rede
	former	ehemalige, ehemaliger, ehemaliges
	slave	Sklave
	slave owner	Sklavenhalter
	cheer	jubeln
	join hands	sich an den Händen fassen
	God Almighty	Allmächtiger Gott
	Congress	der Kongress
	pass	(Gesetz) verabschieden
	racial	Rassen-
	discrimination	Diskriminierung
	illegal	illegal
	negro	Neger, Negerin
	engage	sich beteiligen
	creative	kreativ
	battle	Schlacht, Kampf
	injustice	Ungerechtigkeit
	balcony	Balkon

Workshop

64	**surprising**	überraschend
	shocking	schockierend
	disappoint	enttäuschen
	embarrassing	peinlich
65	**comparison**	Vergleich
	frozen	gefroren, tiefgekühlt
	meter (AE)	Meter
	liter (AE)	Liter
	taboo	Tabu
	colored (AE)	farbig
	nigger	Nigger
	Afro-/African-American	Afro-Amerikaner, Afro-Amerikanerin

Checklist

Ich kann	
... erklären, warum jemand etwas getan hat.	Feeling tired after a long day's work, she sat down at the front of the bus.
... persönliche Zusammenhänge erklären.	He was too new to have made any enemies.
... sagen, wenn ich mir einer Sache sicher bin.	I'm sure the bus boycott will work.
... ausdrücken, dass etwas Erfolg hatte.	King's ideas and hard work made a difference.
... Enttäuschung ausdrücken.	I'm disappointed that you can't come with me.
... Überraschung ausdrücken.	I'm surprised about the good result.

Holidays

Picture-based task

In diesem Teil der mündlichen Prüfung erhältst du Bildmaterial, zu dem du sprechen sollst. Im Gespräch mit dem Prüfer – bei einer Zweier-Prüfung mit einem Partner – sollst du Bilder beschreiben, Informationen dazu geben, Stellung nehmen und abschließend deine Meinung äußern.

1 General lead-in tasks

You've won a one-week holiday in a competition.

a) *Choose between the offers in the pictures. Give reasons for your choice.*
b) *Talk to your parents about the holiday. Give reasons why you are old enough to go on holiday alone.*

2 Follow-up questions

a) *Talk about what you think is positive and negative in the pictures.*
b) *Tell us why you think people spend a lot of money on their holidays.*
c) What was your best holiday? What was your worst holiday? *Give reasons.*

3 Holiday situations

Situation 1:
You are on a camping holiday. Unfortunately it's been raining every day for the last four days.

Situation 2:
You are on a beach holiday. Unfortunately the sand is so hot you can't walk over it and the sea is like a hot bath.

How can you make the best of these situations?

4 Closing remark

Which of the pictures would you mail to a friend or use as a screen saver?
Give reasons for your answer.

Fashion and lifestyle

5 General lead-in task

Look at the pictures. Choose two pictures you want to talk about.
Work in pairs and make dialogues.

A: I have chosen pictures one and three. In picture 1 I can see … .
B: Can you describe the persons?
A: Well, the boy … . He has … . He's wearing … .
B: The persons in picture 3 look … . The girl's hairstyle is … .
Her boyfriend is … .

6 Follow-up questions

a) You're going to have a party. Which of the persons would you invite? *Give reasons.*
b) Imagine you liked someone who looks totally different from you. Would you go out with him or her? Would you try to change his or her clothes?
c) What do you know about punk culture? Think about music, clothes, hairstyle, …
d) In which of these two situations would you feel more comfortable – at a party for rich people or in the street among a group of punks?

7 Lifestyle situations

a) It's stylish to have a tattoo or a piercing. What do you think about this trend? Will you still feel the same about it in 20 years? What would your parents say if you came home with a lip-piercing, a belly-piercing or a tattoo?
b) Think about punk, hippie, emo, gothic lifestyles. Is there one you like even if your lifestyle is different? What do you like about it?
c) Most models are very slim. What do you think about that? Would you go on a diet to look good in the latest fashion trends?

8 Closing remark

Look at the pictures again. Who would you give your mobile number to?

Topic-based task

Du hast in diesem Schuljahr zahlreiche Themenbereiche kennen gelernt. Bereite zwei davon für den ersten Teil der mündlichen Prüfung vor. Im *Opening Talk* wird dich der Prüfer danach fragen.

Bereich	**Thema**
Stars/Famous people (Units 1, 2, 4, 7)	Avril Lavigne/Orlando Bloom/Robbie Williams Serena and Venus Williams/Ellen MacArthur Johnny Depp/Whoopi Goldberg Helen Clark/Hillary Clinton Martin Luther King/Rosa Parks
India (Unit 3)	Culture and economy New Delhi – capital of India Bollywood – film industry in India
Ireland (Unit 5)	History and religious conflict Tourism and sights Music and sports
Our changing planet (Unit 6)	Rising sea levels/Wildlife and plants Natural disasters/Tropical rain forest

Du musst natürlich nicht alle Unterthemen zu einem Gebiet vorbereiten.

a) Nenne zuerst deine Bereiche und ziehe dann dazu eine Karte. Danach hast du Zeit, dich mit dem genauen Thema vertraut zu machen.

b) Beginne nun, über die Themen zu sprechen. Es wird erwartet, dass du ca. 20 bis 25 Sätze frei sprichst. Aber keine Angst. Wenn du ins Stocken gerätst, wird der Prüfer dir einige *follow-up questions* stellen. So hilft er dir weiter und du kannst darauf reagieren.

Beispiele für Karten:

Martin Luther King

Headline in a newspaper

"Free at last! Free at last! Thank God Almighty, we are free at last!"

Martin Luther King

Speech at the Lincoln Memorial in August 1963

"I have a dream that one day on the red hills of Georgia, the sons of former slaves and the sons of former slave owners will be able to sit down together at the same table."

Rosa Parks

Leaflet in Montgomery, Alabama, in December 1955

"Don't ride the buses to work, to town or to school on Monday, December 5."

Rosa Parks

Questions

- What do you remember about Rosa Parks and the American civil-rights movement?
- What do you think about black people's fight for racial equality?

Beispiele für einen möglichen *report*:

In December 1955 a group of black people in Montgomery, Alabama, handed out some leaflets. They didn't want people to use the buses on Monday, December 5. In a film about the civil-rights movement in the USA we saw a black woman named Rosa Parks on a bus in Montgomery. She was on her way home after work and I think she was very tired. So she sat down on a seat reserved for white people. The bus conductor told her to sit on a seat for black people in the back of the bus. But Rosa Parks refused. Then the bus driver called the police. When the police arrived, Rosa was arrested because she had broken the segregation law.

At that time black people in the USA had fewer rights than white people. They weren't allowed to use the same schools, swimming pools or restaurants as the Whites. They didn't earn the same money for the same work. This was the result of slavery. Many black people hated this situation, but they had no chance to change anything.

After Rosa Parks had been arrested, the Blacks started a boycott. They asked Martin Luther King to become their leader. He accepted and became the leader of the black civil-rights movement in the USA. The boycott lasted for 382 days. After that both Whites and Blacks could use all seats in all buses.

I am sure Rosa Parks' action was important for racial justice in the USA. I think she was a brave woman. Many people have probably forgotten Rosa Parks, who died at the age of 92 in 2005. Her courage helped the Blacks to end racial discrimination in the USA. I hope people will never forget her.

Sierra Wave

a Joe's home was high up on a hill. They sat outside and looked out over Echo Park. Steve liked Echo Park because here everything he enjoyed about Los Angeles was more extreme. The hills were steeper, the houses older, more mysterious.
At night the streets still belonged to the gangs. They talked for a while, about sports. Steve had been a big swimmer in college but he hadn't talked to anyone about it for a long time. He missed sports.
"Let me show you something," Joe said. "I think you'll be interested."

b Steve followed him into the garage. Hanging from the roof was a hang-glider.
"This is what I'm into now," Joe said. Then Joe told him about hang-gliding up north, in the Sierras – not just floating a hundred feet above the beach, but standing on the top of a mountain and catching the Sierra Wave, a thermal that could take you up to fourteen thousand feet, or higher, so high you had to carry an oxygen bottle. He showed Steve a picture he'd taken of himself, hanging in his harness and grinning, the tops of the mountains far below.
The moment Steve saw that picture, he knew he had to learn.

c Joe gave Steve lessons on the beach near Palos Verdes for three months during the summer vacation. In June, Joe started talking about taking a trip up north, to the Owens Valley, so Steve could do some real gliding. They drove north in Joe's pickup until the Sierras rose up on their left.
They spent that night in a campground outside of Bishop. The wind woke Steve just before morning. He looked out at the mountains. He felt this was the day they had been waiting for.
As they drove up the dirt road to the top of Gunter Peak, Joe said it was going to be a hot day, a good day for soaring.

d The top of the mountain was a dry world of rock and bright sunlight. Steve walked around and stopped to watch a kid who was putting his glider together.
"How you doing?" the kid asked him.
"Fine," Steve said. "Going to catch one of those big thermals today."
"You'd better be careful of those thermals. They're nothing to play around with."

e "Maybe you'd better not try for a thermal yet," Joe said. "Just take a short hop. It's up to you."
"All right," Steve said.
"Then you won't need the oxygen bottle. Do you want the parachute?"
"No, I won't need the parachute either."
Steve hooked in to the glider. He felt warm air on his face. Then he ran forward until it caught the glider, and lifted off into the air.

f The sunlight was blinding. The mountain fell away. A mile ahead, he could see several gliders, and flew towards them. It was a thermal.

He knew it the moment he felt the strong upward push. He forgot everything and he gave himself to it completely.
Slowly the other gliders dropped out. Then there was only a bird, perhaps an eagle, and together they spiraled for thousands of feet, straight up into the sun.

g When the cold began to bite, even through his jacket, Steve pulled the control bar back towards him. But the glider did not respond. The thermal was too strong.
He tried everything, but the glider went higher and higher. Then he did what he had been afraid to do until now.

He looked down. Thousands of square miles lay below him, like a map. He was higher than the highest mountains now. Looking south, he saw Mount Whitney. He could follow the highway back down through the valley.
He could see all the way to China Lake.

h But something was wrong.
He had flown so high he was suffering from lack of oxygen.
He was losing consciousness. But he could see so far, and so much, that he felt a joy stronger than any he had ever known. Hanging in the sun, he felt tears running down his face, and knew only that he was floating, he was flying.

by William Hauptman (adapted)

1 Look at a map

Look at a map of the USA. Collect information about the geography and climate from the text. Where do you think the story happened?

2 Questions about the story

Answer these questions in your exercise book.

1. How did Steve first find out about hang-gliding?
2. Why did Steve want to learn to hang-glide?
3. What was the weather like when they went to the Sierras?
4. Why did Joe suggest that Steve shouldn't try for a thermal? Give two reasons.
5. How did Steve get caught in the thermal?
6. What happens to Steve at the end of the story?

3 Dangers and joys!

In 'Sierra Wave' we learn something about the dangers and joys of hang-gliding. You should be very careful if you do sports like these.

Put the information from the text under the right heading.

- see so far / see so much
- floating / flying
- suffering / lack of oxygen
- losing consciousness
- something wrong
- thermal too strong
- mountains far below
- cold even through jacket
- no control of glider
- hanging in the sun
- strong upward push
- alone with a bird

I like this poem because ...

The Man Who Invented Football

by Kit Wright

The man who invented football,
He must have been dead clever,
He hadn't even a football shirt
Or any clothes whatever.

The man who invented soccer,
He hadn't even a ball
Or boots, but only his horny feet
And a bison's skull, that's all.

The man who invented football,
To whom our hats we doff,
Had only the sun for a yellow card
And death to send him off.

The cave-mouth was the goal-mouth,
The wind was the referee,
When the man who did it did it
In 30,000 BC!

For Word

by Benjamin Zephaniah

Thank you for the *words* I read
Thank you for the words I need
Thank you for the **WORDS** so great
Thanks for *words* that raise debate,
Thanks for the **words** on my bookshelf
Thanx for the **words** I make myself
Thank you for words that make me cry
And words that leave me feeling dry.

Thanks for WORDS that do inspire
And those words that burn like fire
Thanks for all the *words* I note
Thank you for all the words I quote,
I thank you for the words like me
Thanks for WORDS that set me free
And I thank you for ***words*** like you
I always need a word or two.

Thanks for words that make things plain
And **words** that help me to explain
Thanks for words that make life fun
And words that help me overcome,
Thanks for words that make me rap
Thanks for **words** that make me clap
Thanks for *words* that make me smile
Thanks for *words* with grace and style.

Thanks for all those **words** that sing
Thanks for **words** are everything
Thanks for all the words like this
And little sloppy words like kiss,
Thanks for words like hip-hooray
And those cool words I like to say
Thanks for ***words*** that reach and touch
Thank you very, very much.

The Want-Want Twins

by Jackie Kay

We are the Want-Want Twins.
We go from shop to shop.
We are the Want-Want Twins.
We don't know how to stop.
One day it's a bow and arrow.
Another it's a dinosaur.
What are we going to get tomorrow?
More. More. More.

We are the Want-Want Twins.
Our eyes sharp shiny pins.
Our hands quick shark's fins.
We go from shop to shop.
One day it's the game Frustration.
We don't know what we need.
Another it is compensation.
Greed. Greed. Greed.

We are the Want-Want Twins.
We're completely over the top.
We are the Want-Want Twins.
We don't know how to stop.
We send our parents every night
A list that goes like this:
2 new bikes. Don't be tight.
X.X.X.

We are the Want-Want Twins.
Money grows on trees.
We are the Want-Want Twins.
We are the bee's knees.
All we want is everything.
We don't know how to stop.
We will be the Want-Want Twins till we
drop
drop
drop.

1 Three poems

Read these three poems. Do not worry if you do not know all the words. Just try to understand what the three authors (Wright, Zephaniah and Kay) are trying to say.

2 Your ideas

Decide which poem you like best and say why. Write three or four sentences. The words below can help you.

sounds nice
makes me happy/laugh
funny
describes life today
because I like football
see pictures in my head

1 A company's website

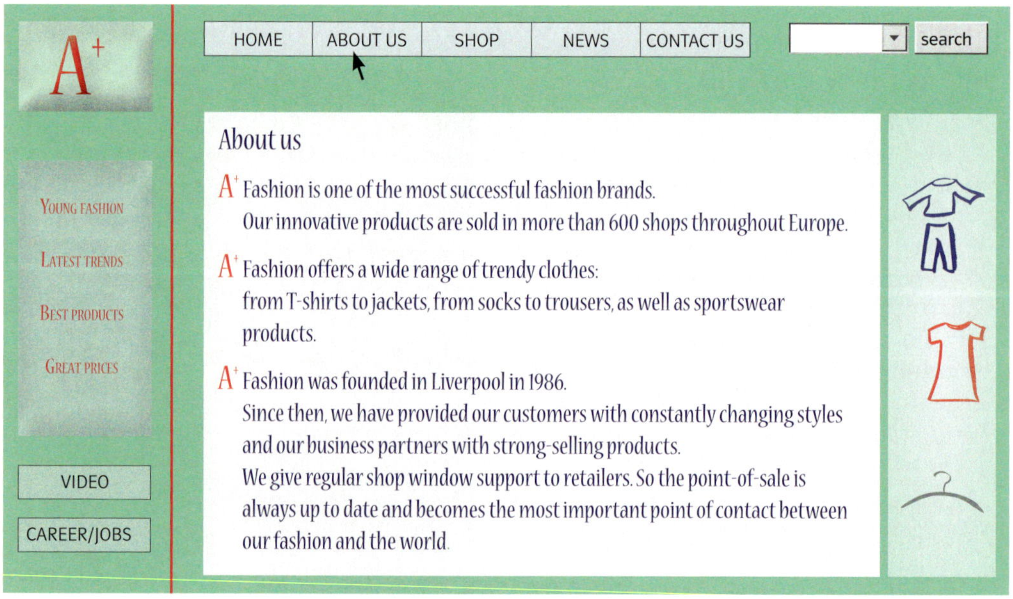

a) *Answer the questions.*

1. Where was the company founded?
2. What products are made?
3. What is special about the company?
4. What kind of jobs does A+ Fashion offer? What do you think?

b) Why is it a good idea to know something about the company?
Find reasons and discuss them in class.

2 Presenting a company

Is there a company you would like to work for? *Look at the company's website and make a short presentation about the company.*

location   staff   sector   products   slogan   history

3 Skills

Here are some skills which are important to companies.

a) *What do they mean in German? You can use a dictionary.*

b) *Find the adjective for each noun.*

talent   flexibility   experience
reliability   creativity   friendliness
enthusiasm   punctuality   honesty

4 Tips

You have an interview for a job. Your friend gives you some tips.
More than one answer is possible. *Make sentences.*

Make sure you	go to bed early the night before.
Don't forget to	go to the hairdresser's.
Remember to	put on clean clothes.
Just be	wear a short top or mini-skirt.
Don't just	have a look at the company's website before the interview.
You shouldn't	get there on time.
	yourself!
	answer 'yes' or 'no'.

5 Questions for the interview

a) Here are some questions which the interviewer may ask.
Read the questions. What would you answer? Make notes.

1. What are your hobbies?
2. Why do you want to work for us?
3. Why do you think you would enjoy this job?
4. Do you have any questions about the company?
5. What are your strengths and weaknesses?

b) During an interview you can also ask questions.

Will I have the chance of making more money? Will I … ?

chance of	make more money
opportunity of	meet new people
	do other projects
	…

c) *Ask more questions about the job.*

- what kind of work
- pay
- working hours
- holidays
- training
- colleagues

6 The interview

Work with a partner. One of you is the interviewer and the other one is the applicant.
Use the questions from exercise 5 and the phrases in the box.

I'm interested in …
I'd like/enjoy this job because …
I know a lot about …
I'm good at …
I don't like …
One question I have is …

Grammar words

adjective *Eigenschaftswort*	It was a **terrific** day.
adverb *Adverb*	They dance **wildly**.
article *Artikel*	the, a
cardinal numbers *Kardinalzahlen*	one, two, three, …
comparison *Vergleich*	Tom is **faster than** Susie.
comparative *Steigerung*	This building is **taller**.
future *Zukunft*	It**'ll be** sunny tomorrow.
genitive *Genitiv*	Ben is Carol**'s** brother.
-ing form *-ing-Form*	**Making** a video is much fun.
if-clause *Bedingungssatz*	**If** it's cold, we'll need our jackets.
irregular verb *unregelmäßiges Verb*	buy – **bought** – **bought**
modal *Modalverb*	can, have to, should, must, need, could, mustn't, …
negative sentence *Verneinung*	I **don't** like kiwis.
noun *Hauptwort*	house, bag, winter
object pronoun *Objektpronomen*	They always help **us**.
order *Aufforderung, Verbot*	**Open** the door!
ordinals *Ordnungszahlen*	first, second, third, …
passive *Passiv*	Houses **were built** out of wood.
past perfect *Vorvergangenheit*	After they **had released** him, he became president.
past progressive *Verlaufsform in der Vergangenheit*	They **were having** breakfast.
personal pronoun *persönliches Fürwort*	Where's Lester? **He**'s in the park.
phrasal verb *Verb + Präposition*	Why do you **put up with** that?
plural *Mehrzahl*	two books, ten **sheep**
possessive pronoun *besitzanzeigendes Fürwort*	**my** book, **his** computer, **her** dog
preposition *Präposition, Verhältniswort*	in, on, under, …
present perfect simple *Perfekt*	I**'ve** just **surfed** the internet.
present perfect progressive *Verlaufsform im Perfekt*	It **has been raining** for three hours!
present progressive *Verlaufsform in der Gegenwart*	He**'s talking** to Lester.
question *Frage*	Where are my CDs?
question tag *Bestätigungsfrage*	**You're** in a band, **aren't you**?
question word *Fragewort*	what, where, who, …
reflexive pronoun *Reflexivpronomen*	I did it **myself**. We drove there **ourselves**.
regular verb *regelmäßiges Verb*	walk – walk**ed**
relative clause *Relativsatz*	The car **which my father bought three weeks ago** was very expensive. The guy **who we saw** told me about it.
reported speech *indirekte Rede*	He said that he went home happy.
sentence *Satz*	Your CDs are in your bag.
short answer *Kurzantwort*	Are you happy? – **Yes, I am.**
short form *Kurzform*	I'm, you're, he's, …
simple past *einfache Vergangenheit*	They **went** to the bus stop.
simple present *einfache Gegenwart*	We always **meet** after school.
singular *Einzahl*	one book
statement *Aussagesatz*	It's hot today.
superlative *Superlativ*	Mrs Blake is **the best** teacher.
verb *Verb, Zeitwort*	come, ask, be, have, …
word order *Wortstellung*	Peter *(S)* enters *(V)* the house *(O)*.

Englische Laute *(English sounds)*

Selbstlaute (Vowels)

[ɑ:] car, father; ähnlich wie in *Bahn*
[ʌ] number, cut, mother; ähnlich wie in *Dach*
[e] yes, pen, friend; ähnlich wie in *nett*
[ə] a book, a pen; ähnlich wie der Endlaut in *bitte*
[3:] girl, her; ähnlich wie in *mögen*
[æ] bag, map, that; ähnlich wie in spät
[ɪ] it, list, six; ähnlich wie in *Kind*
[i:] she, see, please; ähnlich wie in *tief*
[i] funny, History, Australian
[ɒ] on, dog, what; ähnlich wie in *Kopf*
[ɔ:] morning, horse, four; ähnlich wie in *Horn*, aber lang
[ʊ] foot, look; ähnlich wie in *Schutt*
[u:] you, two, blue; ähnlich wie in *du*

Doppellaute (Diphthongs)

[aɪ] biro, five, my; ähnlich wie in *kein*
[aʊ] pound, now; ähnlich wie in *Frau*
[eə] there, chair, their
[eɪ] name, say, table
[ɪə] here, hear
[ɔɪ] boy; ähnlich wie in *Heu*
[əʊ] go, know, road
[ʊə] tourist

Mitlaute (Consonants)

[j] yes, you; wie das deutsche j in *ja*
[l] let's, blue; school, twelve
[ŋ] morning, song; wie in *singen*, kein [g] sprechen!
[ŋg] English, single; wie in [ŋ], jedoch mit nachfolgendem [g]
[r] ruler, red, road
[s] see, sister; stimmloses, d. h. hartes s wie in *reißen*
[z] is, dogs, cars, stimmhaftes, d. h. weiches s wie in *brausen*
[ʒ] television; wie in *Jalousie* und *Gelee*
[dʒ] Germany, jeans; wie in *Dschungel*
[ʃ] she, station; wie in *Tisch*
[tʃ] child, teacher; wie in *deutsch*
[ð] the, this, mother; stimmhafter, d. h. weicher Lispellaut
[θ] thank you, Thursday; stimmloser, d. h. harter Lispellaut
[v] volleyball, video, of; wie in *Wasser*
[w] one, what, sandwich

[:] bedeutet, dass der vorangehende Laut lang ist, z. B. you [ju:]
['] bedeutet, dass die folgende Silbe betont ist, z. B. hello [hə'ləʊ]

Das englische Alphabet *(The English alphabet)*

a	[eɪ]	b	[bi:]	c	[si:]	d	[di:]	e	[i:]	f	[ef]	g	[dʒi:]
h	[eɪtʃ]	i	[aɪ]	j	[dʒeɪ]	k	[keɪ]	l	[el]	m	[em]	n	[en]
o	[əʊ]	p	[pi:]	q	[kju:]	r	[ɑ:]	s	[es]	t	[ti:]	u	[ju:]
v	[vi:]	w	['dʌblju:]	x	[eks]	y	[waɪ]	z	[zed]				

Numbers

Cardinal numbers

1 = one	10 = ten	20 = twenty	30 = thirty
2 = two	11 = eleven	21 = twenty-one	40 = forty
3 = three	12 = twelve	22 = twenty-two	50 = fifty
4 = four	13 = thirteen	23 = twenty-three	60 = sixty
5 = five	14 = fourteen	24 = twenty-four	70 = seventy
6 = six	15 = fifteen	25 = twenty-five	80 = eighty
7 = seven	16 = sixteen	26 = twenty-six	90 = ninety
8 = eight	17 = seventeen	27 = twenty-seven	100 = one hundred
9 = nine	18 = eighteen	28 = twenty-eight	200 = two hundred
	19 = nineteen	29 = twenty-nine	1,000 = one thousand

Ordinal numbers

1st	first	11th	eleventh	21st	twenty-first
2nd	second	12th	twelfth	22nd	twenty-second
3rd	third	13th	thirteenth	23rd	twenty-third
4th	fourth	14th	fourteenth	24th	twenty-fourth
5th	fifth	15th	fifteenth	…	
6th	sixth	16th	sixteenth		
7th	seventh	17th	seventeenth	30th	thirtieth
8th	eighth	18th	eighteenth	…	
9th	ninth	19th	nineteenth		
10th	tenth	20th	twentieth	100th	(one) hundredth

- *first, second* und *third* sind unregelmäßige Formen.
  Sie enden nicht wie die anderen Ordnungszahlen auf *-th.*
- Beispiele: das dritte Mal = *the third time,* der 80. Geburtstag = *the eightieth birthday*

The year

1998 kann eine normale Zahl *(number)* oder eine Jahreszahl *(year)* sein. Man sagt:
1,998: one thousand nine hundred and ninety-eight *(number)*
1998: nineteen ninety-eight *(year)*

Ab 2000 werden normale Zahlen und Jahreszahlen gleich gesprochen:
2000 = two thousand
2001 = two thousand and one
2002 = two thousand and two

Man schreibt die Zahlen aber unterschiedlich:
– 2,012 *(number)*
– 2012 *(year)*

The date

Schreibung und Aussprache des Datums unterscheiden sich:

- Man schreibt in Großbritannien: *9th June*
  in den USA: *June 9th*
- Man spricht in Großbritannien: *the ninth of June*
  in den USA: *June (the) ninth*

The time

quarter = (ein) Viertel   *half* = halb

- Bei Zeitangaben verwendet man für die ersten 30 Minuten nach der vollen Stunde *past*, z. B.:

7:05 *five past seven* (oder *seven oh five*)	7:15 *quarter past seven* (oder *seven fifteen*)	7:30 *half past seven* (oder *seven thirty*)

Nach *half past* zählt man zur nächsten Stunde hin:

7:40 *twenty to eight* (oder *seven forty*)	7:45 *quarter to eight* (oder *seven forty-five*)	7:55 *five to eight* (oder *seven fifty-five*)

- Bei vollen Stunden benutzt man *o'clock*, z. B. *8 o'clock, 10 o'clock*
- *am* bedeutet *in the morning*
- *pm* bedeutet *in the afternoon* bzw. *in the evening*

Decimal numbers

Bei Zahlen mit Stellen hinter dem Komma benutzt man im Englischen einen Punkt, z. B.:

12.42 *twelve point four two*   16.8 *sixteen point eight*

Zero (oh, nil)

Für die Zahl Null gibt es im Englischen verschiedene Ausdrücke. Man sagt:

zero	beim Zählen: 0, 1, 2, … *(zero, one, two, …)* oder bei Temperaturangaben: 0° *(zero degrees)*
oh	beim Telefonieren *(My number is 82044. = eight two oh double four)* oder bei Jahreszahlen *(1905 = nineteen oh five)* oder bei der Uhrzeit *(7:05 = seven oh five)*
nil	bei Fußballergebnissen: *We won 1:0. (= one nil)*
love	beim Tennis *(15:0 = fifteen love)*

List of irregular verbs

Grundform (Infinitive)		**Vergangenheit** (past tense)		**Perfekt** (past participle)		
be	[bi:]	was, were	[wɒz, wɜ:]	been	[bɪn]	*sein*
become	[bɪ'kʌm]	became	[bɪ'keɪm]	become	[bɪ'kʌm]	*werden*
begin	[bɪ'gɪn]	began	[bɪ'gæn]	begun	[bɪ'gʌn]	*beginnen, anfangen*
break	[breɪk]	broke	[brəʊk]	broken	['brəʊkn]	*(zer-)brechen*
bring	[brɪŋ]	brought	[brɔ:t]	brought	[brɔ:t]	*bringen*
build	[bɪld]	built	[bɪlt]	built	[bɪlt]	*bauen*
buy	[baɪ]	bought	[bɔ:t]	bought	[bɔ:t]	*kaufen*
catch	[kætʃ]	caught	[kɔ:t]	caught	[kɔ:t]	*fangen*
choose	[tʃu:z]	chose	[tʃəʊz]	chosen	[tʃəʊzn]	*(aus-)wählen*
come	[kʌm]	came	[keɪm]	come	[kʌm]	*kommen*
cut	[kʌt]	cut	[kʌt]	cut	[kʌt]	*schneiden*
deal	[di:l]	dealt	[delt]	dealt	[delt]	*geben, verteilen*
do	[du:]	did	[dɪd]	done	[dʌn]	*machen, tun*
draw	[drɔ:]	drew	[dru:]	drawn	[drɔ:n]	*zeichnen*
drink	[drɪŋk]	drank	[dræŋk]	drunk	[drʌŋk]	*trinken*
drive	[draɪv]	drove	[drəʊv]	driven	[drɪvn]	*fahren*
eat	[i:t]	ate	[eɪt]	eaten	[i:tn]	*essen, fressen*
fall	[fɔ:l]	fell	[fel]	fallen	[fɔ:ln]	*fallen*
feed	[fi:d]	fed	[fed]	fed	[fed]	*füttern*
feel	[fi:l]	felt	[felt]	felt	[felt]	*fühlen*
fight	[faɪt]	fought	[fɔ:t]	fought	[fɔ:t]	*kämpfen*
find	[faɪnd]	found	[faʊnd]	found	[faʊnd]	*finden*
fly	[flaɪ]	flew	[flu:]	flown	[fləʊn]	*fliegen*
forget	[fə'get]	forgot	[fə'gɒt]	forgotten	[fə'gɒtn]	*vergessen*
get	[get]	got	[gɒt]	gotten	['gɒtn]	*bekommen, werden*
give	[gɪv]	gave	[geɪv]	given	[gɪvn]	*geben*
go	[gəʊ]	went	[went]	gone	[gɒn]	*gehen, fahren*
grow	[greʊ]	grew	[gru:]	grown	[grəʊn]	*wachsen*
have	[hæv]	had	[hæd]	had	[hæd]	*haben*
hear	[hɪə]	heard	[hɜ:d]	heard	[hɜ:d]	*hören*
hide	[haɪd]	hid	[hɪd]	hid	[hɪd]	*sich verstecken*
hit	[hɪt]	hit	[hɪt]	hit	[hɪt]	*schlagen*
hold	[həʊld]	held	[held]	held	[held]	*halten*
hurt	[hɜ:t]	hurt	[hɜ:t]	hurt	[hɜ:t]	*(sich) verletzen*
keep	[ki:p]	kept	[kept]	kept	[kept]	*behalten*
know	[nəʊ]	knew	[nu:]	known	[nəʊn]	*wissen*
lead	[li:d]	led	[led]	led	[led]	*führen*
leave	[li:v]	left	[left]	left	[left]	*verlassen*
lie	[laɪ]	lay	[leɪ]	lain	[leɪn]	*liegen*
light	[laɪt]	lit	[lɪt]	lit	[lɪt]	*anzünden*
lose	[lu:z]	lost	[lɒst]	lost	[lɒst]	*verlieren*
make	[meɪk]	made	[meɪd]	made	[meɪd]	*machen*
meet	[mi:t]	met	[met]	met	[met]	*treffen*
pay	[peɪ]	paid	[peɪd]	paid	[peɪd]	*bezahlen*
put	[pʊt]	put	[pʊt]	put	[pʊt]	*setzen, stellen, legen*
read	[ri:d]	read	[red]	read	[red]	*lesen*

Grundform (Infinitive)		Vergangenheit (past tense)		Perfekt (past participle)		
ride	[raɪd]	rode	[rəʊd]	ridden	[rɪdn]	*reiten, fahren*
rise	[raɪz]	rose	[rəʊz]	risen	[rɪzn]	*aufgehen (Sonne)*
run	[rʌn]	ran	[ræn]	run	[rʌn]	*rennen*
say	[seɪ]	said	[sed]	said	[sed]	*sagen*
see	[si:]	saw	[sɔ:]	seen	[si:n]	*sehen*
sell	[sel]	sold	[səʊld]	sold	[səʊld]	*verkaufen*
send	[send]	sent	[sent]	sent	[sent]	*schicken*
shake	[ʃeɪk]	shook	[ʃʊk]	shaken	['ʃeɪkn]	*schütteln*
shoot	[ʃu:t]	shot	[ʃɒt]	shot	[ʃɒt]	*schießen*
sing	[sɪŋ]	sang	[sæŋ]	sung	[sʌŋ]	*singen*
sink	[sɪŋk]	sank	[sæŋk]	sunk	[sʌŋk]	*(ein-)sinken*
sit	[sɪt]	sat	[sæt]	sat	[sæt]	*sitzen*
sleep	[sli:p]	slept	[slept]	slept	[slept]	*schlafen*
speak	[spi:k]	spoke	[spəʊk]	spoken	[spəʊkn]	*sprechen*
spend	[spend]	spent	[spent]	spent	[spent]	*verbringen*
stand	[stænd]	stood	[stʊd]	stood	[stʊd]	*stehen*
steal	[sti:l]	stole	[stəʊl]	stolen	['stəʊln]	*stehlen*
strike	[straɪk]	struck	[strʌk]	struck	[strʌk]	*einschlagen*
take	[teɪk]	took	[tʊk]	taken	['teɪkn]	*nehmen*
teach	[ti:tʃ]	taught	[tɔ:t]	taught	[tɔ:t]	*unterrichten*
tell	[tel]	told	[təʊld]	told	[təʊld]	*sagen, erzählen*
think	[θɪŋk]	thought	[θɔ:t]	thought	[θɔ:t]	*denken*
throw	[θrəʊ]	threw	[θru:]	thrown	[θrəʊn]	*werfen*
wear	[weə]	wore	[wɔ:]	worn	[wɔ:n]	*tragen (Kleidung)*
win	[wɪn]	won	[wʌn]	won	[wʌn]	*gewinnen*
write	[raɪt]	wrote	[rəʊt]	written	[rɪtn]	*schreiben*

In der alphabetischen Wortliste findest du das Vokabular von *Let's go*. Namen von Menschen und Orten sind am Ende des Vokabulars gesammelt.
Wendungen, die aus mehreren Wörtern bestehen, werden unter mehreren Stichworten aufgeführt. So findest du *all day* zum Beispiel unter *all* und *day*.
Die Zahlen hinter den Wörtern sagen dir, wo das Wort zum ersten Mal vorkommt:
apple I 2 33 = Band I, Unit 2, Seite 33
Wörter mit einem Kreis musst du zwar verstehen, aber nicht anwenden:
°**arrow**

A

a [ə] ein/eine **I 1** 11
a bit [ə 'bɪt] ein wenig **V 4** 46
a day [ə 'deɪ] pro Tag **II 1** 9
a few [ə 'fjuː] ein paar **II 3** 44
a little [ə 'lɪtl] etwas **II 3** 45
a lot [ə 'lɒt] viel **II 3** 48
a lot of [ə 'lɒt əv] viele **I 4** 66
a pair of … [ə 'peər əv] ein Paar … **II 3** 44
be able to [biː 'eɪbl tə] können, in der Lage sein **III 4** 51
aboard [ə'bɔːd] an Bord **III 7** 90
°**Aboriginal** [æbə'rɪdʒənəl] den Ureinwohnern Australiens zugehörig **V 2** ER
about [ə'baʊt] über **I 4** 68; etwa °**III 6** 79
above [ə'bʌv] über, oberhalb **III 5** 65
above all [ə'bʌv 'ɔːl] vor allem **VI 2** 15
abroad ['əbrɔːd] im Ausland **V 1** 8
absolutely [æbsə'luːtli] absolut, total **V 6** 72
accept [ək'sept] akzeptieren **IV 2** 25
accident ['æksɪdnt] Unfall **II 4** 54
account [ə'kaʊnt] Konto **III 5** 62
acid rain ['æsɪd reɪn] saurer Regen **VI 6** 51
across [ə'krɒs] über, hinüber **II 4** 54
°**act** [ækt] (schau-)spielen **I 2** 40
act like ['ækt laɪk] sich benehmen wie **III ER** 31
action ['ækʃn] Aktion **IV 4** 50
active ['æktɪv] aktiv **VI 4** 34
activity [æk'tɪvəti] Beschäftigung, Aktivität **I 1** 20
activity centre [æk'tɪvəti sentə] Freizeitzentrum **I 1** 22
actor/actress ['æktə 'æktrəs] Schauspielerin, Schauspieler **III 7** 86
°**adapter** [ə'dæptə] Adapter **II 7** 112
add [æd] hinzufügen **II 1** 12
addicted [ə'dɪktɪd] süchtig **V 6** 70
addiction [ə'dɪkʃn] Sucht **V 6** 70
address [ə'dres] Adresse **II 7** 106
admirer [əd'maɪərə] Verehrerin, Verehrer **IV 1** 8
adult ['ædʌlt] Erwachsener **V 6** ER
adventure [əd'ventʃə] Abenteuer **II 5** 72
advert ['ædvɜːt] Anzeige **V 4** 44
advertise ['ædvətaɪz] Reklame machen **IV 5** 61
advertising poster ['ædvətaɪzɪŋ 'pəʊstə] Werbeplakat **IV 7** 90
advertisement [əd'vɜːtɪsmənt] Anzeige **V 3** 36
°**advice** [əd'vaɪs] Ratschlag **V 6** 69
adviser [əd'vaɪzə] Beraterin, Berater **V 4** ER
aerobics [eə'rəʊbɪks] Aerobic **I 5** 84
affect [ə'fekt] sich auswirken auf, beeinflussen **VI 6** 53
afford [ə'fɔːd] sich leisten **III 6** 77
be afraid of [biː ə'freɪd əv] Angst haben vor **II 5** 76
African ['æfrɪkən] Afrikaner, Afrikanerin **IV 6** 79
Afro-/ African-American [æfrəʊ-/ 'æfrɪkən -ə'merɪkən] Afro-Amerikanerin, Afro-Amerikaner **VI 7** 65
after ['ɑːftə] nach **II 1** 9; nachdem **VI 1** 8
after all ['ɑːftə ɔːl] schließlich **VI 2** 15
afternoon [ɑːftə'nuːn] Nachmittag **II 1** 9
again [ə'gen] wieder **I 6** 104
against [ə'genst] gegen **II 1** 12
be against [biː ə'genst] gegen etwas sein **V 2** 19
age [eɪdʒ] Alter **III 6** 76
agent ['eɪdʒnt] Agent, Manager **III 2** 24
°estate agent [ɪ'steɪt 'eɪdʒnt] Immobilienmaklerin, Immobilienmakler **V 4** 44
aggressive [ə'gresɪv] aggressiv **VI 3** 26
… years ago [jɪəz ə'gəʊ] vor … Jahren **II 3** 46
agricultural [ægrɪ'kʌltʃərəl] landwirtschaftlich **VI 5** 44
aid [eɪd] Hilfe **V 4** 43
AIDS [eɪdz] Aids **V 3** 36
air [eə] Luft **V 7** 88
air-conditioning system [eə kən'dɪʃnɪŋ 'sɪstəm] Klimaanlage **III 7** 91
airport ['eəpɔːt] Flughafen **III 5** 66
°**alarm system** [ə'lɑːm 'sɪstəm] Alarmanlage **IV 5** 66
°**album** ['ælbəm] Album **I 4** 70
alcohol ['ælkəhɒl] Alkohol **V 5** 60
alcoholic [ælkə'hɒlɪk] Alkoholikerin, Alkoholiker **V 6** 70
be alive [bɪ 'əlaɪv] am Leben sein **IV 4** 50
all [ɔːl] alle, alles **I 1** 20
after all ['ɑːftə ɔːl] schließlich **VI 2** 15
all day [ɔːl 'deɪ] den ganzen Tag **I 4** 70
all night [ɔːl 'naɪt] die ganze Nacht **I 4** 70
all over the world [ɔːl əʊvə ðə 'wɜːld] auf der ganzen Welt **VI 1** 10
all the time [ɔːl ðə 'taɪm] die ganze Zeit **IV 5** 60
at all [ət 'ɔːl] überhaupt **IV 1** 12
allowance (AE) [ə'laʊəns] Taschengeld **IV 1** 9
almost ['ɔːlməʊst] beinahe, fast **II 5** 72
alone [ə'ləʊn] allein **III 4** 50
along [ə'lɒŋ] entlang **I 8** 134
alphabet ['ælfəbet] Alphabet **I LS** 13
already [ɔːl 'redi] schon **III 3** 34
also ['ɔːlsəʊ] auch **III 1** 9
alternative [ɔːl'tɜːnətɪv] Alternative **VI 5** 45
although [ɔːl'ðəʊ] obwohl **IV 3** 35
altogether [ɔːltə'geðə] insgesamt **IV 2** 24
always ['ɔːlweɪz] immer **I 5** 84
amateur ['æmətə] Amateur **IV ER** 82
amazing [ə'meɪzɪŋ] erstaunlich, toll **V 5** 60
ambassador [æm'bæsədə] Botschafter **VI 1** 9

amber list ['æmbə lɪst] Gelbe Liste **III 4** 51
ambulance ['æmbjʊləns] Krankenwagen **II 4** 54
°**American** [ə'merɪkən] amerikanisch; Amerikanerin, Amerikaner **II 6** 91
and [ænd] und **I LS** 11
anecdote ['ænɪkdəʊt] Anekdote, lustige Geschichte **IV 7** 90
be angry [bɪ 'æŋgri] verärgert sein **III 1** 13
animal ['ænɪml] Tier **I B2** 48
animal home ['ænɪml həʊm] Tierheim **IV 5** 62
announcement [ə'naʊnsmənt] Ansage **IV 7** 94
annoy someone [ə'nɔɪ 'sʌmwʌn] jemandem auf die Nerven gehen **V 6** 71
anorak ['ænəræk] Anorak **II 7** 111
°**anorexia** [ænər'eksiə] Magersucht **V 6** 73
another [ə'nʌðə] noch ein (e) **I 3** 59; weiterer, weitere, weiteres **V 6** 72
answer ['ɑ:nsə] Antwort **I 2** 45; antworten, beantworten **II 3** 47
anti ['ænti] anti- **V 3** 36
any ['eni] einige, irgendwelche **II 3** 41
Any potatoes? ['eni pə'teɪtəʊz] (Möchten Sie) Kartoffeln? **II 3** 41
anybody ['enibɒdi] (irgend-) jemand **II 4** 54
°anyone ['eniwʌn] (irgend-)jemand **III 7** 92
anything ['eniθɪŋ] irgendetwas **IV 5** 61
Anything else? ['eniθɪŋ 'els] Noch etwas? **I 8** 133
anywhere ['eniweə] irgendwo **VI 3** 26
apartheid [ə'pɑ:teɪd] Apartheid **V 3** 34
apartment (AE) [ə'pɑ:tmənt] Wohnung **III 7** 86
appear [ə'pɪə] erscheinen **IV 5** 64
apple ['æpl] Apfel **I 2** 33
applicant ['æplɪkənt] Bewerberin, Bewerber **IV 5** 69
application [æplɪ'keɪʃn] Bewerbung **IV 5** 69
apply [ə'plaɪ] sich bewerben um **IV 5** 61
apprenticeship [ə'prentɪʃɪp] Lehre, Ausbildung **V 4** 43
April ['eɪprɪl] April **I 8** 132
archery ['ɑ:tʃri] Bogenschießen **VI 1** 8
area ['eəriə] Gebiet **II 6** 88
argument [ɑ:gjəmənt] Streit, Auseinandersetzung **V 4** 46
have an argument [hæv ən 'ɑ:gjəmənt] Streit haben **V 4** 46
arm [ɑ:m] Arm **II 4** 54
around [ə'raʊnd] um … herum **II 7** 108
look around [lʊk ə'raʊnd] sich umsehen **IV 1** 9
arrest [ə'rest] festnehmen **V 3** 35
arrive [ə'raɪv] ankommen **I 6** 105
°**arrow** ['ærəʊ] Pfeil **II 5** 72
Art [ɑ:t] Kunst **II 1** 9
article ['ɑ:tɪkl] Bericht, Artikel **II 5** 72
artist ['ɑ:tɪst] Künstlerin, Künstler **IV 5** 60
as [æz] als, wie **II 2** 24
as … as [æz] so … wie **II 6** 90
Asian ['eɪʃn] Asiatin, Asiat; asiatisch **V 1** 10
ask [ɑ:sk] fragen **I 3** 54
ask for ['ɑ:sk fə] fragen nach, bitten um **II 7** 106
assembly line [ə'sembli laɪn] Montageband **III 6** 77
°**assistant** [ə'sɪstənt] Assistentin, Assistent **II 5** 72
clerical assistant ['klerɪkl ə'sɪstənt] Büroangestellte, Büroangestellter **V 4** 44
at [æt, ət] im, in **I 1** 22; an, bei **I 2** 32
at all [ət 'ɔ:l] überhaupt **IV 1** 12
at first [æt 'fɜ:st] zuerst **IV 1** 12
at home [ət 'həʊm] zu Hause **I B6** 116
at last [æt lɑ:st] endlich **VI 7** 62
at least [æt 'li:st] wenigstens **IV 1** 12
at night [ət 'naɪt] nachts **III ER** 23
at that time [ət ðæt taɪm] damals **V 1** 10
at the end of [æt ði 'end əv] am Ende von **II 1** 17
at the moment [æt ðə 'məʊmənt] jetzt gerade **III 2** 24
athlete ['æθli:t] Sportlerin, Sportler **I 8** 134
atmosphere ['ætməsfɪə] Atmosphäre **III 5** 64
attachment [ə'tætʃmənt] Anlage **III 5** 62
attack [ə'tæk] angreifen **VI 6** 51
attention [ə'tenʃn] Aufmerksamkeit **VI 2** 14
attraction [ə'trækʃən] Attraktion, Anziehungspunkt **II 7** 106
attractive [ə'træktɪv] attraktiv, gut aussehend **VI 3** 27
audience ['ɔ:diəns] Publikum **IV ER** 82
August ['ɔ:gəst] August **I 8** 132
aunt [ɑ:nt] Tante **II 8** 120
Aussie ['ɒzi] Spitzname für eine Australierin/ einen Australier **V 2** 16
Australian [ɒs'treɪliən] Australierin, Australier; australisch **V 2** 16
auto-rickshaw [ɔ:təʊ 'rɪkʃɒ:] Auto-Rickscha **VI 3** 26
automatically [ɔ:tə'mætɪkli] automatisch **III 6** 76
autopilot ['ɔ:teʊpaɪlət] Autopilot **VI 2** 15
autumn ['ɔ:təm] Herbst **I 8** 132
avoid [ə'vɔɪd] vermeiden **VI 3** 26
award [ə'wɔ:d] Preis, Auszeichnung **VI 1** 8
away [ə'weɪ] weg **I 5** 86

B

baby, babies ['beɪbi] Baby, Babys **I 6** 107
babysit ['beɪbɪsɪt] babysitten **V 6** 68
back [bæk] zurück **I 7** 122; Rückseite **III ER** 118
°**backpack (AE)** ['bækpæk] Rucksack **IV 1** 15
bacon ['beɪkn] Schinkenspeck **I 7** 120
bad [bæd] schlecht **II 6** 87; schlimm **III 1** 10
bad luck [bæd 'lʌk] Pech **V 4** 46
badminton ['bædmɪntən] Federball, Badminton **II 1** 10
bag [bæg] Tasche **I B1** 30; Tüte **II 2** 29
bagpipes ['bægpaɪps] Dudelsack **III ER** 49
bait [beɪt] Köder **IV 5** 65
bake [beɪk] backen **V 4** 49
baker ['beɪkə] Bäckerin, Bäcker **II 3** 40
balance ['bæləns] Gleichgewicht **II 5** 76
balcony ['bælkəni] Balkon **VI 7** 63
ball [bɔ:l] Ball **I B1** 30
balloon [bə'lu:n] Ballon **I B4** 82
banana [bə'nɑ:nə] Banane **I 6** 102
band [bænd] Band, Gruppe **I 5** 84
bandage ['bændɪdʒ] Verband **II 4** 58
°**bang** [bæŋ] Knall **I 8** 134
Bangladeshi [bæŋglə'deʃi] Einwohner Bangladeschs **IV 6** 79
bank [bæŋk] Bank (Geldinstitut) **I B5** 98
bar [bɑ:] Tafel (Schokolade) **I 8** 133; Bar **III ER** 56

°**bar chart** ['bɑ: tʃɑ:t] Säulendiagramm **IV6** 78
°**barbecue** ['bɑ:bɪkju:] Grillfest **II5** 80
bare [beə] bloß **V2** 21
°**barge** [bɑ:ʤ] Hausboot **IV5** 61
baseball ['beɪsbɔ:l] Baseball **III ER** 108
basket ['bɑ:skɪt] Korb **III7** 92
basketball ['bɑ:skɪtbɔ:l] Basketball **I1** 18
bat [bæt] Schläger **III ER** 108
bathroom ['bɑ:θrʊm] Badezimmer **I B3** 64
°**battery** ['bætri] Batterie **II7** 112
battle ['bætl] Schlacht, Kampf **VI7** 63
bay [beɪ] Bucht **IV ER** 112
be [bi:] sein **II2** 27
be able to [bi: 'eɪbl tə] können, in der Lage sein **III4** 51
be afraid of [bi: ə'freɪd əv] Angst haben vor **II5** 76
be against [bi: ə'genst] gegen etwas sein **V2** 19
be alive [bɪ ə'laɪv] am Leben sein **IV4** 50
be allowed to [bi: ə'laʊd tə] dürfen **III4** 51
be angry [bɪ 'æŋgri] verärgert sein **III1** 13
be bored [bɪ bɔ:d] gelangweilt sein, Langeweile haben **IV7** 90
be cold [bɪ 'kəʊld] frieren **III3** 36
be fascinated [bɪ 'fæsɪneɪtɪd] fasziniert sein **IV4** 51
be frightened [bɪ 'fraɪtnd] Angst haben **V2** 20
be furious [bɪ 'fjʊəriəs] wütend sein **IV ER** 57
°be lost [bɪ 'lɒst] sich verlaufen **I6** 102
be lucky [bɪ 'lʌki] Glück haben **II1** 12
be right [bɪ raɪt] Recht haben **II5** 76
be scared [bɪ 'skeəd] Angst haben **II8** 122
be sick [bɪ 'sɪk] krank sein, sich übergeben **V4** 42
be surprised [bɪ sə'praɪzd] überrascht/erstaunt sein **III3** 38
be tired [bɪ 'taɪəd] müde sein **V2** 20
be unlucky [bɪ ʌn'lʌki] kein Glück haben **II1** 19
be worried [bɪ 'wʌrid] sich Sorgen machen **III1** 12
beach [bi:tʃ] Strand **III5** 60
bear [beə] Bär **II7** 108
grizzly bear ['grɪzli beə] Grizzlybär **IV3** 35
polar bear ['pəʊlə beə] Eisbär **VI6** 51
beard [bɪəd] Bart **V2** 21
beautiful ['bju:tɪfl] schön **II7** 104
because [bɪ'kɒz] weil **I7** 118
become [bɪ'kʌm] werden **IV2** 25
bed [bed] Bett **I B3** 64
bed and breakfast [bed ənd 'brekfəst] (Privat-)Zimmer mit Frühstück **II8** 117
bedroom ['bedrʊm] Schlafzimmer **I B3** 64
before [bɪ'fɔ:] vor (zeitlich), bevor **II1** 9
begin [bɪ'gɪn] beginnen, anfangen **II6** 90
beginner's luck [bɪ'gɪnəz lʌk] Anfängerglück **III ER** 109
beginning [bɪ'gɪnɪŋ] Anfang **IV1** 12
behind [bɪ'haɪnd] hinter **I2** 34
believe [bɪ'li:v] glauben **IV1** 8
bell [bel] Glocke, Klingel **II1** 12
belong to [bɪ'lɒŋ tə] gehören **V1** 8
besides [bɪ'saɪdz] außerdem **V6** 70
best [best] bester, beste, bestes **II6** 87
best thing ['best θɪŋ] Allerbeste **V5** 60
bestseller [best'selə] Bestseller **VI4** 34
better ['betə] besser **II6** 87
between [bɪ'twi:n] zwischen **II5** 72
big [bɪg] groß **I2** 36
bike [baɪk] Fahrrad **I3** 50
by bike [baɪ 'baɪk] mit dem Fahrrad **II1** 8
ride a bike [raɪd ə 'baɪk] Fahrrad fahren **I3** 50
bingo ['bɪŋgəʊ] Bingo **I1** 25
binoculars [bɪ'nɒkjʊləz] Fernglas **II8** 127
Biology [baɪ'ɒlədʒi] Biologie **II1** 9
bird [bɜ:d] Vogel **I B2** 48
birdwatching ['bɜ:dwɒtʃɪŋ] Beobachten von Vögeln **III4** 50
biro ['baɪrəʊ] Kugelschreiber **I2** 33
birth [bɜ:θ] Geburt **V3** 34
birthday ['bɜ:θdeɪ] Geburtstag **I5** 88
birthplace ['bɜ:θpleɪs] Geburtsort **III ER** 119
a bit [ə 'bɪt] etwas **III ER** 31
black [blæk] schwarz **I LS** 10
Blacks [blæks] Schwarze **V3** 34
°**block** [blɒk] Häuserblock **V6** 71
blond [blɒnd] blond **III1** 10
blood [blʌd] Blut **IV ER** 112
blow [bləʊ] blasen **IV ER** 112
blue [blu:] blau **I LS** 10
board [bɔ:d] Tafel **I2** 32; Bord **IV2** 25; (ins Flugzeug) einsteigen **IV7** 87
board game ['bɔ:d geɪm] Brettspiel **I B2** 48
°**boarding school** ['bɔ:dɪŋ sku:l] Internat **V3** 34
boat [bəʊt] Boot **I3** 51
racing boat ['reɪsɪŋ bəʊt] Rennboot **IV3** 49
body ['bɒdi] Körper, Leiche **IV4** 51
bomb [bɒm] Bombe **IV6** 77
bone [bəʊn] Knochen **IV ER** 113
book [bʊk] Buch **I B1** 30; buchen **II8** 118
bookshelf, bookshelves ['bʊkʃelf 'bʊkʃelvz] Bücherregal, Bücherregale **I4** 68
boots [bu:ts] Stiefel **II5** 73
border [bɔ:də] Grenze **V7** 88
boring ['bɔ:rɪŋ] langweilig **I3** 56
be bored [bɪ bɔ:d] gelangweilt sein, Langeweile haben **V4** ER
born [bɔ:n] geboren **III6** 76
borrow (from) ['bɒrəʊ frɒm] ausleihen (von) **III3** 34
boss [bɒs] Chefin, Chef, Vorgesetzte, Vorgesetzer **IV5** 61
both ['bəʊθ] beide **VI1** 9
bottle ['bɒtl] Flasche **I8** 133
bottom ['bɒtəm] Boden, Unterseite **IV7** 101
boutique [bu:'ti:k] Boutique **II5** 81
°**bow** [bəʊ] Bogen **II5** 72
bowl [bəʊl] Schüssel, Schälchen **II2** 22
box [bɒks] Schachtel, Kasten **I6** 109
telephone box ['telɪfəʊn bɒks] Telefonzelle **I6** 104
boxer ['bɒksə] Boxer **V2** 20
boy [bɔɪ] Junge **I1** 20
boyfriend ['bɔɪfrend] Freund **V6** 73
boycott ['bɔɪkɒt] Boykott **VI7** 62
boycott ['bɒɪkɒt] boykottieren **VI7** 62
brave [breɪv] mutig, tapfer **II7** 109
broken ['brəʊkn] zerbrochen, kaputt **III4** 53
bread [bred] Brot **II3** 40
break [breɪk] Pause **II1** 9; (zer-)brechen **III ER** 23
break (an arm, ...) ['breɪk ən 'ɑ:m] sich (einen Arm,...) brechen **IV7** 91
break (down) [breɪk 'daʊn] (zusammen-)brechen, kaputtgehen **III3** 36
break laws [breɪk lɔ:z] gegen Gesetze verstoßen **V3** 35

breakfast ['brekfəst] Frühstück **I 7** 120
for breakfast [fə 'brekfəst] zum Frühstück **I 7** 120
have breakfast [hæv 'brekfəst] frühstücken **I 5** 84
bridge [brɪdʒ] Brücke **II 5** 74
bright [braɪt] hell **V 4** 47
bring [brɪŋ] bringen **II 5** 65
bring along [brɪŋ ə'lɒŋ] mitbringen **V 6** 68
British ['brɪtɪʃ] Britin, Brite; britisch **III 2** 25
brochure ['brəʊʃə] Broschüre **II 7** 105
brother ['brʌðə] Bruder **I 1** 20
brown [braʊn] braun **I LS** 10
brush one*s teeth [brʌʃ wʌnz tiːθ] sich die Zähne putzen **VI 6** 53
bucket ['bʌkɪt] Eimer **I 7** 122
buffalo ['bʌfələʊ] Büffel **IV 2** 24
build [bɪld] bauen **V 1** 9
building ['bɪldɪŋ] Gebäude **III 5** 66
building site ['bɪldɪŋ saɪt] Baustelle **IV 7** 88
electric light bulb [ɪ'lektrɪk laɪt bʌlb] Glühbirne **III 6** 76
bulkhead ['bʌlkhed] Trennwand, Schott **VI 2** 15
bull [bʊl] Stier, Bulle **VI 4** 33
bump [bʌmp] Beule **II 4** 58
burn [bɜːn] brennen, verbrennen **IV ER** 113
bury ['beri] vergraben, begraben **IV ER** 113
bus [bʌs] Bus **I B5** 98
bus stop ['bʌs stɒp] Bushaltestelle **II 3** 40
by bus [baɪ 'bʌs] mit dem Bus **II 1** 8
bush [bʊʃ] Busch (-land) **V 2** 20
business ['bɪznɪs] Geschäft **III 2** 26
businessman ['bɪznɪsmæn] Geschäftsmann **V 1** 8
businesswoman ['bɪznɪs wʊmən] Geschäftsfrau **V 1** 8
do business [dʊ 'bɪznɪs] Geschäft/Geschäfte machen **V 1** 9
busy ['bɪzi] beschäftigt **I 7** 118; belebt, voll **III ER** 30
but [bʌt] aber **I 1** 18
butcher ['bʊtʃə] Metzger, Metzgerin; Schlachter **II 3** 40
butter ['bʌtə] Butter **I 7** 120
button ['bʌtn] Knopf **III 5** 64
buy [baɪ] kaufen **I 5** 88
by [baɪ] mit **I 3** 61
by bike [baɪ 'baɪk] mit dem Fahrrad **II 1** 8
by boat [baɪ 'bəʊt] mit dem Boot **I 3** 61
by bus [baɪ 'bʌs] mit dem Bus **II 1** 8
Bye [baɪ] Tschüs **I 1** 17

C

cab [kæb] Taxi **III 7** 93
°**cable car** ['keɪbl kɑː] Straßenbahn in San Francisco **II 6** 90
cafe ['kæfeɪ] Cafe **I B5** 98
cafeteria [kæfə'tɪərɪə] Cafeteria **I B1** 30
cage [keɪdʒ] Käfig **IV 3** 39
°**calendar** ['kæləndə] Kalender **II 4** 56
call [kɔːl] (an-)rufen; nennen; Anruf **II 4** 54
caller ['kɔːlə] Anruferin, Anrufer **II 6** 90
calory ['kæləri] Kalorie **V 6** 73
camcorder ['kæmkɔːdə] Camcorder **III 1** 10
camera ['kæmrə] Kamera, Fotoapparat **I 3** 55
cameraman ['kæmərə'mæn] Kameramann **IV 5** 60
video camera [vɪdɪəʊ 'kæmrə] Videokamera **I 3** 55
camp [kæmp] zelten; (Zelt-)Lager **II 7** 104
camper ['kæmpə] Camperin, Camper **III 8** 103
campfire ['kæmpfaɪə] Lagerfeuer **II 7** 108
camping site ['kæmpɪŋ saɪt] Zeltplatz, Campingplatz **II 8** 119
training camp [treɪnɪŋ kæmp] Trainingslager **III 8** 105
campaign [kæm'peɪn] Kampagne **V 3** 36
can, could [kæn kʊd] können; konnte (n) **I 1** 18
Can you pass me ...? [kæn jə 'pɑːs miː] Kannst du mir ... geben/reichen? **I 7** 120
can't/cannot [kɑːnt 'kænɒt] kann/kannst/könnt/können nicht **I 1** 18
Canadian [kə'neɪdiən] Kanadierin, Kanadier; kanadisch **V 7** 87
candle ['kændl] Kerze **III 3** 38
cap [kæp] Kappe, Mütze **II 5** 73
capital ['kæpɪtəl] Hauptstadt **V 1** 10
captain ['kæptɪn] Kapitän **IV 2** 25
car [kɑː] Auto **I 6** 104
car mechanic [kɑːr mɪ'kænɪk] Automechanikerin, Automechaniker **V 1** 8
car park ['kɑː pɑːk] Parkplatz **I B5** 98
used car [juːzd 'kɑː] Gebrauchtwagen **IV ER** 56
carbon dioxide ['kɑːbən daɪ'ɒksaɪd] Kohlendioxid **VI 6** 52
card [kɑːd] Karte **I 1** 18
°report card (AE) [rɪ'pɔːt kɑːd] Zeugnis **V 6** 73
care for [keə fɔː] sich kümmern um **III ER** 118
take care [teɪk 'keə] aufpassen **IV 1** 10
career [kə'rɪə] Karriere **V 2** 31
careful ['keəfl] vorsichtig **III 2** 26
cargo bay ['kɑːgəʊ beɪ] Frachtraum **III 5** 64
Caribbean [kærɪ'biːən] Karibin, Karibe; karibisch **IV 6** 76
carnival ['kɑːnɪvl] Karneval **IV 6** 76
carrot ['kærət] Karotte **II 3** 41
carry ['kæri] tragen **I 3** 51
cartoon [kɑː'tuːn] Zeichentrickfilm **II 6** 94
cartridge ['kɑːtrɪdʒ] Tintenpatrone **I 2** 33
cash machine ['kæʃ məʃiːn] Geldautomat **IV 7** 94
°**casino** [kə'siːnəʊ] Kasino **II 6** 90
cassette [kə'set] Kassette **I 5** 91
castle ['kɑːsl] Schloss, Burg **II 8** 122
cat [kæt] Katze **I B1** 30
catch [kætʃ] fangen **I 6** 105
catchy [kætʃi] eingängig, zündend **VI 1** 8
cathedral [kə'θiːdrəl] Dom, Kathedrale **III 1** 8
catholic ['kæθlɪk] katholisch **VI 5** 44
cattle ['kætl] Rinder **V 2** 17
cause [kɔːz] verursachen **IV 3** 35
cave [keɪv] Höhle **V 2** 20
CD [siː'diː] CD **I LS** 15
celebrate ['selɪbreɪt] feiern **III 7** 95
celebration [selə'breɪʃn] Feier **V 1** 10
cell [sel] Zelle **V 3** 37
cell phone (AE) ['sel foʊn] Handy, Mobiltelefon **IV 3** 34
cent [sent] Cent **III 7** 88
center (AE) ['sentə] Zentrum **III 5** 60
centimetre ['sentɪmiːtə] Zentimeter **VI 6** 50
°**central locking system** ['sentrəl 'lɒkɪŋ 'sɪstəm] Zentralverriegelung **III 5** 61
century ['sentʃəri] Jahrhundert **IV 2** 25
certainly ['sɜːtnli] bestimmt, gewiss **VI 3** 27
°**food chain** ['fuːd tʃeɪn] Nahrungskette **III 4** 53
chair [tʃeə] Stuhl **I 2** 32

challenge ['tʃælɪndʒ] Herausforderung **V 5** 61
champagne [ʃæm'peɪn] Champagner **VI 2** 19
champion ['tʃæmpiən] Meisterin, Meister, Champion **VI 4** 33
chance [tʃæns] Chance, Gelegenheit **IV 5** 62
chancellor ['tʃɑ:nsələ] Kanzlerin, Kanzler **VI 4** 33
change [tʃeɪndʒ] ändern **V 3** 34
change [tʃeɪndʒ] Veränderung **VI 6** 51
change money [tʃeɪndʒ 'mʌni] Geld wechseln **IV 7** 94
change parts [tʃeɪndʒ 'pɑ:ts] Rollen wechseln **II 7** 112
change trains [tʃeɪndʒ 'treɪnz] umsteigen **III 1** 12
chaotic [keɪ'ɒtɪk] chaotisch **VI 3** 26
character ['kærəktə] Charakter **IV 4** 52; Figur **VI 1** 8
°**charity** ['tʃærəti] Wohlfahrtsorganisation **V 4** 43
charming ['tʃɑ:mɪŋ] charmant **VI 1** 8
charts [tʃɑ:ts] Hitparade **II 6** 94
chassis ['ʃæsi] Karosserie **III 6** 77
chat [tʃæt] Geplauder **II 2** 28; chatten **III 8** 103
chatroom ['tʃætru:m] Chatroom **III 8** 103
cheap [tʃi:p] billig **II 3** 48
check [tʃek] kontrollieren, prüfen **II 7** 112
check in [tʃek 'ɪn] einchecken (am Flughafen) **IV 7** 87
°checklist ['tʃeklɪst] Checkliste **I 1** 29
°checkout ['tʃekaʊt] Abschlusskontrolle, Auschecken **I 1** 29
safety check ['seɪfti tʃek] Sicherheitsüberprüfung **V 6** 62
cheer [tʃɪə] jubeln **VI 7** 63
cheerleader ['tʃɪəli:də] Cheerleader **IV 1** 16
cheese [tʃi:z] Käse **I B1** 30
cheeseburger ['tʃi:zbɜ:gə] Cheeseburger **III 1** 16
°**chew** [tʃu:] kauen **V 2** 21
chicken ['tʃɪkɪn] Huhn, Hähnchen **II 2** 26
chicken curry ['tʃɪkɪn kʌri] indisches Gericht mit Hühnerfleisch **II 2** 26
chief [tʃi:f] Oberhaupt **III ER** 49
child [tʃaɪld] Kind **I 6** 107
children ['tʃɪldrən] Kinder **I 2** 32
childcare ['tʃaɪldkeə] Kinderbetreuung **VI 4** 32
Chinese [tʃaɪ'ni:z] Chinesin, Chinese; chinesisch **III 7** 87
chocolate ['tʃɒklət] Schokolade **I 8** 133
chocolate pudding ['tʃɒklət pʊdɪŋ] Schokoladenpudding **II 2** 23
choice [tʃɔɪs] Wahl, Auswahl **IV 5** 61
choose [tʃu:z] (aus-)wählen **II 6** 90
Christmas ['krɪsməs] Weihnachten **II 3** 45
church [tʃɜ:tʃ] Kirche **I B5** 98
cigarette [sɪgər'et] Zigarette **V 6** 70
cinema ['sɪnəmə] Kino **I B5** 98
°**circle** ['sɜ:kl] Kreis **I 2** 36
circus ['sɜ:kəs] Zirkus **I 1** 20
city ['sɪti] Stadt **I 6** 87
civil-rights movement [sɪvl 'raɪts 'mu:vmənt] Bürgerrechtsbewegung **VI 7** 63
claim [kleɪm] fordern, behaupten **IV 7** 88
clan [klæn] Clan, Sippe, Sippschaft **III ER** 49
clap [klæp] klatschen **III ER** 118
class [klɑ:s] Klasse **I 2** 32
classroom ['klɑ:srʊm] Klassenzimmer **I B1** 30
clean [kli:n] sauber **I 7** 118; reinigen, putzen **II 8** 124
clean up ['kli:n ʌp] sauber machen **V 4** 42
clear [klɪə] klar **IV 5** 65
clerical assistant ['klerɪkl ə'sɪstənt] Büroangestellte, Büroangestellter **V 4** 44
clever ['klevə] klug **VI 7** 62
click [klɪk] (an-)klicken **II 7** 106
cliff [klɪf] Klippe **III 4** 50
climate ['klaɪmət] Klima **VI 6** 51
climb [klaɪm] klettern **I 3** 54
°**clip-on ring** ['klɪp ɒn rɪŋ] Ring als Clip **IV 1** 12
cloak [kləʊk] Umhang **II 5** 73
clock [klɒk] Uhr **I B5** 98
°**close** [kləʊz] schließen **I 5** 86; nah **III 7** 90
cloth [klɒθ] Stoff **III ER** 49
clothes [kləʊðz] Kleider, Kleidung **I B4** 82
°**clothing** ['kləʊðɪŋ] Kleidung **V 4** 47
cloud [klaʊd] Wolke **V 2** 20
cloudy ['klaʊdi] wolkig **I B6** 116
clown [klaʊn] Clown **I 3** 57
club [klʌb] Club, Verein **II 1** 10
coach [kəʊtʃ] Trainer **II 6** 95
coal [kəʊl] Kohle **IV ER** 101
coast [kəʊst] Küste **V 2** 16
cockpit ['kɒkpɪt] Cockpit **III 5** 64
coconut ['kəʊkənʌt] Kokusnuss **VI 5** 47
country code ['kʌntri kəʊd] Verhaltensregeln in der freien Natur **III 4** 50
coffee ['kɒfi] Kaffee **I 7** 120
coin [kɔɪn] Münze **III 6** 76
coke [kəʊk] Cola **I 6** 108
cold [kəʊld] kalt **II 4** 56
be cold [bɪ 'kəʊld] frieren **III 3** 36
collage [kɒl'ɑ:ʒ] Collage **III ER** 56
°**radio collar** ['reɪdiəʊ 'kɒlə] Funkhalsband **IV 3** 38
colleague ['kɒli:g] Kollegin, Kollege **IV 5** 65
collect [kə'lekt] sammeln **II 3** 42; (ab-)holen **III 3** 36
collection [kə'lekʃn] Sammlung **II 6** 86
college ['kɒlɪdʒ] College, Universität **III 2** 24
colonist ['kɒlənɪst] Kolonistin, Kolonist **IV 2** 25
colony ['kɒləni] Kolonie **IV 2** 25
colored (AE) ['kʌləd] farbig **VI 7** 65
colour ['kʌlə] Farbe **I LS** 10
come [kʌm] kommen **I 5** 89
come in [kʌm 'ɪn] hereinkommen **I 2** 36
Come in, please. [kʌm 'ɪn pli:z] Herein! **I 2** 36
Come on! [kʌm 'ɒn] Komm (t) schon! **III 2** 25
come up [kʌm ʌp] aufgehen **V 5** 62
°**comfortable** ['kʌmpftəbl] bequem **III 5** 61
comic ['kɒmɪk] Comicheft **I 3** 51
comment ['kɒment] kommentieren, sagen **V 5** 61
communicate [kə'mju:nɪkeɪt] kommunizieren **VI 2** 15
community [kə'mju:nəti] Gemeinde, Gemeinschaft **IV 6** 76
company ['kʌmpəni] Firma **III 2** 24
°Internet services company [ɪntənet sɜ:vɪsɪz 'kʌmpəni] Internetagentur **V 4** 46
music company ['mju:zɪk 'kʌmpəni] Musikfirma, Plattenfima **III 2** 24
°**compare** [kəm'peə] vergleichen **II 1** 14
comparison [kəm'pærɪsn] Vergleich **VI 7** 65
compass ['kʌmpəs] Kompass **III 4** 50
competition [kɒmpə'tɪʃn] Konkurrenz; Wettbwerb **V 4** 46
complain [kəm'pleɪn] sich beschweren **IV 5** 61
°**complete** [kəm'pli:t] vervollständigen **I 4** 72; vollständig **II 3** 45
completely [kəm'pli:tli] völlig **VI 6** 50

computer [kəm'pju:tə] Computer **I LS** 11
computer freak [kəm'pju:tə fri:k] Computerfreak **V 6** 69
computer room [kəm'pju:tə rʊm] Computerraum **I B1** 30
concentrate ['kɒntsəntreɪt] sich konzentrieren **V 6** 73
concert ['kɒnsət] Konzert **I 5** 92
confession [kən'feʃn] Konfession, Glaubensrichtung **VI 5** 44
confident ['kɒnfɪdnt] zuversichtlich, selbstsicher **VI 4** 34
conflict ['kɒnflɪkt] Konflikt, Auseinandersetzung **VI 5** 44
confused [kən'fju:zd] verwirrt **IV 1** 12
congratulate [kən'grætʃʊleɪt] beglückwünschen **IV ER** 56
congratulations [kəngrætʃʊ'leɪʃnz] herzlichen Glückwunsch **IV ER** 56
Congress ['kɒŋgres] Der Kongress **VI 7** 63
°**connection** [kə'nekʃn] Verbindung **II 7** 112
pros and cons [prəʊz ənd 'kɑ:nz] Vorteile und Nachteile **III 5** 61
construct [kɒn'strʌkt] bauen **V 4** 43
contact ['kɒntækt] Kontakt **III 5** 62
Contact us. ['kɒntækt ʌs] Kontaktiert uns. / Setzt euch mit uns in Verbindung. **II 7** 106
contest ['kɒntest] Wettbewerb **IV 3** 34
continent ['kɒntɪnənt] Erdteil, Kontinent **III 5** 64
contract ['kɒntrækt] Vertrag **V 4** 46
control [kən'trəʊl] Kontrolle **IV 5** 64
remote control [rɪ'məʊt kəntrəʊl] Fernbedienung **II 8** 123
°**convict** ['kɒnvɪkt] Sträfling **V 2** 19
°convict ship ['kɒnvɪkt ʃɪp] Sträflingsschiff **V 2** 19
cook [kʊk] kochen **II 1** 10; Köchin, Koch **IV 5** 60
cooker ['kʊkə] Herd **II 2** 23
cool [ku:l] cool, locker **IV 1** 8
copper ['kɒpə] Polizistin, Polizist **IV 5** 64
copy ['kɒpi] kopieren **III 6** 79; Kopie **VI 2** 17
coral reef ['kɒrəl ri:f] Korallenriff **VI 6** 51
corn [kɔ:n] Mais **IV 2** 26
corner ['kɔ:nə] Ecke **I 7** 123
cornflakes ['kɔ:nfleɪks] Cornflakes **I 7** 120
°**correct** [kə'rekt] korrigieren; richtig, korrekt **I 6** 109
corridor ['kɒrɪdɔ:] Gang, Flur **II 1** 12
cost [kɒst] kosten **IV 1** 12
cottage ['kɒtɪdʒ] Ferienhaus **III 3** 38
could [kʊd] konnte (n), könnte (n) **II 7** 104
countdown ['kaʊntdaʊn] Countdown **III 5** 64
counter ['kaʊntə] Kasse, Ladentheke **V 4** 47
country ['kʌntri] Land **I 8** 134
country code ['kʌntrɪ kəʊd] Verhaltensregeln in der freien Natur **III 4** 50
countryside ['kʌntrɪsaɪd] Landschaft **IV 5** 61
courage ['kʌrɪdʒ] Mut **VI 2** 15
courier ['kʊrɪə] Kurier **III 7** 86
course [kɔ:s] Weiterbildung, Lehrgang **V 4** ER
of course [əv 'kɔ:s] natürlich, selbstverständlich **II 1** 8
take a course [teɪk ə 'kɔ:s] eine Weiterbildung machen **V 4** ER
cousin ['kʌzn] Cousin, Cousine **II 8** 118
cow [kaʊ] Kuh **I B6** 116
cowboy ['kaʊbɔɪ] Cowboy **I LS** 11
cowgirl ['kaʊgɜ:l] weiblicher Cowboy **VI 4** 33
°**crack** [kræk] Crack (Droge) **IV 5** 64
°**cracker** ['krækə] (salziger) Keks **II 5** 80
craft [krɑ:ft] Handwerk **IV 2** 26
°**crag** [kræg] Klippe **IV 3** 49
crane [kreɪn] Kran **IV ER** 101
crazy ['kreɪzi] verrückt **III 7** 86
crazy about ['kreɪzi ə'baʊt] verrückt nach **V 2** 16
creative [kri'eɪtɪv] kreativ **VI 7** 63
crime [kraɪm] Kriminalität, Verbrechen **V 1** 9
°**crimes unsolved** [kraɪmz ʌn'sɒlvd] unaufgeklärte Verbrechen **II 6** 94
crisps [krɪsps] Chips **I 8** 133
cross [krɒs] überqueren **IV 4** 51
cross country skiing ['krɒs 'kʌntri 'ski:ɪŋ] Skilanglauf **IV 3** 43
crowd [kraʊd] Menge **IV ER** 112
cry [kraɪ] weinen, schreien **II 2** 27
cub [kʌb] Jungtier **VI 6** 51
culture ['kʌltʃə] Kultur **IV 6** 76
cup [kʌp] Tasse **I 7** 120; Pokal **II 6** 95
cupboard ['kʌbəd] Schrank **I 2** 32
°**cure** [kjʊər] heilen **V 6** 73
°be cured of [bi kjʊərd əv] geheilt sein von **V 6** 73
curve [kɜ:rv] Kurve **IV 7** 90
customer ['kʌstəmə] Kundin, Kunde **III 7** 87
cut [kʌt] schneiden **II 4** 58
cut costs [kʌt 'kɒsts] Kosten senken **V 4** 46
°cut out [kʌt 'aʊt] ausschneiden **I 7** 126
cute [kju:t] süß, niedlich, nett **IV 1** 8
cycle ['saɪkl] Fahrrad fahren, radeln **IV 7** 90
°cycling equipment ['saɪklɪŋ ɪ'kwɪpmənt] Fahrradausrüstung **V 4** 47
°cyclist ['saɪklɪst] Radfahrerin, Radfahrer **V 4** 47

D

dad [dæd] Vati, Vater **I 7** 118
daily ['deɪli] täglich **V 7** 89
damage ['dæmədʒ] Schaden **IV 3** 35; beschädigen **IV ER** 112
damaged ['dæmədʒd] beschädigt **IV 7** 90
damn [dæm] verdammt **VI 1** 8
dance [dɑ:ns] tanzen **III 3** 38; Tanz, Tanzveranstaltung **IV 4** 8
dancer ['dɑ:nsə] Tänzerin, Tänzer **III 3** 38
danger ['deɪndʒə] Gefahr **VI 6** 50
dangerous ['deɪndʒərəs] gefährlich **I 3** 50
dark [dɑ:k] dunkel **II 7** 108
in the dark [ɪn ðə 'dɑ:k] im Dunkeln **V 5** 60
date [deɪt] Datum **II 5** 74; Verabredung **IV 1** 9
daughter ['dɔ:tə] Tochter **I 5** 89
day [deɪ] Tag **I 4** 70
all day [ɔ:l 'deɪ] den ganzen Tag **I 4** 70
in the daytime [ɪn ðə 'deɪtaɪm] tagsüber, bei Tag **III ER** 23
the other day [ði: 'ʌðə deɪ] neulich; vor kurzem **IV 5** 64
daylight ['deɪlaɪt] Tageslicht **V 2** 20
DDT [di: di: 'ti:] Insektizid **III 4** 53
°**dead** [ded] tot **I 4** 67
deal [di:l] Abmachung **IV ER** 82
deal with [di:l 'wɪð] sich befassen mit **VI 2** 17
Dear Sir or Madam [dɪə sɜ: ɔ: 'mædəm] Sehr geehrte Damen und Herren **VI 2** 17
Dear ... [dɪə] Liebe/Lieber ... (Anrede im Brief) **I 5** 91
death [deθ] Todesopfer, Todesfall **V 3** 36
December [dɪ'sembə] Dezember **I 8** 132
decide [dɪ'saɪd] entscheiden **III 1** 8
decision [dɪ'sɪʒn] Entscheidung **IV 1** 9
deck [dek] Deck **V 2** 19

E

east [i:st] Osten **IV6** 77
eastern Europe ['i:stən 'jʊərəp] Osteuropa **IV6** 77
easy ['i:zi] leicht **I8** 132
eat [i:t] essen, fressen **I3** 51
economical [i:kə'nɒmɪkl] sparsam **III5** 61
economy [ɪ'kɒnəmi] Wirtschaft **V3** 35
education [edʒʊ'keɪʃn] Bildung **V3** 34
egg [eg] Ei **I7** 120
eight [eɪt] acht **ILS** 10
eighteen [eɪ'ti:n] achtzehn **I2** 32
eighty ['eɪti] achtzig **I6** 101
elbow ['elbəʊ] Ellbogen **II4** 55
elbow pad ['elbəʊ pæd] Ellbogenschützer **II4** 58
elect [ɪ'lekt] wählen **VI4** 32
election [ɪ'lekʃn] Wahl **V3** 36
electric [ɪ'lektrɪk] elektrisch **III7** 91
electric light bulb [ɪ'lektrɪk laɪt bʌlb] Glühbirne **III6** 76
electricity [ɪlek'trɪsəti] Strom, Elektrizität **III3** 38
elephant ['elɪfənt] Elefant **I7** 122
elevation [elə'veɪʃn] Anhebung **IVER** 101
eleven [ɪ'levn] elf **ILS** 10
elf [elf] Elfin, Elf; Elbin, Elb **VI1** 8
elk, elk [elk elk] Rothirsch, Rothirsche; Elch **IV3** 35
°**else** [els] anders, sonst **V2** 27
someone else ['sʌmwʌn els] jemand anderes **V4** 45
embarrassed [ɪm'bærəst] verlegen **II4** 56
embarrassing [ɪm'bærəsɪŋ] peinlich **VI7** 64
employee [ɪmplɔɪ'i:] Angestellte, Angestellter **V1** 9
employer [ɪm'plɔɪə] Arbeitgeberin, Arbeitgeber **V4** ER
employment [ɪm'plɔɪmənt] Arbeit, Beschäftigung **IVER** 75
empty ['emti] leer **II2** 27
enclose [ɪn'kləʊz] beifügen **VI2** 17
encyclopedia [ɪnsaɪklə'pɪdɪə] Enzyklopädie **VI2** 17
end [end] enden; Ende **II1** 16; beenden **V3** 35
°end in ['end ɪn] enden auf **I8** 132
enemy ['enəmi] Feindin, Feind **IV4** 52
energetic [enə'dzetɪk] voller Energie **VI1** 8
energy ['enədʒi] Energie **V4** 46
engage [ɪn'geɪdʒ] sich beteiligen **VI7** 63
engine ['endʒɪn] Motor **III5** 61
engineer [endʒɪ'nɪə] Ingenieurin, Ingenieur **IIIER** 75
English ['ɪŋglɪʃ] Englisch, englisch **ILS** 11; Engländerin, Engländer **II1** 9
enjoy [ɪn'dʒɔɪ] etwas gern tun, genießen **III1** 10
enough [ɪ'nʌf] genug **III5** 64
entertainment [entə'teɪnmənt] Unterhaltung **VI3** 27
enthusiasm [in'θju:ziæzm] Enthusiasmus, Begeisterung **VI1** 8
environment [ɪn'vaɪrnmənt] Umwelt **VI6** 51
environmental [ɪnvaɪrən'mentl] Umwelt-, die Umwelt betreffend **VI6** 53
equal ['i:kwəl] gleich **VI4** 32
equator [ɪ'kweɪtə] Äquator **VI2** 19
°**equipment** [ɪ'kwɪpmənt] Ausrüstung **V4** 47
escape [es'keɪp] fliehen, flüchten **V3** 35
especially [ɪ'speʃli] besonders **IVER** 112
essay ['eseɪ] Essay, Aufsatz **III8** 104
°**estate agent** [ɪ'steɪt 'eɪdʒənt] Immobilienmaklerin, Immobilienmakler **V4** 44
EU (European Union) [i: ju: (jʊərə'pi:ən 'ju:njən)] EU, Europäische Union **IV6** 78
euro ['jʊərəʊ] Euro **I6** 101
even ['i:vən] sogar **II6** 88
evening ['i:vnɪŋ] Abend **II2** 26
event [ɪ'vent] Veranstaltung, Ereignis **III3** 42
ever ['evə] jemals, schon einmal **III4** 52
ever after ['evə 'ɑ:ftə] bis an ihr Lebensende **VI3** 27
ever since [evə 'sɪns] seitdem, seit **VI1** 8
every ['evri] jeder, jede, jedes **V2** 21
everybody ['evribədi] jeder, alle **III3** 39
everyone ['evriwʌn] jeder, alle **III1** 12
everything ['evriθɪŋ] alles **II7** 108
everywhere ['evriweə] überall **VI2** 16
exact [ɪg'zækt] genau **III4** 52
example [ɪk'sɑ:mpl] Beispiel **IV3** 35
except for [ɪk'sept fɔ:r] außer **VI4** 37
excited [ɪk'saɪtɪd] aufgeregt **III7** 90
exciting [ɪk'saɪtɪŋ] spannend **II5** 72
°**excuse** [ɪk'skju:s] Entschuldigung (Ausrede) **II7** 111
Excuse me. [ɪk'skju:z mi:] Entschuldigung. **I5** 85
exercise book ['eksəsaɪz bʊk] (Übungs-)Heft **I2** 33
exhibition [eksɪ'bɪʃn] Ausstellung **II8** 122
exotic [ɪg'zɒtɪk] exotisch **V1** 10
expensive [ɪk'spensɪv] teuer **III1** 15
experience [ɪks'pɪəriəns] Erfahrung **IV1** 10
expert ['ekspɜ:t] Experte **IV5** 60
explain [ɪk'spleɪn] erklären **III4** 51
explorer [ɪks'plɔ:rə] Entdeckerin, Entdecker **V2** 19
extra ['ekstrə] Extra-, extra **VI4** 35
eye [aɪ] Auge **III1** 12
eyebrow ['aɪbraʊ] Augenbraue **IV1** 9
keep an eye on [ki:p ən 'aɪ ɒn] aufpassen, beobachten **IV5** 64

F

face [feɪs] Gesicht **III1** 13
fact [fækt] Tatsache **IV1** 12
in fact [ɪn 'fækt] tatsächlich **IV6** 76
factory ['fæktəri] Fabrik **V1** 9
faint [feɪnt] ohnmächtig werden **III7** 91
fair [feə] hell, blond; fair, gerecht **III1** 12; Kirmes **IIIER** 108
falcon ['fɔ:lkən] Falke **II7** 113
(peregrine) falcon ['perɪgrɪn 'fɔ:lkən] (Wander-)Falke **III4** 51
fall [fɔ:l] fallen **I6** 105
fall apart [fɔ:l ə'pɑ:t] auseinander fallen **IVER** 31
fall asleep [fɔ:l ə'sli:p] einschlafen **V2** 20
fall in love [fɔ:l ɪn 'lʌv] sich verlieben **IV1** 8
fall out ['fɔ:l aʊt] ausgehen **V6** 73
fall over [fɔ:l 'əʊvə] stolpern über **II4** 58
fall (AE) [fɒ:l] Herbst **V6** 68
false [fɔ:ls] falsch **VI4** 32
fame ['feɪm] Ruhm **IIIER** 101
family ['fæmli] Familie **I4** 68
family name ['fæmli neɪm] Nachname **I4** 72
famous ['feɪməs] berühmt **II5** 72
fan [fæn] Fan, Anhänger **I5** 93
fantastic [fæn'tæstɪk] fantastisch **II6** 90
°**fantasy** ['fæntəsi] Fantasie **IIIER** 75
fanzine ['fænzi:n] Fanzeitung **IIIPR6** 125
far [fɑ:] weit **III3** 38
farm [fɑ:m] Farm, Bauernhof **IB6** 116

farmer ['fɑ:mə] Viehzüchterin, Viehzüchter **V 2** 20
be fascinated [bɪ 'fæsɪneɪtɪd] fasziniert sein **IV 4** 51
fashion ['fæʃn] Mode **IV 6** 77
fashion ['fæʃn] Modedesign **VI 1** 9
fast [fɑ:st] schnell **I 3** 50
°fast food [fɑ:st 'fu:d] Schnellimbiss **I LS** 12
father ['fɑ:ðə] Vater **I 4** 72
favourite ['feɪvrɪt] Lieblings- **I B2** 48
February ['febrʊəri] Februar **I 8** 132
feed [fi:d] füttern **II 7** 109
feel [fi:l] fühlen **IV 5** 64
feel responsible [fi:l rɪ'spɒnsəbl] sich verantwortlich fühlen **V 4** 42
feel sorry [fi:l 'sɒri] Leid tun **IV 5** 64
feet, foot [fi:t, fʊt] Füße, Fuß **II 4** 55
°fell-racing ['fel 'reɪsɪŋ] Geländerennen **IV 3** 49
felt tip [felt 'tɪp] Filzstift **I 2** 33
female ['fi:meɪl] weiblich **V 5** 61
fence [fens] Zaun **III 4** 51
ferry ['feri] Fähre **VI 5** 45
festival ['festɪvl] Festival, Gedenktag **III 7** 88
fetch [fetʃ] holen **III ER** 109
few [fju:] wenig, wenige **III 7** 86
field [fi:ld] Feld **I B6** 116
fifteen [fɪf'ti:n] fünfzehn **I 2** 32
fifty ['fɪfti] fünfzig **I 5** 85
fight [faɪt] kämpfen **II 5** 72
file [faɪl] Ordner **III 6** 79
film [fɪlm] filmen; Film **I 3** 55
°fin [fɪn] Flosse **IV 7** 94
finally ['faɪnəli] schließlich **III 5** 64
find [faɪnd] finden **I 3** 58
find out [faɪnd 'aʊt] herausfinden **VI 1** 8
find that [faɪnd ðæt] zu dem Ergebnis kommen **V 6** ER
fine [faɪn] schön, gut **V 5** 60
finger ['fɪŋgə] Finger **II 4** 52
finish ['fɪnɪʃ] beenden, fertig machen **III 3** 35
fir tree ['fɜ: tri:] Nadelbaum **II 7** 113
fire ['faɪə] Feuer **II 4** 54; abfeuern, schießen **IV ER** 113
start a fire [stɑ:t ə 'faɪə] Feuer legen **IV 3** 35
fireworks ['faɪəwɜ:ks] Feuerwerk **III 3** 39
firm [fɜ:m] Firma **VI 2** 17
first [fɜ:st] erster, erste, erstes **II 1** 8
at first [æt 'fɜ:st] zuerst **IV 1** 12
fish [fɪʃ] Fisch, Fische **I B2** 48; angeln, fischen **IV 3** 36
fish fingers [fɪʃ 'fɪŋgəz] Fischstäbchen **II 2** 24
fishburger ['fɪʃbɜ:gə] Fischburger **I LS** 12
fit in [fɪt ɪn] hineinpassen **III ER** 75
fitness ['fɪtnəs] Fitness **VI 6** 51
five [faɪv] fünf **I LS** 10
fix [fɪks] regeln, arrangieren **III 2** 26; reparieren **VI 2** 15
flag [flæg] Flagge, Fahne **VI 5** 44
flame [fleɪm] Flamme **III 5** 64
°flashcard ['flæʃkɑ:d] Bildkarte **I 2** 36
flat [flæt] Wohnung **I 4** 68; flach **IV 2** 24
flea market ['fli: mɑ:kɪt] Flohmarkt **II 3** 44
flight [flaɪt] Flug **III 5** 64
flip out [flɪp 'aʊt] ausflippen **IV 1** 9
flood [flʌd] überschwemmen **VI 6** 50; Überschwemmung, Hochwasser **VI 6** 51
floor [flɔ:] Fußboden **V 4** 42
florist ['flɒrɪst] Floristin, Florist **V 4** 50
flower ['flaʊə] Blume **III 4** 50
fly [flaɪ] fliegen **II 7** 113
fly [flaɪ] Fliege **V 2** 21
fog [fɒg] Nebel **II 4** 56
foggy ['fɒgi] neblig **II 4** 56
°fold over [fəʊld 'əʊvə] umknicken **IV 1** 17
folder ['fəʊldə] Ordner **I 2** 33
follow ['fɒləʊ] folgen **I 6** 104
following ['fɒləʊɪŋ] folgender, folgende, folgendes **V 2** 20
food [fu:d] Essen **I B4** 82
°food chain ['fu:d tʃeɪn] Nahrungskette **III 4** 53
foot [fʊt] Fuß (Maßeinheit) **V 7** 89
foot, feet [fʊt fi:t] Fuß, Füße **II 4** 55
football ['fʊtbɔ:l] Fußball **I LS** 12
footsteps ['fʊtsteps] Fußstapfen **III ER** 101
for [fɔ:] für **I 5** 88; seit (Zeitraum) **IV 3** 35
for ages [fə 'eɪdʒɪs] seit einer Ewigkeit **IV 7** 87
for life [fə 'laɪf] lebenslänglich **V 3** 35
What for? [wɒt 'fɔ:] Wofür? Wozu? **IV 3** 36
°force oneself [fɒ:s wʌn'self] sich zwingen **V 6** 72
foreign ['fɒrɪn] ausländisch, fremd **V 1** 8
forest ['fɒrɪst] Wald **IV 3** 38
rain forest [reɪn 'fɒrɪst] Regenwald **III 5** 62
forget [fə'get] vergessen **I 3** 50
fork [fɔ:k] Gabel **II 2** 22
form [fɔ:m] Form **II 2** 30; bilden **III 4** 52
order form ['ɔ:də 'fɔ:m] Bestellformular **VI 2** 17
formal [fɔ:ml] förmlich **VI 2** 17
former ['fɔ:mə] ehemalige, ehemaliger, ehemaliges **VI 7** 63
°Formula One ['fɔ:mjʊlə wʌn] Formel 1 **V 5** 63
fortunate ['fɔ:tʃnət] glücklicher, glückliche, glückliches **V 2** 20
°fortune ['fɔ:tʃu:n] Schicksal **I 7** 126
°fortune teller ['fɔ:tʃu:n telə] Wahrsagerin, Wahrsager **I 7** 126
forty ['fɔ:ti] vierzig **I 5** 85
forward ['fɒ:wəd] vorwärts **VI 4** 32
four [fɔ:] vier **I LS** 10
four-seater [fɔ: si:tə] Viersitzer **III ER** 75
fourteen [fɔ:'ti:n] vierzehn **I 2** 32
fourth [fɔ:θ] vierte, vierter, viertes **V 7** 88
°frame [freɪm] Rahmen **V 4** 47
freak [fri:k] Freak **V 6** 69
free [fri:] frei; befreien **V 3** 36
free climber [fri: 'klaɪmə] Freeclimber **V 5** 62
free climbing [fri: 'klaɪmɪŋ] Klettern **V 5** 62
free time ['fri: taɪm] Freizeit **IV 1** 17
freedom ['fri:dəm] Freiheit **III 7** 90
French [frentʃ] die Franzosen; französisch **III 7** 90
frequently ['fri:kwentli] häufig **IV 3** 49
Friday ['fraɪdeɪ] Freitag **I 1** 20
fridge [frɪdʒ] Kühlschrank **II 2** 23
friend [frend] Freundin, Freund **I 3** 51
make friends [meɪk 'frendz] Freundschaften schließen **II 1** 10
friendly ['frendli] freundlich **V 4** 46
°frog [frɒg] Frosch **I 2** 37
°toy frog ['tɔɪ frɒg] Spielzeugfrosch **I 2** 37
from [frɒm] von **I 1** 16
front door [frʌnt 'dɔ:] Haustür **III 3** 35
in front of [ɪn 'frʌnt əv] vor **III 1** 10
frozen ['frəʊzn] gefroren, tiefgekühlt **VI 7** 65
fruit [fru:t] Obst **I B5** 98
frustrated [frʌs'treɪtɪd] frustriert **VI 1** 9
fuel ['fju:əl] Kraftstoff, Benzin **III ER** 75
full [fʊl] voll **III 7** 90
full-time job ['fʊl taɪm dʒɒb] Vollzeitbeschäftigung **IV ER** 75
fun [fʌn] Spaß **I B6** 116
fun fair [fʌn feə] Kirmes **III ER** 108

make fun [meɪk 'fʌn] Spaß machen **VI 1** 8
funny ['fʌni] lustig, seltsam **IV ER** 112
fur [fɜː] Fell, Pelz **IV 2** 24
be furious [bɪ 'fjʊəriəs] wütend sein **IV ER** 57
further ['fɜːðə] weiter (weg) **II 7** 109
future ['fjuːtʃə] (zu-)künftig **III ER** 75
future ['fjuːtʃə] Zukunft **IV 5** 61

G

Gaelic ['geɪlɪk] gälisch **VI 5** 44
game [geɪm] Spiel **I 1** 18
game show host ['geɪm ʃəʊ həʊst] Moderator **II 6** 90
gang [gæŋ] Bande, Gang **IV 5** 64
garage ['gærɑːʒ] Autowerkstatt **IV 5** 61
garden ['gɑːdn] Garten **I 4** 66
gas (AE) [gæs] Benzin **III 5** 61
gate [geɪt] Ausgang **III 5** 68
genius ['ʤiːniəs] Genie **III 6** 77
Geography [dʒɪ'ɒgrəfi] Erdkunde **II 1** 9
German ['dʒɜːmən] deutsch **I 6** 109; Deutsch (Fach) **II 1** 9
get [get] holen **I 7** 125; bekommen **II 1** 8; besorgen **III 2** 24
get addicted [get ə'dɪktɪd] süchtig werden **V 6** 70
get divorced [get dɪ'vɔːst] sich scheiden lassen **V 6** 71
get in [get 'ɪn] einsteigen **III 3** 36
get off [get 'ɒf] aussteigen **III 1** 12
get off [get ɒf] absteigen **V 2** 20
get on [get 'ɒn] einsteigen **III 1** 12
get on [get ɒn] aufsteigen **V 2** 20
get ready [get 'redɪ] fertig machen **III 5** 64
get someone wrong [get 'sʌmwʌn rɒŋ] jemanden falsch verstehen **V 4** 42
get up [get 'ʌp] aufstehen **I 5** 84
get wet [get 'wet] nass werden **IV 1** 9
geyser ['giːzə] Geysir **IV 3** 34
ghost [gəʊst] Geist, Gespenst **V 6** 74
giant ['dʒaɪənt] Riesin, Riese **VI 5** 45
gift [gɪft] Geschenk **IV 2** 26
girl [gɜːl] Mädchen **I 1** 20
Girl Guide [gɜːl gaɪd] Pfadfinderin **VI 4** 34
girlfriend ['gɜːlfrend] Freundin **II 5** 72
give [gɪv] geben **I 8** 134
give a lift [gɪv ə 'lɪft] (im Auto) mitnehmen **IV 5** 64
give birth [gɪv 'bɜːθ] zur Welt bringen **IV 2** 25
give in [gɪv 'ɪn] nachgeben **IV 1** 9
give up [gɪv 'ɒp] aufgeben **IV 1** 16
glacier ['gleɪʃə] Gletscher **IV 3** 49
glad [glæd] froh **IV 1** 12
glass [glɑːs] Glas **I 6** 108
glasses ['glɑːsɪz] Brille **II 7** 108
glitter ['glɪtə] glitzern, funkeln **III 7** 92
global warming ['gləʊbəl wɒːmɪŋ] Erderwärmung **VI 6** 50
gloves [glʌvz] Handschuhe **V 7** 89
°**glue** [gluː] Klebstoff **I 7** 126
go [gəʊ] gehen **I 1** 20; fahren **I 6** 106
go camping [gəʊ 'kæmpɪŋ] zelten gehen **II 8** 119
go crazy [gəʊ 'kreɪzi] durchdrehen **III 8** 104
go for a pizza [gəʊ fər ə 'piːtsə] Pizza essen gehen **II 2** 26
go for a ride ['gəʊ fə ə raɪd] eine Spritztour machen **IV ER** 56
go for a walk [gəʊ fər ə 'wɔːk] spazieren gehen **III ER** 118
go from bad to worse [gəʊ frəm bæd tə wɜːs] immer schlimmer werden **IV 7** 90
go home [gəʊ 'həʊm] heimgehen **I 5** 85
go off [gəʊ 'ɒf] ausgehen **II 7** 111
go on [gəʊ 'ɒn] weitergehen/-machen **I 8** 134
go on a diet [gəʊ ɒn ə daɪət] eine Diät machen **V 6** 72
go on tour ['gəʊ ən 'tʊə] auf Tournee gehen **IV ER** 83
go out with [gəʊ 'aʊt wɪð] hinausgehen, ausgehen (mit) **I 5** 88
go shopping [gəʊ 'ʃɒpɪŋ] einkaufen gehen **I 5** 88
go skiing [gəʊ 'skiːɪŋ] Ski fahren gehen **II 6** 88
go to the limit [gəʊ tə ðə 'lɪmɪt] bis zum Äußersten gehen **V 5** 61
go to war [gəʊ tə 'wɔː] Krieg führen **IV 2** 25
go wild [gəʊ 'waɪld] toben **IV 1** 8
go with [gəʊ wɪð] passen zu **II 2** 27
°**go-cart track** ['gəʊ kɑːt træk] Gokart-Bahn **V 5** 63
God [gɒd] Gott **III 5** 65
God Almighty ['gɒd ɒːl'maɪti] Allmächtiger Gott **VI 7** 63
gold [gəʊld] Gold **IV 1** 12
°**golf** [gɒlf] Golf **II 6** 94
good [gʊd] gut **I 1** 16
in good shape [ɪn gʊd 'ʃeɪp] in guter Form **V 6** 62
government ['gʌvənmənt] Regierung **IV 2** 25
governor ['gʌvənə] Gouverneur, Gouverneurin **VI 4** 34
grade [greɪd] Klassenstufe **II 7** 104
grade (AE) [greɪd] Note **V 6** 73
°**grammar** ['græmə] Grammatik **I 1** 28
grandma ['grændmɑː] Oma **I 4** 66
grandmother ['grændmʌðə] Großmutter, Oma **V 2** 20
grandpa ['grændpɑː] Opa **I 4** 67
grandparents ['grændpeərənts] Großeltern **V 1** 10
grass [grɑːs] Gras **III 7** 86
grateful ['greɪtfl] dankbar **VI 2** 17
great [greɪt] großartig **I 1** 20
green [griːn] grün **I LS** 10
greenhouse gas ['griːnhaʊs gæs] Treibhausgas **VI 6** 52
greeting ['griːtɪŋ] Gruß, Grußformel **VI 2** 17
grey [greɪ] grau **V 4** 46
grey whale [greɪ 'weɪl] Grauwal **V 7** 89
grizzly bear ['grɪzli beə] Grizzlybär **IV 3** 35
grocer ['grəʊsə] Lebensmittelhändlerin, Lebensmittelhändler **II 3** 40
grocery store ['grəʊsəri stɔː] Lebensmittelgeschäft **III 7** 87
ground [graʊnd] Boden **III ER** 75
°**ground someone** [graʊnd 'sʌmwʌn] jemandem Hausarrest erteilen **V 6** 68
group [gruːp] Gruppe **II ER** 118
grow [grəʊ] wachsen **IV 4** 52
grow up [grəʊ ʌp] aufwachsen **V 6** 68
guard [gɑːd] Wärterin, Wärter **V 3** 37
°**guess** [ges] raten **IV 3** 43
guest [gest] Gast **III 1** 17
guide [gaɪd] Führerin, Führer; führen **III 7** 88
pocket guide ['pɒkɪt gaɪd] Taschenführer **III 4** 52
guinea pig ['gɪni pɪg] Meerschweinchen **I B2** 48
guitar [gɪ'tɑː] Gitarre **I 1** 18
gun [gʌn] Waffe **III 7** 90
guy [gaɪ] Kerl, Typ **III 8** 102
guys [gaɪz] Leute **III 1** 8
gym [dʒɪm] Turnhalle **II 1** 10

H

habitat ['hæbɪtæt] Lebensraum, Heimat **VI 6** 51
hair [heə] Haar **III 1** 12
haircut ['heəkʌt] Frisur **IV 5** 60
hairdresser ['heədresə] Friseurin, Friseur **IV 5** 60
half [hɑ:f] halb **IV 5** 61
half a year [hɑ:f ə 'jɪə] ein halbes Jahr **IV 5** 61
half of ['hɑ:f əv] Hälfte von **IV ER** 30
hall [hɔ:l] Halle, Saal **III ER** 118
hallway ['hɔ:lweɪ] Flur, Korridor **III ER** 82
hamburger ['hæmbɜ:gə] Hamburger **I LS** 11
hamster ['hæmstə] Hamster **I 4** 66
hand [hænd] Hand **I 6** 105
join hands [dʒɔɪn hændz] sich an den Händen fassen **VI 7** 63
handout ['hændaʊt] Arbeitsblatt **VI 2** 16
hang (up) ['hæŋ ʌp] (auf-)hängen **II 7** 109
hang on ['hæŋ ɒn] (noch) warten **III 2** 24
hang out ['hæŋ aʊt] herumhängen **IV 1** 9
happen ['hæpən] passieren, geschehen **II 4** 55
happy ['hæpi] glücklich **II 2** 26
hard [hɑ:d] hart **III 3** 39; schwierig **IV 6** 77
hardly ['hɑ:dli] kaum **IV 1** 12
hardware store (AE) ['hɑ:dweə stɔ:] Baumarkt **IV 2** 24
hat [hæt] Hut **I 6** 100
hate [heɪt] hassen **III 1** 10; Hass **VI 3** 27
have [hæv] nehmen **III 1** 16
have a break [hæv ə 'breɪk] (eine) Pause machen **III 2** 24
have a party [hæv ə 'pa:ti] eine Party feiern **I B4** 83
have a shower [hæv ə 'ʃaʊə] duschen **I 4** 70
have an argument [hæv ən 'ɑ:gjəmənt] Streit haben **V 4** 46
have breakfast [hæv 'brekfəst] frühstücken **I 5** 84
have (got) [hæv 'gɒt] haben, besitzen **I 2** 33
have got on [hæv gɒt 'ɒn] anhaben, tragen **II 1** 12
have lunch [hæv 'lʌntʃ] Mittag essen **I 5** 84
have to ['hæv tu:] müssen **II 7** 106
he [hi:] er **I 1** 17
head [hed] Kopf **II 4** 54
°heading ['hedɪŋ] Überschrift **I 8** 135
headmaster [hed'mɑ:stə] Schulleiterin, Schulleiter; Rektorin, Rektor **II 1** 12
headphones ['hedfəʊnz] Kopfhörer **III 1** 9
heal [hi:l] heilen **IV 1** 12
°Health class ['helθ klɑ:s] Gesundheitserziehung **V 6** 70
hear [hɪə] hören **III 3** 36
heart [hɑ:t] Herz **VI 5** 47
heat [hi:t] erhitzen, Hitze **III 3** 39
heavy ['hevi] schwer **III 5** 64
height [haɪt] Größe **V 6** 73
height [haɪt] Höhe **V 7** 88
helicopter ['helɪkɒptə] Hubschrauber **III 7** 90
Hello. [hə'ləʊ] Hallo./Guten Tag. **I LS** 9
helmet ['helmət] Helm **II 4** 59
help [help] helfen, Hilfe **I 3** 54
Help yourself. ['help jɔ:'self] Bedien* dich./Bedient euch. **V 4** 46
hen [hen] Henne **I B6** 116
her [hɜ:] ihr, ihre **I 4** 66
herd [hɜ:d] Herde **IV 2** 24
here [hɪə] hier **I 2** 32
Here you are. ['hɪə ju: ɑ:] Bitte schön. **I 2** 38
hero ['hɪərəʊ] Held **V 5** 61
heroine ['herəʊɪn] Heldin **V 5** 61
hers [hɜ:z] ihre, ihrer, ihres **IV 7** 88
Hi! [haɪ] Hallo! **I LS** 9
hide [haɪd] (sich) verstecken **I 4** 71
high [haɪ] hoch **II 6** 88
high-tech [haɪ'tek] Hightech- **VI 2** 15
highway ['haɪweɪ] Landstraße, Autobahn **V 1** 9
°information highway [ɪnfə'meɪʃn 'haɪweɪ] Datenautobahn **V 1** 9
hike [haɪk] wandern **II 7** 104; Wanderung **°II 7** 110
hill [hɪl] Hügel **V 2** 20
him [hɪm] ihn, ihm **I 3** 54
himself [hɪm'self] sich selbst **V 2** 20
hippo (potamus) ['hɪpəʊ] Nilpferd, Flusspferd **I 7** 122
hire ['haɪə] mieten **III 3** 36; anheuern **IV 5** 60
his [hɪz] sein, seine **I 4** 66
History ['hɪstri] Geschichte **II 1** 9
hit [hɪt] schlagen, treffen **II 4** 58; Hit **III 2** 27; Klick, Besucher **V 4** 46
HIV [eɪtʃaɪ'vi:] HIV **V 3** 36
hobby ['hɒbi] Hobby **I B2** 48
hockey ['hɒki] Hockey **I LS** 12
ice hockey [aɪs 'hɒki] Eishockey **V 7** 87
hold [həʊld] halten **IV 1** 8
hole [həʊl] Loch **III 6** 76
holidays ['hɒlədeɪz] Ferien **II 8** 118
holiday flat ['hɒlədeɪ flæt] Ferienwohnung **II 8** 118
°on holiday [ɒn 'hɒlədeɪ] im Urlaub, in den Ferien **II 8** 118
home [həʊm] Heim, Zuhause **I 5** 85
animal home ['ænɪml həʊm] Tierheim **IV 5** 62
at home [æt 'həʊm] zu Hause **I B6** 116
homeless ['həʊmləs] obdachlos **VI 6** 51
homework ['həʊmwɜ:k] Hausaufgaben **I 5** 85
°old people*s home [əuld 'pi:plz 'həʊm] Altenheim **V 4** 45
°homeroom (AE) [həʊmru:m] Klassenzimmer **V 6** 72
hood (AE) [hʊd] Motorhaube **IV ER** 56
hope [həʊp] hoffen, Hoffnung **III 5** 65
horoscope ['hɒrəskəʊp] Horoskop **III PR6** 125
horror ['hɒrə] Schrecken, Entsetzen **III ER** 82
horse [hɔ:s] Pferd **I 4** 75
horse riding [hɔ:s 'raɪdɪŋ] Reiten **VI 1** 8
horsepower ['hɔ:spaʊə] Pferdestärke (PS) **III 6** 77
hospital ['hɒspɪtl] Krankenhaus **II 4** 54
hospitality [hɒspɪ'tæləti] Bewirtung **V 4** ER
hot [hɒt] heiß, scharf **II 2** 23
hot dog ['hɒt dɒg] Hotdog **I LS** 12
hotel [həʊ'tel] Hotel **II 8** 119
hotel manager [həʊ'tel 'mænɪdʒə] Hoteldirektorin, Hoteldirektor **V 1** 8
hour ['aʊə] Stunde **I 5** 84
house [haʊs] Haus **I B3** 64
housework ['haʊswɜ:k] Hausarbeit **VI 4** 32
how [haʊ] wie **I 1** 17
How are you? [haʊ 'ɑ: ju:] Wie geht es dir/Ihnen? **II 4** 56
How much is it? [haʊ 'mʌtʃ ɪz ɪt] Was kostet das?/Was macht das? **I 8** 133
however [haʊ'evə] wie dem auch sei **V 4** 46
huge [hju:ʤ] riesig **IV 4** 51
hundred ['hʌndrəd] hundert **I 6** 101
Hungarian [hʌŋ'geəriən] Ungarin, Ungar; ungarisch **IV 6** 78

hungry ['hʌŋgri] hungrig **I 8** 134
hunt [hʌnt] jagen **IV 2** 24
°**Hurray!** [hə'reɪ] Hurra! **I 1** 20
hurricane ['hʌrɪkən] Orkan, Hurrikan **VI 6** 51
hurt [hɜ:t] sich verletzen, weh tun **II 4** 54
husband ['hʌzbənd] Ehemann **III 7** 87
hut [hʌt] Hütte **VI 4** 33

I

I [aɪ] ich **I LS** 9
I don't mind. [aɪ dəʊnt 'maɪnd] Es macht mir nichts aus. **IV 5** 62
I look forward to hearing from you. [aɪ lʊk 'fɔ:wəd tə 'hɪərɪŋ frɒm 'ju:] Ich freue mich darauf, von Ihnen zu hören. **IV 5** 74
I'd like … (I would like …) [aɪd 'laɪk] Ich möchte/hätte gern … **I 6** 100
ice [aɪs] Eis, Glatteis **II 4** 56
ice age ['aɪs eɪʤ] Eiszeit **IV 3** 49
ice cream [aɪs 'kri:m] Eis (Speiseeis) **I 3** 51
ice hockey [aɪs 'hɒki] Eishockey **V 7** 87
iced tea [aɪst ti:] Eistee **III 1** 16
icy ['aɪsi] eisig **II 4** 56
iceberg ['aɪsbɜ:g] Eisberg **VI 2** 14
idea [aɪ'dɪə] Idee **I 3** 50
ideal weight [aɪ'dɪəl weɪt] Idealgewicht **V 6** 73
idol ['aɪdl] Idol, Vorbild **IV ER** 23
if [ɪf] wenn **III 4** 51
ill [ɪl] krank **IV 2** 25
illegal [ɪ'li:gl] illegal **VI 7** 63
I'm cold. [aɪm 'kəʊld] Mir ist kalt. **II 8** 122
I'm fine, thank you. [aɪm 'faɪn θæŋk ju] (Mir geht es) gut, danke. **II 4** 56
I'm (I am) [aɪm (aɪ 'æm)] ich bin **I LS** 9
I'm sorry. [aɪm 'sɒri] Es tut mir Leid. **II 4** 56
image ['ɪmɪdʒ] Bild **VI 2** 15
imagine [ɪ'mæʤɪn] sich ausdenken **III ER** 75
immediately [ɪ'mi:diətli] sofort **VI 2** 17
immense [ɪ'ments] viel, immens **V 5** 60
immigrant ['ɪmɪgrənt] Einwanderin, Einwanderer **V 1** 10
important [ɪm'pɔ:tənt] wichtig **V 2** 25
impress ['ɪmpres] beeindrucken **V 6** 68
in [ɪn] in, im; auf **I B1** 30; hinein **I 3** 50
in 1975 [ɪn naɪnti:n sevnti'faɪv] (im Jahr) 1975 **II 3** 40
in front of [ɪn 'frʌnt əv] vor **III 1** 10
°in the end [ɪn ðɪ 'end] schließlich **II 3** 42
in the morning [ɪn ðə 'mɔ:nɪŋ] morgens **II 1** 8
in good shape [ɪn gʊd 'ʃeɪp] in guter Form **V 6** 62
in one sense [ɪn 'wʌn 'sens] in einer Hinsicht **VI 2** 14
in-line skates ['ɪnlaɪn 'skeɪts] Inliner **II 3** 44
include [ɪn'klu:d] einschließen **VI 6** 50
including [ɪn'klu:dɪŋ] einschließlich **III 6** 76
increase ['ɪnkri:s] steigen, ansteigen **VI 6** 50; Anstieg **VI 6** 51
independence [ɪndɪ'pendəns] Unabhängigkeit **IV 2** 25
independent [ɪndɪ'pendənt] unabhängig **VI 3** 29
Indian ['ɪndiən] Indianerin, Indianer; indianisch **I 1** 20; Inderin, Inder; indisch **II 2** 26
industry ['ɪndəstri] Industriezweig **IV ER** 23
infection [ɪn'fekʃn] Infektion **IV 1** 12
information [ɪnfə'meɪʃn] Information (en) **II 7** 104
°information highway [ɪnfə'meɪʃn 'haɪweɪ] Datenautobahn **V 1** 9
°tourist information centre ['tʊərɪst ɪnfə'meɪʃn 'sentə] Touristeninformation **III 3** 42
ingredient [ɪn'gri:diənt] Bestandteil **VI 3** 27
injured ['ɪndʒəd] verletzt **V 6** 62
injustice [ɪn'dʒʌstɪs] Ungerechtigkeit **VI 7** 63
inquire [ɪn'kwaɪə] sich erkundigen **VI 2** 17
insect ['ɪnsekt] Insekt **III 4** 53
inside [ɪn'saɪd] hinein **V 4** 47
inspiration [ɪnspər'eɪʃn] Inspiration **III 6** 77
°**Instead** [ɪn'sted] stattdessen **II 4** 60
instruction [ɪn'strʌkʃn] Anweisung **III 4** 52
instrument ['ɪntstrəmənt] Maschine, Instrument **III 6** 76
interested ['ɪntrəstɪd] interessiert **II 5** 77
interesting ['ɪntrəstɪŋ] interessant **II 1** 8
international [ɪntə'næʃnəl] international **III 8** 105
°**Internet** ['ɪntənet] Internet **II 6** 88
°Internet services company [ɪntənet sɜ:vɪsɪz 'kʌmpəni] Internetagentur **V 4** 46
surf the Internet [sɜ:f ðɪ 'ɪntənet] im Internet surfen **II 7** 105
interview ['ɪntəvju:] Interview **I 8** 133; interviewen **II 6** 93; Bewerbungsgespräch **V 4** ER
interviewer ['ɪntəvju:ə] Interviewerin, Interviewer **I 8** 133
into ['ɪntʊ] in, hinein **I 6** 102
introduce someone [ɪntrə'dju:s 'sʌmwʌn] jemanden vorstellen **VI 4** 34
invent [ɪn'vent] erfinden **III 6** 76
invention [ɪn'venʃn] Erfindung **III 6** 76
inventor [ɪn'ventə] Erfinderin, Erfinder **III 6** 76
invest [ɪn'vest] investieren **VI 5** 45
°**invitation** [ɪnvɪ'teɪʃn] Einladung **II 5** 80
invite [ɪn'vaɪt] einladen **V 6** 72
involve [ɪn'vɒlv] jemanden an etwas beteiligen **VI 4** 32
Irish ['aɪrɪʃ] Irin, Ire; irisch **III 7** 88
Ironman ['aɪənmæn] Ironman **V 5** 61
is [ɪz] ist **I LS** 9
…is/are off the menu [ɪz/ɑ: ɒf ðə 'menju:] … ist/sind ausgegangen (auf einer Speisekarte) **II 2** 24
island ['aɪlənd] Insel **I 3** 51
it [ɪt] es **I LS** 10
its [ɪts] sein, seine **I 4** 78

J

jacket ['dʒækɪt] Jacke **II 5** 73
jail [ʤeɪl] Gefängnis **IV 5** 64
jam [dʒæm] Marmelade **I 7** 120
January ['dʒænjuəri] Januar **I 8** 132
jeans [dʒi:nz] Jeanshose **II 5** 79
jelly baby ['dʒeli beɪbi] Gummibärchen **I 8** 133
jewelry ['ʤu:əlri] Schmuck **IV 1** 12
jigsaw puzzle ['dʒɪgsɔ: pʌzl] Puzzle **II 6** 86
job [dʒɒb] Aufgabe, Arbeit, Beruf **I 7** 118
job centre [dʒɒb 'sentə] Arbeitsamt **V 4** ER
full-time job [fʊl taɪm 'ʤɒb] Vollzeitbeschäftigung **IV ER** 75
part-time job [pɑ:t taɪm 'ʤɒb] Teilzeitbeschäftigung **IV ER** 75
jog [ʤɒg] joggen, laufen **III 7** 86
join hands [dʒɔɪn hændz] sich an den Händen fassen **VI 7** 63

joke [dʒəʊk] Witze machen, nicht ernst meinen **III 8** 104
journey ['dʒɜ:nɪ] Reise **V 2** 19
July [dʒʊ'laɪ] Juli **I 8** 132
jump [dʒʌmp] springen **I 3** 54
June [dʒu:n] Juni **I 8** 132
jungle ['dʒʌŋgl] Dschungel **IV 4** 50
just [dʒʌst] nur, gerade **III 1** 8
just in time [dʒʌst ɪn 'taɪm] rechtzeitig **III ER** 119

K

kangaroo [kæŋəru:] Känguru **V 2** 20
keep [ki:p] behalten **V 4** 45
keep an eye on [ki:p ən 'aɪ ɒn] aufpassen, beobachten **IV 5** 64
keep away [ki:p ə'weɪ] wegbleiben **III 4** 50
keep separate [ki:p 'seprət] trennen **V 3** 34
ketchup ['ketʃʌp] Ketchup **II 2** 23
key [ki:] Schlüssel **I 3** 59; Taste **II 7** 106
key word ['ki: wɜ:d] Schlüsselwort **I 5** 86
°keyboard ['ki:bɔ:d] Tastatur **II 7** 106
shift key ['ʃɪft ki:] Umschalttaste **II 7** 106
kick someone off ['kɪk sʌmwʌn ɒf] jemanden hinauswerfen **V 6** 70
kid [kɪd] Kind **IV 1** 8
kidnap ['kɪdnæp] entführen, kidnappen **IV 4** 52
kill [kɪl] töten **IV 2** 24
killer ['kɪlə] Mörderin, Mörder **V 6** 69
kilo ['ki:ləʊ] Kilo **II 3** 41
kilometre ['kɪləmi:tə] Kilometer **III 8** 102
kind [kaɪnd] Art **III 7** 87
°**kindergarten** ['kɪndəgɑ:tn] Kindergarten **I 2** 36
kindergarten assistant ['kɪndəgɑ:tn ə'sɪstənt] Kindergärtnerin, Kindergärtner **V 4** 42
°**kinetoscope** ['kɪnətəskəʊp] Kinematograph **III 6** 76
king [kɪŋ] König **IV 4** 52
kiss [kɪs] küssen **VI 5** 45
kitchen ['kɪtʃɪn] Küche **I B3** 64
kite [kaɪt] Drachen **VI 5** 47
kiwi ['ki:wi:] Kiwi **II 3** 41
km² (square kilometre) [skweə 'kɪləmi:tə] Quadratkilometer **II 6** 88
knee [ni:] Knie **II 4** 55
knee pad ['ni: pæd] Knieschützer **II 4** 58
knife, knives [naɪf, naɪvz] Messer **II 2** 22
knock [nɒk] Klopfen **III ER** 82
know [nəʊ] wissen, kennen **I 8** 133
well-known ['welnəʊn] bekannt **V 4** 46
°**kph (kilometres per hour)** [kɪ'lɒmɪtəz pə aʊə] km/h **V 5** 61

L

label ['leɪbl] Marke, Label **VI 1** 9
lady ['leɪdi] Dame **III 7** 90
lake [leɪk] See **I 3** 51
land [lænd] landen **III 7** 90; Land **V 2** 16
language ['læŋgwɪdʒ] Sprache **IV 2** 24
large [lɑ:dʒ] groß **III ER** 49
lasagne [lə'zænjə] Lasagne **III 1** 16
last [lɑ:st] letzter, letzte, letztes **I 3** 54; dauern **V 5** 60
at last [æt lɑ:st] endlich **VI 7** 62
the very last [ðə veri 'lɑ:st] der/die/das allerletzte **IV 3** 43
late [leɪt] spät **II 3** 42
Latin ['lætɪn] lateinisch; Latein **III 4** 51
laugh [lɑ:f] lachen **II 2** 27
laught at ['lɑ:f ət] auslachen **V 6** 73
launch [lɔ:nʃ] vom Stapel lassen **VI 2** 15
law [lɔ:] Gesetz **V 3** 34
law firm ['lɔ: fɜ:m] Anwaltskanzlei **V 3** 34
lawyer [lɔ:jə] Rechtsanwältin, Rechtsanwalt **V 3** 34
lay the table [leɪ ðə 'teɪbl] den Tisch decken **II 2** 22
layout ['leɪaʊt] Layout **III PR6** 125
lead [li:d] führen **V 2** 21
leader ['li:də] Anführerin, Anführer **IV ER** 82
leaflet ['li:flət] Flugblatt **VI 7** 62
league [li:g] Liga **II 6** 87; Verein, Verband °**V 3** 35
learn [lɜ:n] lernen **I 8** 132
least [li:st] mindestens **V 6** ER
leather ['leðə] Leder **IV 2** 24
leave [li:v] verlassen, zurücklassen **I 7** 108
left [left] links **I 6** 102
leg [leg] Bein **II 4** 54
legend ['ledʒənd] Legende **IV ER** 112
lemonade [lemə'neɪd] Limonade **I 8** 133
°**length** [leŋθ] Länge **III 5** 61
less [les] weniger **V 5** 62
lesson ['lesn] (Unterrichts-)Stunde **II 1** 9
let [let] lassen **III 1** 10
let down [let 'daʊn] enttäuschen **IV ER** 83
letter ['letə] Brief **II 2** 24; Buchstabe **II 6** 90
°capital letters ['kæpɪtl letəz] Großbuchstaben **II 7** 106
library ['laɪbrərɪ] Bibliothek **I B1** 30
licence ['laɪsəns] (Führer-)Schein **III 8** 103
lie [laɪ] liegen **III 7** 86; Lüge, lügen **III ER** 119
lie down ['laɪ daʊn] sich hinlegen **V 2** 20
°**life, lives** [laɪf laɪvz] das Leben **I 5** 84
for life [fə 'laɪf] lebenslänglich **V 3** 35
°way of life [weɪ əv 'laɪf] Lebensstil, Lebensart **V 1** 10
lift [lɪft] heben **V 6** 70; Mitfahrgelegenheit **VI 7** 62
lift weights [lɪft 'weɪts] Gewichte heben **V 6** 70
lift-off ['lɪftɒf] Start (bei Raumfähren) **III 5** 64
light [laɪt] Licht **I 6** 104; leichter, leichte, leichtes **V 7** 89; anzünden **V 2** 31
lightning ['laɪtnɪŋ] Blitz **V 2** 20
like [laɪk] mögen; wie **I 4** 76
act like ['ækt laɪk] sich benehmen wie **III ER** 31
look (like) … [lʊk 'laɪk] aussehen (wie) … **II 8** 123
What would you like? [wɒt wʊd ju: 'laɪk] Was möchtest du?/Was hättest du/hätten Sie gern? **I 6** 100
limit ['lɪmɪt] Grenze **V 5** 61
go to the limit [gəʊ tə ðə 'lɪmɪt] bis zum Äußersten gehen **V 5** 61
line [laɪn] Zeile **II 1** 13
link [lɪŋk] Link **II 7** 106; Verbindung **VI 3** 27
lion ['laɪən] Löwe **I 7** 127
lip [lɪp] Lippe **IV 1** 9
list [lɪst] Liste **I 1** 17
listen (to) ['lɪsən tu:] anhören **V 6** ER; (zu-)hören **I 3** 57
liter (AE) ['li:tə] Liter **VI 7** 65
litter ['lɪtə] Abfall **III 4** 50
little ['lɪtl] klein **I 1** 20; wenig **V 6** 72
live [laɪv] live, direkt **IV ER** 82
live [lɪv] leben, wohnen **I 4** 70
°**liver** ['lɪvə] Leber **V 2** 21
living room ['lɪvɪŋ ru:m] Wohnzimmer **I B3** 64

local ['ləʊkl] örtlich, lokal **III 7** 88
locate [ləʊ'keɪt] befinden **V 7** 88; orten, ausfindig machen **VI 2** 15
location [ləʊ'keɪʃən] Lage **V 7** 88
lock [lɒk] abschließen **III 3** 35
locker ['lɒkə] Schließfach **V 6** 75
locomotive [ləʊkə'məʊtɪv] Lokomotive **IV ER** 101
lonely ['ləʊnli] einsam **II 1** 9
long [lɒŋ] lang **I 5** 84
look [lʊk] sehen, schauen **I 1** 20
look after [lʊk 'ɑ:ftə] aufpassen auf, sich kümmern um **V 4** 42
look at ['lʊk ət] anschauen **I 6** 104
look for ['lʊk fɔ:] suchen nach **I 6** 106
look forward to [lʊk 'fɔ:wəd tu:] sich freuen auf **V 3** 36
look like ... [lʊk 'laɪk] aussehen wie ... **I 8** 123
°look up [lʊk 'ʌp] nachschauen, nachschlagen **II 5** 72
lord [lɔ:d] Herr, Lord **VI 1** 8
lorry ['lɒri] Laster, LKW **IV 6** 77
lose [lu:z] verlieren **II 5** 76
°be lost [bi: 'lɒst] sich verlaufen **I 6** 102
lots of [lɒts əv] viel, viele **II 6** 90
loud [laʊd] laut **V 2** 19
love [lʌv] lieben **I LS** 12; liebe Grüße **V 6** 71
fall in love [fɔ:l ɪn 'lʌv] sich verlieben **IV 1** 8
lovers ['lʌvə] Liebende, Liebespaar(e) **VI 3** 27
low-paid [ləʊ-peɪd] schlecht bezahlt **VI 4** 35
luck [lʌk] Glück **V 4** 46
bad luck [bæd 'lʌk] Pech **V 4** 46
be lucky [bi: 'lʌki] Glück haben **II 1** 12
lunch [lʌntʃ] Mittagessen **II 1** 9
have lunch [hæv 'lʌntʃ] Mittag essen **I 5** 84
lunchtime ['lʌntʃtaɪm] Mittagszeit **II 4** 59

M

machine [mə'ʃi:n] Maschine **VI 4** 35
time machine [taɪm mə'ʃi:n] Zeitmaschine **III 5** 62
mad [mæd] wütend, böse **V 6** 74
be mad at someone [bi 'mæd ət sʌmwʌn] wütend auf jemanden sein **V 6** 74
magazine [mægə'zi:n] Zeitschrift **II 5** 86
magic ['mædʒɪk] Zauberei, Magie **V 2** 17
magical ['mædʒɪkl] magisch **VI 5** 45
magnet ['mægnət] Magnet **IV ER** 101
magnetic [mæg'netɪk] magnetisch **IV ER** 101
mail [meɪl] schreiben, mailen **V 6** 71
main course ['meɪn kɔ:s] Hauptgericht **II 2** 25
majority [mə'dʒɒrəti] Mehrheit **VI 5** 45
make [meɪk] machen, tun **II 2** 37
make a record ['meɪk ə rekɔ:d] eine Aufnahme machen **VI 1** 8
make fun [meɪk 'fʌn] Spaß machen **VI 1** 8
make it ['meɪk ɪt] es schaffen **IV ER** 23
make money [meɪk 'mʌni] Geld verdienen **V 2** ER
make-up ['meɪkʌp] Schminke **II 1** 12
make-up artist ['meɪk ʌp 'ɑ:tɪst] Visagistin, Visagist **IV 5** 60
male [meɪl] männlich **V 5** 61
mall (AE) [mɔ:l] Einkaufszentrum **IV 1** 9
man [mæn] Mann **I 3** 52
manage ['mænɪdʒ] etwas schaffen, bewältigen **VI 2** 14
many ['meni] viele **I 2** 39
map [mæp] Landkarte, Stadtplan **I 2** 32
March [mɑ:tʃ] März **I 8** 132
march [mɑ:tʃ] marschieren **VI 7** 63
market ['mɑ:kɪt] Markt **I B5** 98
flea market ['fli: mɑ:kɪt] Flohmarkt **II 3** 44
marketing ['mɑ:kɪtɪŋ] Werbung, Marketing **IV 5** 61
marketing assistant ['mɑ:kɪtɪŋ ə'sɪstənt] Marketingassistentin, Marketingassistent **IV 5** 61
marry ['mæri] heiraten **VI 4** 33
mast [mɑ:st] Mast **VI 2** 14
match [mætʃ] Spiel **II 6** 87; zuordnen **III 1** 15
Maths [mæθs] Mathe (matik) **II 1** 9
matter ['mætə] Angelegenheit **VI 2** 17
May [meɪ] Mai **I 8** 132
may [meɪ] vielleicht **VI 6** 50
maybe ['meɪbi:] vielleicht **V 1** 8
me [mi:] mir, mich **I 3** 54
°meal [mi:l] Mahlzeit **II 2** 22
mean [mi:n] meinen **III 7** 86
means of transport [mi:nz əv 'trænspɔ:t] Verkehrsmittel **III 6** 79
measure ['meʃə] messen **VI 2** 15
meat [mi:t] Fleisch **IV 2** 24
mechanic [mɪ'kænɪk] Mechanikerin, Mechaniker **IV 5** 61
car mechanic [kɑ:r mɪ'kænɪk] Automechanikerin, Automechaniker **V 1** 8
medal ['medəl] Medaille **V 2** ER
medication [medɪ'keɪʃən] Medikamente **V 6** 70
meet [mi:t] treffen, sich treffen **I 3** 50
meeting ['mi:tɪŋ] Treffen, Sitzung, Besprechung **V 1** 8
melt [melt] schmelzen **III 5** 64
member ['membə] Mitglied **VI 1** 9
men [men] Männer **I 6** 104
menu ['menju:] Speisekarte **II 2** 24
message ['mesɪdʒ] Nachricht **III 5** 62
text message [tekst 'mesɪdʒ] SMS **VI 2** 16
meter (AE) ['mi:tə] Meter **VI 7** 65
metre ['mi:tə] Meter **I 8** 134
mid [mɪd] in der Mitte **VI 5** 45
middle ['mɪdl] Mitte **II 5** 76
migrant worker ['maɪgrnt 'wɜ:kə] Wanderarbeiter **VI 4** 34
migrate [maɪ'greɪt] wegziehen, umsiedeln **VI 6** 50
mile [maɪlz] Meile **III 5** 65
square mile [skweə 'maɪl] Quadratmeile **IV 3** 35
°military ['mɪlɪtri] militärisch **V 3** 35
milk [mɪlk] Milch **I 7** 120
milkshake ['mɪlkʃeɪk] Milchshake **I LS** 12
million ['mɪljən] Million **II 6** 88
millionaire [mɪljə'neə] Millionärin, Millionär **V 4** 50
I don't mind. [aɪ dəʊnt 'maɪnd] Es macht mir nichts aus. **IV 5** 62
mine [maɪn] Bergwerk **III ER** 101; meine, meiner, meines **IV 7** 88
miner ['maɪnə] Bergmann **III ER** 101
minerals ['mɪnərəl] Mineralien **VI 6** 51
minimum wage ['mɪnɪməm weɪdʒ] Mindestlohn **VI 4** 35
minute ['mɪnɪt] Minute **II 6** 90
mirror ['mɪrər] Spiegel **V 6** 72
miss [mɪs] vermissen **IV 6** 78
miss out on something [mɪs 'aʊt ɒn sʌmθɪŋ] (etwas) verpassen **II 5** 76
°missing ['mɪsɪŋ] fehlend **II 2** 30
moan [məʊn] motzen, stöhnen **IV 7** 90
°mobile phone [məʊbaɪl 'fəʊn] Mobiltelefon, Handy **II 2** 28

model ['mɒdl] Modell **III5** 69; Model **°IV1** 16
°model car ['mɒdl kɑ:] Modellauto **II6** 87
modern ['mɒdən] modern **II3** 40
modernize ['mɒdənaɪz] modernisieren **VI5** 45
mom (AE) [mɒm] Mama, Mutti **IV1** 12
moment ['məʊmənt] Augenblick, Moment **IV7** 90
at the moment [ət ðə 'məʊmənt] jetzt gerade **III2** 24
Monday ['mʌndeɪ] Montag **I1** 20
money ['mʌni] Geld **I6** 101
make money [meɪk 'mʌni] Geld verdienen **V2** ER
pocket money ['pɒkɪt mʌni] Taschengeld **II3** 44
monkey ['mʌŋki] Affe **I7** 122
Monopoly [mə'nɒpli] Monopoly **I1** 18
monster ['mɒnstə] Ungeheuer, Monster **IB4** 82
month [mʌnθ] Monat **I8** 132
moon [mu:n] Mond **IVER** 101
moose, moose [mu:s, mu:s] Elch, Elche **IV3** 35
more [mɔ:] mehr **II5** 72
morning ['mɔ:nɪŋ] Morgen, Vormittag **I1** 16
mosque [mɒsk] Moschee **V1** 10
most [məʊst] die meisten **V1** 8
mother ['mʌðə] Mutter **I4** 72
motor bike ['məʊtə baɪk] Motorrad **II4** 61
motorhome ['məʊtəhəʊm] Wohnmobil **IIIER** 75
mountain ['maʊntən] Berg **IV7** 90
mountain bike ['maʊntɪn baɪk] Mountainbike **ILS** 11
°mouse [maʊs] (Computer-)Maus **II7** 106; Maus **IV4** 50
move [mu:v] umziehen **IIIER** 56
Bewegung, Tanzschritt **IV1** 22
move up [mu:v‿ʌp] aufsteigen **VI4** 34
movie (AE) ['mu:vi] Film **II6** 94; Kino **V6** 78
Mr ['mɪstə] Herr (Anrede) **I1** 17
Mrs ['mɪsɪz] Frau (Anrede) **I2** 36
Ms [mɪz] Frau (Anrede) **II1** 13
much [mʌtʃ] viel **II7** 106
muesli ['mju:zli] Müsli **I7** 120
mum [mʌm] Mama, Mutti **II2** 23
°murder ['mɜ:də] Mord **II6** 94
museum [mju:'zi:əm] Museum **II6** 88
music ['mju:zɪk] Musik **I6** 86
music company ['mju:zɪk 'kʌmpəni] Musikfirma **III2** 24
musical ['mju:zɪkl] Musical **IV4** 50
musician [mju:'zɪʃən] Musikerin, Musiker **V3** 36
Muslim ['mʊzlɪm] Moslemin, Moslem; moslemisch **V1** 10
must [mʌst] müssen **II6** 90
a must see [ə 'mʌst si:] ein Muss **IV1** 11
mustn't ['mʌsnt] nicht dürfen **II8** 123
my [maɪ] mein, meine **ILS** 9
myself [maɪ'self] mich, selbst **V4** 44
°mysterious [mɪ'stɪəriəs] rätselhaft **II6** 94

N

nachos ['nɑ:tʃəʊz] Nachos **III1** 16
nail [neɪl] Nagel **IVER** 112
name [neɪm] Name **ILS** 9; nennen, ernennen **VI4** 34
°name card ['neɪm kɑ:d] Namensschild **ILS** 9
family name ['fæmli neɪm] Nachname **I4** 72
nasty ['nɑ:sti] gemein **IVER** 31
national holiday ['næʃnl 'hɒlədeɪ] Nationalfeiertag **III7** 95
national park ['næʃnl pɑ:k] Nationalpark **II7** 104
°national strike ['næʃənəl straɪk] Generalstreik **V3** 35
nationality [næʃən'æləti] Nationalität, Staatsangehörigkeit **V1** 10
native ['neɪtɪv] Eingeborene, Eingeborener **IVER** 112
natural ['nætʃərəl] natürlich **V5** 62
nature ['neɪtʃə] Natur **IV3** 35
near [nɪə] in der Nähe **II7** 104
°nearly ['nɪəli] fast **III7** 92
need [ni:d] brauchen **II2** 22
needle ['ni:dl] Nadel **IV1** 12
needn't [ni:dnt] nicht müssen **II7** 105
negro ['ni:grəʊ] Neger, Negerin **VI7** 63
neighbour ['neɪbə] Nachbarin, Nachbar **III3** 34
neighbourhood ['neɪbəhʊd] Nachbarschaft **III7** 86
nervous ['nɜ:vəs] angespannt, nervös **V5** 60
nest [nest] Nest **III4** 51
netball ['netbɔ:l] Korbball **VI4** 37
never ['nevə] niemals **I5** 84
never-never land ['nevə 'nevə lænd] Niemandsland **V2** 17
new [nju:] neu **I2** 32
New Year's Day [nju: jɪəz deɪ] Neujahr **III3** 39
New Year's Eve [nju: jɪəz i:v] Silvester **III3** 38
news [nju:z] Nachrichten, Neuigkeiten **II6** 94
newspaper ['nju:speɪpə] Zeitung **I5** 93
newspaper advert ['nju:speɪpə 'ædvɜ:t] Zeitungsanzeige **V4** 44
next [nekst] nächster, nächste, nächstes **II1** 10
°next door [nekst 'dɔ:] nebenan **IV5** 66
next to ['nekst tə] neben **IB5** 98
nice [naɪs] nett, hübsch **I3** 54
Nice to meet you. ['naɪs tə mi:t ju:] Schön dich zu treffen. **I2** 40
nigger ['nɪgə] Nigger **VI7** 65
night [naɪt] Nacht, Abend **I4** 70
all night [ɔ:l 'naɪt] die ganze Nacht **I4** 70
at night [ət 'naɪt] nachts **IIIER** 23
nine [naɪn] neun **ILS** 10
nineteen [naɪn'ti:n] neunzehn **I2** 32
ninety ['naɪnti] neunzig **I6** 101
no [nəʊ] nein; kein, keine, keines **I1** 18
no signal [nəʊ 'sɪgnəl] kein Empfang **IV7** 90
No vacancies. [nəʊ 'veɪkənsi:z] Belegt/Keine Zimmer frei. **III3** 42
No way. ['nəʊ 'weɪ] Absolut nicht. **II6** 87
nobody ['nəʊbədi] niemand, keiner **III3** 39
°Nobel Peace Prize [nəʊbel 'pi:s praɪz] Friedensnobelpreis **V3** 36
noise [nɔɪz] Lärm **V2** 27
noisy ['nɔɪzi] laut **III2** 27
non-stop [nɒn'stɒp] non-stop **VI2** 14
nonetheless [nʌnðə'les] trotzdem **IV6** 76
normal ['nɔ:məl] normal **IIIER** 75
north [nɔ:θ] Norden; nördlich **V2** 16
nose [nəʊs] Nase **IV1** 9
not [nɒt] nicht **I2** 36
not even [nɒt 'i:vən] nicht einmal **V2** 20
not yet [nɒt 'jet] noch nicht **III3** 36
not … either [nɑt 'aɪðər] auch nicht **V6** 73
notebook ['nəʊtbʊk] Notizbuch **III4** 52
°notes [nəʊts] Notizen **III6** 79
nothing ['nʌθɪŋ] nichts **V4** 46
notice ['nəʊtɪs] Hinweis **II7** 109; bemerken **IV5** 65

notice board ['nəʊtɪs bɔ:d] schwarzes Brett **II1** 10
November [nəʊ'vembə] November **I8** 132
now [naʊ] nun, jetzt **IB1** 30
nowadays ['naʊədeɪz] heutzutage **III8** 104
number ['nʌmbə] Zahl, Nummer **ILS** 10

O

ocean ['əʊʃn] Ozean **III5** 64
... o'clock [ə'klɒk] ... Uhr **I5** 84
October [ɒk'təʊbə] Oktober **I8** 132
of [ɒv/əv] von **I5** 84
of course [əv 'kɔ:s] natürlich, selbstverständlich **II1** 8
offer ['ɒfə] anbieten **IV5** 61; Angebot **IV7** 86
special offer [speʃl 'ɒfə] Sonderangebot **II3** 44
office ['ɒfɪs] Büro **III7** 86
official [ə'fɪʃl] offiziell **III6** 79
often ['ɒfn] oft **I5** 84
oh [əʊ] null (bei Telefonnummern) **ILS** 10
°**oil** [ɔɪl] ölen **II7** 112; Öl **VI6** 52
OK [əʊ'keɪ] okay, in Ordnung **ILS** 10
old [əʊld] alt **I1** 17
°old people*s home [əuld 'pi:plz 'həʊm] Altenheim **V4** 45
Olympic Games [əʊ'lɪmpɪk geɪmz] Olympische Spiele **V2** 16
on [ɒn] am **I1** 21; auf **I2** 34; an, eingeschaltet **I6** 104
on a bus [ɒn ə 'bʌs] im Bus **I6** 109
on a train [ɒn ə 'treɪn] im Zug **I6** 109
on his/her own [ɒn hɪs/hɜ: 'əʊn] alleine **IV1** 12
°on holiday [ɒn 'hɒlɪdeɪ] im Urlaub, in den Ferien **II8** 118
on record [ɒn 'rekɔ:d] bekannt, belegt **VI6** 51
on top [ɒn 'tɒp] oben **III7** 90
on TV [ɒn ti:'vi:] im Fernsehen **VI1** 8
onboard ['ɒnbɔ:d] Bord- **VI2** 15
°**once** [wʌns] einmal **III PR3** 122
one [wʌn] eins **ILS** 10
one day [wʌn 'deɪ] eines Tages **II5** 72
onion ['ʌnjən] Zwiebel **II3** 41
online banking [ɒn'lain bæŋkɪŋ] Onlinebanking **V1** 9
online forum ['onlaɪn 'fɔ:rəm] Internetforum **V1** 9
only ['əʊnli] nur **I6** 100; erst **III1** 12
open ['əʊpən] offen; öffnen **I2** 36
°**opening ceremony** [əʊpənɪŋ 'serɪməni] Eröffnungsfeier **V2** ER
opera ['ɒprə] Oper **V2** 16
°**operator** ['ɒpəreɪtə] Vermittlung **II4** 54
°**opinion** [ə'pɪnjən] Meinung **IV1** 12
opportunity [ɒpə'tju:nəti] Chance, Möglichkeit **VI3** 26
opposite ['ɒpəzɪt] Gegenteil **I3** 61; gegenüber **IB5** 98
opposition [ɒpə'zɪʃn] Opposition **VI4** 32
optimist ['ɒptɪmɪst] Optimistin, Optimist **V1** 9
or [ɔ:] oder **I1** 20
orange ['ɒrɪndʒ] Orange, Apfelsine **II3** 41
orbit ['ɔ:bɪt] Umlaufbahn **III5** 64
°**order** ['ɔ:də] Reihenfolge **I6** 102; bestellen **VI2** 17
order form ['ɔ:də 'fɔ:m] Bestellformular **VI2** 17
organisation [ɔ:gənaɪ'zeɪʃn] Organisation **V2** ER
organise ['ɔ:genaɪz] organisieren **V3** 35
original [ə'rɪdʒənəl] einst, ursprünglich, original **V4** 43
other ['ʌðə] anderer, andere, anderes **IV5** 64
the other day [ðɪ 'ʌðə deɪ] neulich **IV5** 64
our ['aʊə] unser, unsere **I3** 50
ours [aʊəz] unsere, unserer, unseres **IV7** 88
out [aʊt] aus, heraus **III2** 25; unterwegs **V5** 62
outback ['aʊtbæk] Hinterland **V2** 16
outlaw ['aʊtlɔ:] Gesetzloser, Bandit **II5** 72
outside [aʊt'saɪd] draußen, außerhalb, außen, vor **II3** 40
outsider [aʊt'saɪdə] Außenseiterin, Außenseiter **V6** 72
oven ['ʌvn] Ofen, Backofen **IV2** 26
over ['əʊvə] über **II6** 88
over there [əʊvə 'ðeə] dort drüben **I5** 88
own [əʊn] eigener, eigene, eigenes **IV2** 24
owner ['əʊnə] Besitzerin, Besitzer **IV5** 64

P

pack [pæk] packen **III3** 35
package ['pækɪdʒ] Paket **III7** 86
packet ['pækɪt] Packung, Päckchen **I8** 133
°**on page ...** [ɒn 'peɪdʒ] auf Seite ... **I1** 21
paint [peɪnt] malen, streichen **II5** 74
°**pair** [peə] Paar **I6** 111
Pakistani [pɑ:kɪ'stɑ:ni] Pakistanerin, Pakistaner; pakistanisch **IV5** 64
palace ['pælɪs] Palast **III1** 8
panther ['pænθə] Panther **IV2** 52
paper ['peɪpə] (Geschenk-)Papier **III3** 43
recycled paper [ri:'saɪkld 'peɪpə] Recyclingpapier **VI6** 53
paradise ['pærədaɪs] Paradies **IV ER** 112
parent ['peərənt] Elternteil **V6** ER
parents ['peərənts] Eltern **III3** 36
park [pɑ:k] Park **I3** 50; parken °**V2** 17
park ranger [pɑ:k 'reɪndʒə] Wildhüterin, Wildhüter **II7** 109
parliament ['pɑ:ləmənt] Parlament **VI4** 32
parrot ['pærət] Papagei **I4** 66
part [pɑ:t] Teil **I8** 135
part-time job [pɑ:t taɪm 'dʒɒb] Teilzeitbeschäftigung **IV ER** 75
take part in [teɪk 'pɑ:t ɪn] teilnehmen an **V5** 60
partner ['pɑ:tnə] Partnerin, Partner **I3** 50
partner school [pɑ:tnə sku:l] Partnerschule **III ER** 118
change parts [tʃeɪndʒ 'pɑ:ts] Rollen tauschen **II7** 112
party ['pɑ:ti] Party, Fete **IB4** 82
have a party ['hæv ə 'pɑ:ti] eine Party feiern **IB4** 82
pass [pɑ:s] geben **I7** 120; bestehen **IV ER** 56; (Gesetz) verabschieden **VI7** 63
passport ['pɑ:spɔ:t] Reisepass **IV7** 87
past [pɑ:st] Vergangenheit **V1** 8; vergangen **VI4** 33
pay [peɪ] bezahlen **V2** 19
low-paid [ləʊ-peɪd] schlecht bezahlt **VI4** 35
P.E. (Physical Education) [pi: 'i: 'fɪzɪkl edʒʊ'keɪʃn] Sportunterricht **II1** 9
peace [pi:s] Frieden **V3** 36
pedestrian zone [pɪ'destriən zəʊn] Fußgängerzone **II3** 40
pen [pen] Füller **I2** 33
°pen friend [pen frend] Brieffreundin, Brieffreund **III8** 102

pence [pens] Pence (britisches Geld. 100 pence = £1) **I 6** 101
pencil ['pensl] Bleistift **I 2** 33
pencil case ['pensl keɪs] Federmäppchen, Etui **I 2** 34
pencil sharpener ['pensl ʃɑ:pnə] Bleistiftspitzer **I 2** 33
penguin ['peŋgwɪn] Pinguin **VI 6** 51
penny ['peni] ein Pence (britische Münze) **I 6** 101
people ['pi:pl] Leute **I 5** 86
°old people*s home [əuld 'pi:plz 'həʊm] Altenheim **V 4** 45
per ... [pɜ:] pro ... **IV 3** 34
(peregrine) falcon ['perɪgrɪn 'fɔ:lkn] (Wander-)Falke **III 4** 51
perfect ['pɜ:fɪkt] perfekt **IV ER** 30
perform [pə'fɔ:m] auftreten, spielen **III 2** 26
performance [pə'fɔ:məns] Aufführung **II 5** 74
perhaps [pə'hæps] vielleicht **I 7** 119
permit ['pɜ:mɪt] Genehmigung, Erlaubnis **IV 3** 34
person ['pɜ:sn] Person **VI 2** 15
personal ['pɜ:sənl] persönlich **IV 5** 60
personnel manager [pɜ:sən'el 'mænɪʤə] Personalchefin, Personalchef **IV 5** 69
perspiration [pɜ:spər'eɪʃən] Schweiß **III 6** 77
pessimist ['pesɪmɪst] Pessimistin, Pessimist **V 1** 9
pet [pet] Haustier **I 4** 66
pet shop ['pet ʃɒp] Zoohandlung **I 6** 102
phone [fəʊn] anrufen; Telefon **I 6** 104
cell phone (AE) ['sel foʊn] Handy, Mobiltelefon **IV 3** 34
satellite phone ['sætlaɪt fəʊn] Satellitentelefon **VI 2** 15
°**phonograph** ['fəʊnəgrɑ:f] Phonograph (Tonaufnahmegerät) **III 6** 76
photo ['fəʊtəʊ] Foto **I 6** 105
°photo album ['fəʊtəʊ ælbəm] Fotoalbum **I 4** 70
take photos [teɪk 'fəʊtəʊz] fotografieren **II 2** 29
photocopy ['fəʊtəʊkɒpi] Kopie **V 4** 44
°**phrase** [freɪz] Satz, Wendung **I 1** 27
pick [pɪk] pflücken **III 4** 50
pick up [pɪk 'ʌp] abholen **III 7** 86
picnic ['pɪknɪk] Picknick **I 8** 133
picture ['pɪktʃə] Bild **I 2** 39
piece [pi:s] Stück, Teil **II 6** 86
pierced [pɪəst] gepierct **IV 1** 9
piercing ['pɪəsɪŋ] Piercing **IV 1** 9
pig [pɪg] Schwein **IV ER** 112
pill [pɪl] Tablette **V 6** 70
pilot ['paɪlət] Pilot **III 5** 65
pipeline ['paɪplaɪn] Pipeline **V 4** 43
pizza ['pi:tsə] Pizza **II 2** 26
pizza service ['pi:tsə 'sɜ:vɪs] Pizza Service **II 2** 31
place [pleɪs] Ort, Platz **II 8** 119
plan [plæn] planen, Plan **I 7** 123
plane [pleɪn] Flugzeug **II 8** 120
planet ['plænɪt] Planet **VI 6** 50
plant [plɑ:nt] Pflanze **III 3** 35; anbauen, pflanzen **IV 2** 26
plantation [plæn'teɪʃn] Siedlung **IV 2** 26
plastic ['plæstɪk] Plastik **VI 6** 53
plate [pleɪt] Teller **II 2** 22
platform ['plætfɔ:m] Gleis, Bahnsteig **III 1** 12
play [pleɪ] spielen **I 1** 18; Theaterstück **II 5** 72
play tricks [pleɪ 'trɪks] Streiche spielen **I 7** 124
player ['pleɪə] Spielerin, Spieler **II 6** 87
playground ['pleɪgraʊnd] Schulhof **I B1** 30
playoffs ['pleɪɒfs] Endrunde **II 6** 87
please [pli:z] bitte **I LS** 15
plenty ['plenti] viel **IV 3** 49
°**plug** [plʌg] Stecker **II 7** 112
plug into [plʌg 'ɪntə] einstecken, anschließen **III 6** 79
plumber ['plʌmə] Klempnerin, Klempner **V 4** 43
°**plural** ['plʊərəl] Plural, Mehrzahl **I 6** 105
pocket guide ['pɒkɪt gaɪd] Taschenführer **III 4** 52
pocket money ['pɒkɪt mʌni] Taschengeld **II 3** 44
poet ['pəʊɪt] Dichter **IV 3** 49
polar bear ['pəʊlə beə] Eisbär **VI 6** 51
police [pə'li:s] Polizei **I 6** 104
policeman [pə'li:smən] Polizist **I 6** 104
policewoman [pə'li:swʊmən] Polizistin **II 2** 29
polite [pə'laɪt] höflich **VI 2** 17
political [pə'lɪtɪkl] politisch **VI 4** 34
politics ['pɒlətɪks] Politik **VI 4** 32
pollution [pə'lu:ʃn] Umweltverschmutzung **VI 6** 51
pond [pɒnd] Teich **I B6** 116
pony ['pəʊni] Pony **I B6** 116
pool [pu:l] (Schwimm-)Becken **I 7** 122
swimming pool ['swɪmɪŋ pu:l] Schwimmbad **I B5** 98
poor [pɔ:] arm **IV 5** 64
Poor you! [pɔ: 'ju:] Du Armer! **IV 7** 91
popcorn ['pɒpkɔ:n] Popcorn **I LS** 12
popular ['pɒpjələ] beliebt **V 1** 8
population [pɒpjʊ:'leɪʃən] Bevölkerung **VI 3** 27
portrait ['pɒ:trɪt] Porträt **III 7** 88
possibility [pɒsə'bɪləti] Möglichkeit **IV ER** 57
possible ['pɒsəbl] möglich **III 6** 76
post office ['pəʊst ɒfɪs] Postamt **I B5** 98
°**postcard** ['pəʊstkɑ:d] Postkarte **I 8** 136
poster ['pəʊstə] Poster, Plakat **I 2** 32
advertising poster ['ædvətaɪzɪŋ 'pəʊstə] Werbeplakat **IV 7** 90
potato, potatoes [pə'teɪtəʊ pə'teɪtəʊz] Kartoffel, Kartoffeln **II 3** 41
pound [paʊnd] Pfund (britische Währung) **I 6** 101; Pfund (Gewichtseinheit) **V 6** 72
power ['paʊə] Macht, Stärke **IV 2** 25
nuclear power ['nju:kli:ə paʊə] Atomkraft **IV E7** 101
power station [paʊə 'steɪʃn] Kraftwerk **VI 6** 52
°powerful ['paʊəfʊl] kräftig, stark **III 5** 61
solar power ['səʊlə paʊə] Sonnenenergie **VI 6** 54
practical ['præktɪkəl] praktisch, nützlich **V 4** ER
practise ['præktɪs] üben **II 5** 74
prairie ['preəri] Prärie **IV 2** 24
prefer [prɪ'fɜ:] vorziehen, etwas lieber tun **III 1** 15
pregnant ['pregnənt] schwanger **IV 2** 24
prepare [prɪ'peə] vorbereiten **III ER** 75
°**preposition** [prepə'zɪʃn] Präposition **IV 1** 9
present ['preznt] Geschenk **III 3** 38; präsentieren **VI 2** 16
°**presentation** [prezn'teɪʃn] Vortrag, Präsentation **III 2** 28
president ['prezɪdənt] Präsident **II 6** 90
press [pres] drücken **III 5** 64
pretty ['prɪti] nett, hübsch **III ER** 118
price [praɪs] Preis **III 3** 40
priest [pri:st] Priester **IV ER** 112
print ['prɪnt] (aus-)drucken **III PR6** 125
prison ['prɪzən] Gefängnis **V 2** 19

prisoner ['prɪzənə] Gefangene, Gefangener **V2** 19
prize [praɪz] Preis, Gewinn **II3** 45
pro and con ['prəʊ ənd kɒn] Vorteil und Nachteil **III5** 61
probably ['prɒbəbli] wahrscheinlich **II8** 118
problem ['prɒbləm] Problem **I3** 58
produce [prə'dju:s] produzieren **IV4** 50
producer [prə'dju:sə] Produzentin, Produzent **III6** 77
production [prə'dʌkʃn] Produktion **III6** 77
professional [prə'feʃnəl] professionell, fachmännisch **IV1** 12
program (AE) ['proʊgræm] Sendung **VI4** 34
programme ['prəʊgræm] Programm, Fernsehsendung **II6** 90
project ['prɒdʒekt] Projekt **II1** 16
promise ['prɒmɪs] versprechen **IV ER** 83
°pronunciation ['prənʌnsɪ'eɪʃn] Aussprache **III6** 78
propeller [prə'pelə] Propeller **III ER** 75
properly ['prɒpəli] richtig **VI6** 51
protect [prə'tekt] schützen **III8** 107
protest ['prəʊtest] Protest **VI3** 29
protestant ['prɒtɪstnt] evangelisch, protestantisch **VI5** 44
protestor [prəʊ'testə] Protestierende, Protestierender **VI6** 55
proud [praʊd] stolz **V6** 68
pull [pʊl] ziehen **IV5** 65
pullover ['pʊləʊvə] Pullover **II5** 73
pump [pʌmp] Pumpe, pumpen **IV ER** 101
°pumpkin ['pʌmpkɪn] Kürbis **IV2** 26
pupil ['pju:pl] Schülerin, Schüler **I B1** 30
push [pʊʃ] schieben, drücken **III5** 64
put [pʊt] setzen, stellen, legen **I7** 119
put on [pʊt 'ɒn] anlegen **II4** 58
put up [pʊt 'ʌp] aufstellen **II5** 74
put up with [pʊt 'ɒp wɪð] akzeptieren **IV1** 9
°puzzle ['pʌzl] Puzzle, Rätsel **I3** 50

Q

qualified ['kwɒlɪfaɪd] qualifiziert **IV5** 61
qualify ['kwɒlɪfaɪ] in Frage kommen **V4** ER
queen [kwi:n] Königin **III1** 8
question ['kwestʃən] Frage **II4** 55
queue [kju:] Schlange **III1** 8
quick [kwɪk] schnell **III ER** 57
quiet ['kwaɪət] leise, still **III3** 38
quite [kwaɪt] ziemlich **I4** 67
quiz show ['kwɪz ʃəʊ] Quizsendung **II6** 90

R

rabbit ['ræbɪt] Kaninchen **I B2** 48
race [reɪs] rennen, rasen **IV5** 65; Rasse, Ethnie **V1** 10; Rennen, Regatta **VI2** 14
racial ['reɪʃl] Rassen- **VI7** 63
racing ['reɪsɪŋ] Autorennsport **II6** 93
racing boat ['reɪsɪŋ bəʊt] Rennboot **IV3** 49
°fell-racing ['fel 'reɪsɪŋ] Geländerennen **IV3** 49
°racket ['rækɪt] Schläger **IV5** 69
radar ['reɪdɑ: Radar **VI2** 15
radio ['reɪdiəʊ] Radio **III1** 17
°radio collar ['reɪdiəʊ 'kɒlə] Funkhalsband **IV3** 38
rafting ['rɑ:ftɪŋ] Rafting **II6** 90
rail [reɪl] Schiene **IV ER** 101
railroad ['reɪlrəʊd] Eisenbahn **V2** 20
railroad worker ['reɪlrəʊd 'wɜ:kə] Bahnarbeiterin, Bahnarbeiter **V2** 20
rain [reɪn] Regen; regnen **II4** 56
acid rain ['æsɪd reɪn] saurer Regen **VI6** 51
rain forest [reɪn 'fɒrɪst] Regenwald **III5** 64
rainy ['reɪni] regnerisch **I B6** 116
raise [reɪz] sammeln **VI1** 9
ranger ['reɪndʒə] Försterin, Förster; Wildhüterin, Wildhüter **IV3** 34
rap [ræp] Rap; rappen **I LS** 13
rat [ræt] Ratte **III7** 95
R.E. (Religious Education) [ɑ: i: rɪ'lɪdʒəs edʒʊ'keɪʃən] Religionsunterricht **II1** 9
reach [ri:tʃ] erreichen **IV2** 24
read [ri:d] lesen **I2** 36
ready ['redi] bereit, fertig **III5** 65
get ready [get 'redi] fertig machen **III5** 64
real [rɪəl] richtig, echt **III1** 9
realize [rɪə'laɪz] erkennen, feststellen **VI1** 8
really ['rɪəli] wirklich **II5** 76
°rear mechanism [rɪə 'mekənɪzm] Gangschaltung **V4** 46
°reason ['ri:zn] Grund **II7** 110
receive [rɪ'si:v] bekommen **V5** 61
recently ['ri:sntli] vor kurzem **VI6** 53
°receptionist [rɪ'sepʃənɪst] Dame/Herr am Empfang **III5** 60
°recharge [ri:'tʃɑ:dʒ] aufladen **II7** 112
rechargeable [ri:'tʃɑ:dʒəbl] wieder aufladbar **VI6** 53
record ['rekɔ:d] Schallplatte **V3** 36; Rekord **V5** 61
make a record ['meɪk ə rekɔ:d] eine Aufnahme machen **VI1** 8
on record [ɒn 'rekɔ:d] bekannt, belegt **VI6** 51
break a record ['breɪk ə 'rekɔ:d] einen Rekord brechen **IV3** 49
record [rɪ'kɔ:d] aufnehmen **III3** 34
recording contract [rɪ'kɔ:dɪŋ kɒntrækt] Plattenvertrag **III2** 24
recycled paper [ri:'saɪkld 'peɪpə] Recyclingpapier **VI6** 53
red [red] rot **I LS** 10
reference ['refrəns] (Arbeits-) Zeugnis **V4** 46
refugee ['refjʊdʒi:] Flüchtling **IV6** 77
refuse ['refju:s] sich weigern **VI7** 62
reggae ['regeɪ] Reggae **V1** 10
regular ['regjələ] regelmäßig **V5** 60
rehearsal [rɪ'hɜ:sl] Probe **II5** 74
relax [rɪ'læks] entspannen **III7** 90
release [rɪ'li:s] Freilassung; freilassen **V3** 36
reliable [rɪ'laɪəbl] verlässlich **IV4** 51
religion [rɪ'lɪdʒn] Religion **IV1** 12
religious [rɪ'lɪdʒəs] religiös **IV2** 25
remember [rɪ'membə] (sich) erinnern **I8** 132
remote control [rɪ'məʊt kəntrəʊl] Fernbedienung **II8** 123
rent out [rent 'aʊt] vermieten **IV5** 61
repair [rɪ'peə] reparieren **III7** 91
replace [rɪ'pleɪs] ersetzen **V4** 43
report [rɪ'pɔ:t] Bericht **III ER** 75; berichten **V4** 45
°report card (AE) [rɪ'pɔ:t kɑ:d] Zeugnis **V6** 73
reporter [rɪ'pɔ:tə] Reporter **V1** 8
reproduction [ri:prə'dʌkʃn] Reproduktion, Nachbau **IV2** 26
reservation [rezə'veɪʃn] Reservat **IV2** 24
respected [rɪ'spektɪd] respektiert **VI7** 62
responsibility [rɪspɒnsə'bɪləti] Verantwortung **IV5** 62
responsible [rɪ'spɒnsəbl] verantwortlich, zuständig **V4** 42

rest [rest] Rest **IV 3** 38
rest [rest] rasten **V 2** 21
restaurant ['restrɒnt] Restaurant **II 1** 8
result [rɪ'zʌlt] Ergebnis **II 6** 87
return [rɪ'tɜ:n] umkehren **III 5** 65; zurückkehren **V 3** 35
return key [rɪ'tɜ:n ki:] Eingabetaste **II 7** 106
revenge [rɪ'vendʒ] Rache **IV 5** 64
°**revision** [rɪ'vɪʒn] Wiederholung **II 2** 36
rewarding [rɪ'wɔ:dɪŋ] dankbar, schön **V 4** 42
°**rhyme** [raɪm] Reim **II 1** 17
°**rice noodles** [raɪs 'nu:dlz] Reisnudeln **III 7** 87
rich [rɪtʃ] reich **V 2** 23
ride [raɪd] fahren, reiten **II 3** 42
ride a bike [raɪd ə 'baɪk] Fahrrad fahren **I 3** 50
go for a ride [gəʊ fɔ: ə 'raɪd] eine Spritztour machen **IV ER** 56
rider ['raɪdə] Reiter, Reiterin **VI 4** 33
right [raɪt] richtig **I 2** 38; rechts **I 6** 102; genau **IV 3** 38; Recht **V 3** 34
be right [bi: raɪt] Recht haben **II 5** 76
civil-rights movement [sɪvl 'raɪts 'mu:vmənt] Bürgerrechtsbewegung **VI 7** 63
ring [rɪŋ] läuten **II 1** 12; Ring **IV 1** 9
rip [rɪp] reißen **VI 2** 14
rise [raɪz] aufgehen (Sonne) **III 5** 64; ansteigen **VI 6** 50
river ['rɪvə] Fluss **I B6** 116
road [rəʊd] Straße **I B5** 98
°road train [rəʊd treɪn] (langer) Lastwagen **V 2** 17
roar [rɔ:] aufheulen (Motor) **III 7** 90
robber ['rɒbə] Räuberin, Räuber **I 6** 104
robot ['rəʊbɒt] Roboter **I B4** 82
rock [rɒk] Rock; rocken **I 5** 84; Felsen **IV 2** 25
rock star ['rɒk stɑ:] Rockstar **I 5** 84
rocker ['rɒkə] Rocker **I 5** 88
rodeo [rəʊ'deɪəʊ] Rodeo **VI 4** 32
roll [rəʊl] rollen **I 6** 105; Brötchen **II 3** 40
roof [ru:f] Dach **III 1** 8
room [ru:m] Zimmer **I B1** 30
root [ru:t] Wurzel **IV 2** 24
rope [rəʊp] Seil **V 2** 21
rose [rəʊz] Rose **III 7** 92
rough [rʌf] rau, hart **VI 4** 33
round [raʊnd] Runde **II 6** 90; rund **VI 4** 33
route [ru:t] Weg **III 7** 86
row [rəʊ] rudern **IV ER** 113
rubber ['rʌbə] Radiergummi **I 2** 33
rubbish ['rʌbɪʃ] Müll **III ER** 23
rucksack ['rʌksæk] Rucksack **I 8** 134
rugby ['rʌgbi] Rugby **II 1** 10
rule [ru:l] Regel **II 1** 12; beherrschen, regieren **VI 5** 44
ruler ['ru:lə] Lineal **I 2** 33
run [rʌn] laufen, rennen **I 3** 51
run into [rʌn 'ɪntə] zusammenstoßen **II 4** 54
runner ['rʌnə] Sprinterin, Sprinter; Läuferin, Läufer **II 6** 93

S

sacred ['seɪkrɪd] heilig **VI 3** 26
sad [sæd] traurig **IV 1** 13
saddle ['sædl] Sattel **VI 4** 33
safe ['seɪf] sicher **III 5** 67
safety check ['seɪfti tʃek] Sicherheitsüberprüfung **V 6** 62
sail [seɪl] segeln **IV 2** 25; Segel **VI 2** 14
sailor ['seɪlə] Seglerin, Segler **IV ER** 112; Seemann **V 2** 19
salad ['sæləd] Salat **II 2** 23
sale [seɪl] Schlussverkauf **IV ER** 30
salon [sæ'lɔ:ŋ] Haarsalon **IV 5** 60
salt [sɔ:lt] Salz **II 2** 23
same [seɪm] gleich **I 5** 88
sanctuary ['sæŋktʃʊəri] Schutzgebiet **III 4** 51
sand [sænd] Sand **III 5** 60
sandstorm ['sændstɔ:m] Sandsturm **IV 4** 51
sandwich ['sænwɪdʒ] belegtes Brot, Sandwich **I 2** 33
satellite phone ['sætlaɪt fəʊn] Satellitentelefon **VI 2** 15
Saturday ['sætədeɪ] Samstag **I 1** 20
sauce [sɔ:s] Soße **III 7** 87
save [seɪv] sparen **II 3** 45; sichern, speichern **II 7** 106; retten **V 2** 21
say [seɪ] sagen **I 3** 54
say goodbye [seɪ 'gʊdbaɪ] auf Wiedersehen sagen **II 3** 42
°**scale** [skeɪl] Waage **V 6** 73
be scared [bi: 'skeəd] Angst haben **II 8** 122
scene [si:n] Szene **II 5** 74
school [sku:l] Schule **I B1** 30
school bag ['sku:l bæg] Schultasche **I 2** 33
school club ['sku:l klʌb] Schulverein, AG **II 1** 10
school trip ['sku:l trɪp] Klassenfahrt, Schulausflug **II 7** 104
school uniform [sku:l 'ju:nɪfɔ:m] Schuluniform **I 2** 36
science [saɪəns] Wissenschaft **VI 4** 32
science fiction [saɪəns 'fɪkʃn] Science Fiction **II 6** 94
scientist ['saɪəntɪst] Wissenschaftler **VI 6** 50
Scottish ['skɒtɪʃ] schottisch **III 3** 36
scrap-picker [skræp-pɪkə] jemand, der Müll sammelt und wieder verkauft **VI 3** 26
scratch your head ['skrætʃ jɔ: hed] sich am Kopf kratzen **III 8** 105
screen [skri:n] Bildschirm **III 6** 79
screw [skru:] Schraube **V 4** 46
sea [si:] Meer **II 8** 118
sea level [si: 'levl] Meeresspiegel **VI 6** 50
seal [si:l] Seehund **VI 6** 51
search [sɜ:tʃ] (durch-)suchen **IV 5** 64
°search engine [sɜ:tʃ 'endʒɪn] Suchmaschine **V 7** 89
in search of [ɪn 'sɜ:tʃ əv] auf der Suche nach **V 7** 89
season ['si:zn] Jahreszeit **I 8** 132
seat [si:t] Sitz, Sitzgelegenheit **III 7** 90
second ['sekənd] zweite, zweiter, zweites **II 6** 84; Sekunde **III 5** 64
secretary ['sekrətəri] Sekretärin, Sekretär **V 1** 8
see [si:] sehen **I 2** 34; besuchen **I 4** 66
See you. ['si: ju:] Bis später! **I 4** 77
desegregate [di:'segrɪgeɪt] die Rassentrennung aufheben **VI 7** 62
segregation [segrɪ'geɪʃn] Rassentrennung **VI 7** 62
sell [sel] verkaufen **I 6** 100
it is selling fast [ɪt ɪz 'səlɪŋ fa:st] es verkauft sich schnell **IV 7** 86
senator ['senətə] Senatorin, Senator **VI 4** 34
send [send] senden, schicken **I 5** 89
sensitive ['sensətɪv] empfindlich **IV 1** 12
°**sentence** ['sentəns] Satz **I 1** 22
separate ['seprət] trennen, getrennt **V 3** 34
September [sep'tembə] September **I 8** 132
set off [set 'ɒf] aufbrechen, sich auf den Weg machen **III 4** 52
seven ['sevn] sieben **I LS** 10
seventeen [sevn'ti:n] siebzehn **I 2** 32
seventy ['sevnti] siebzig **I 6** 101
several ['sevərəl] einige, mehrere **V 4** 46
sex [seks] Sex **VI 3** 27

shadow ['ʃædəʊ] Schatten **III 3** 38
shake [ʃeɪk] schütteln **V 4** 47
What a shame! [wɒt ə 'ʃeɪm] Wie schade! **III 8** 103
share [ʃeə] teilen **VI 4** 32
°**shark** [ʃɑ:k] Hai **IV 7** 94
she [ʃi:] sie **I 1** 17
sheep [ʃi:p] Schaf, Schafe **I B6** 116
shelf, shelves [ʃelf ʃelvz] Regal, Regale **III 3** 40
shift key ['ʃɪft ki:] Umschalttaste **II 7** 106
shirt [ʃɜ:t] Hemd **II 5** 73
shock [ʃɒk] Schreck, Schock **V 2** 21
shocked [ʃa:kt] geschockt **IV 7** 88
shocking ['ʃɒkɪŋ] schockierend **VI 7** 64
shoe [ʃu:] Schuh **II 5** 73
shoot [ʃu:t] schießen **II 5** 72
shop [ʃɒp] Laden **I B1** 30; einkaufen **I 5** 93
shop assistant ['ʃɒp əsɪstənt] Verkäuferin, Verkäufer **I 8** 133
shop window [ʃɒp 'wɪndəʊ] Schaufenster **II 3** 44
shopping centre ['ʃɒpɪŋ sentə] Einkaufszentrum **I 5** 88
shopping complex ['ʃɒpɪŋ kɒmpleks] Einkaufszentrum **V 7** 88
°shopping list ['ʃɒpɪŋ lɪst] Einkaufsliste **II 3** 41
short [ʃɔ:t] kurz **II 5** 72
should [ʃʊd] sollen, sollten **III 2** 25
shoulder ['ʃəʊldə] Schulter **V 2** 21
shout [ʃaʊt] schreien **II 5** 76
°**show** [ʃəʊ] zeigen **I 7** 119
shower ['ʃaʊə] Dusche **I 4** 70
have a shower ['hæv ə 'ʃaʊə] duschen **I 7** 70
sick [sɪk] krank **V 4** 42
be sick [bɪ 'sɪk] krank sein, sich übergeben **V 4** 42
side [saɪd] Seite **II 5** 76
sight [saɪt] Sehenswürdigkeit **II 6** 88
°**sign** [saɪn] Zeichen, Schild **II 4** 65; unterschreiben **III 2** 24
sign up for [saɪn 'ʌp fə] sich anmelden für **IV 7** 90
signal ['sɪgnəl] Signal **III 6** 76
signature ['sɪgnətʃə] Unterschrift **VI 2** 17
silly ['sɪli] dumm, blöd **II 4** 59
simple ['sɪmpl] einfach **IV ER** 23
since [sɪns] seit (Zeitpunkt) **IV 3** 35
ever since [evə 'sɪns] seitdem, seit **VI 1** 8
sing [sɪŋ] singen **I 5** 90
singer ['sɪŋə] Sängerin, Sänger **I 5** 84
single ['sɪŋgl] Single **III 2** 25
sink [sɪŋk] Spüle, Spülbecken **II 2** 23; einsinken **III 8** 107
sister ['sɪstə] Schwester **I 2** 36
sit [sɪt] sitzen **I 3** 57
sit down [sɪt 'daʊn] sich hinsetzen **I 2** 36
camping site ['kæmpɪŋ saɪt] Zeltplatz, Campingplatz **II 8** 119
situated ['sɪtjueɪtɪd] gelegen **VI 5** 45
situation [sɪtʃu'eɪʃn] Situation **IV ER** 75
six [sɪks] sechs **I LS** 10
sixteen [sɪk'sti:n] sechzehn **I 2** 32
sixty ['sɪksti] sechzig **I 6** 101
size [saɪz] Größe **V 7** 88
skate [skeɪt] Inliner fahren **III 2** 27
skateboard ['skeɪtbɔ:d] Skateboard **I LS** 11
skater [skeɪtə] Skater **III 2** 27
ski [ski:] Ski; Ski laufen **III 3** 36
cross country skiing ['krɒs 'kʌntri 'ski:ɪŋ] Skilanglauf **IV 3** 43
skill [skɪl] Fähigkeit **V 4** 43
skin [skɪn] Haut, Fell **VI 4** 33
skirt [skɜ:t] Rock **I B4** 82
sky [skaɪ] Himmel **V 2** 20
skyscraper ['skaɪskreɪpə] Wolkenkratzer **III 7** 86
slave [sleɪv] Sklave **VI 7** 63
slave owner ['sleɪv əʊnə] Sklavenhalter **VI 7** 63
sleep [sli:p] schlafen **I 4** 70
slob [slɒb] faule Person **V 6** 72
slow [sləʊ] langsam **III 6** 77
slow down [sləʊ daʊn] abbremsen, langsamer fahren **VI 3** 26
small [smɔ:l] klein **I B3** 65
smell [smel] Geruch, riechen **V 1** 10; muffig **IV 7** 88
smile [smaɪl] Lächeln **III 4** 50
smoke [sməʊk] Rauch **III 5** 64; rauchen **V 6** 68
snack [snæk] Snack, Imbiss **III 1** 8
snack bar ['snæk bɑ:] Imbissstube **I 6** 100
snag [snæg] Haken (verborgenes Problem) **IV 7** 86
snake [sneɪk] Schlange **IV 4** 52
°**snapshot** ['snæpʃɒt] Schnappschuss **I 1** 19
snow [snəʊ] Schnee **II 4** 56; schneien **III 3** 36
snowman ['snəʊmæn] Schneemann **III 3** 40
snowmobile ['snəʊməbi:l] Schneemobil **IV 3** 43
snowshoeing ['snəʊʃu:ɪŋ] Schneeschuh laufen **IV 3** 43
so [səʊ] so **I 3** 50; also, deshalb **I 5** 88
so dass **III 3** 38
soap [səʊp] Seife, Seifenoper **II 6** 94
soccer (AE) ['sɒkə] Fußball **III ER** 101
°**socket** ['sɒkɪt] Steckdose **II 7** 112
socks [sɒks] Socken **II 5** 73
sofa ['səʊfə] Sofa **I B3** 64
soft drink machine [sɒft drɪnk mə'ʃi:n] Getränkeautomat **IV 1** 8
software ['sɒfweə] Software **VI 5** 45
soil [sɔil] Boden, Erdreich **VI 6** 51
solar power ['səʊlə paʊə] Sonnenenergie **VI 6** 54
soldier ['səʊldʒə] Soldatin, Soldat **V 2** 20
solo ['səʊləʊ] Solo-, solo **VI 1** 9
some [sʌm] einige, ein paar **I 3** 51
somebody ['sʌmbədi] jemand **II 4** 58
somehow ['sʌmhaʊ] irgendwie **IV 5** 64
°someone ['sʌmwʌn] jemand **III 7** 92
something ['sʌmθɪŋ] etwas **II 2** 26
sometimes ['sʌmtaɪmz] manchmal **I 5** 84
son [sʌn] Sohn **III 1** 12
song [sɒŋ] Lied **IV 1** 8
songwriter ['sɒŋraɪtə] Texterin und Komponistin, Texter und Komponist **VI 1** 10
soon [su:n] bald **III 3** 38
Sorry. ['sɒri] Entschuldigung./Tut mir Leid. **I 2** 33
feel sorry [fi:l 'sɒri] Leid tun **IV 5** 64
sort [sɔ:t] Sorte **III 7** 90
sound [saʊnd] sich anhören, klingen **III 5** 62; Geräusch **V 1** 10
soup [su:p] Suppe **III 1** 16
south [saʊθ] Süden; südlich **V 2** 16
south-west [saʊθ'west] Südwesten; südwestlich **V 2** 20
souvenir [su:vn'ɪə] Andenken, Souvenir **III 1** 9
space [speɪs] Raum, Weltall **III 5** 61
space shuttle [speɪs 'ʃʌtl] Raumfähre **III 5** 64
spaceship ['speɪs ʃɪp] Raumschiff **III 5** 64
spaghetti [spə'geti] Spaghetti **II 2** 23
Spanish ['spænɪʃ] spanisch; Spanierin, Spanier **IV 2** 24
speak [spi:k] sprechen **III 1** 15
Speaking. ['spi:kɪŋ] Am Apparat. (beim Telefonieren) **I 4** 70
special ['speʃl] besonderer, besondere, besonderes **II 7** 106
special offer [speʃl 'ɒfə] Sonderangebot **II 3** 44

spectacular [spek'tækjələ] spektakulär **III ER** 101
speech [spi:tʃ] Rede **VI 7** 63
speed [spi:d] Geschwindigkeit **III 5** 61; schnell fahren **IV 5** 65; Speed **V 6** 70
°**spell** [spel] buchstabieren **I LS** 13
spend [spend] verbringen **IV 1** 12; ausgeben **V 6** 69
spice [spaɪs] Gewürz **VI 3** 28
°**splash** [splæʃ] Platschen, Aufklatschen **V 2** 19
spooky ['spu:ki] gespenstisch, unheimlich **II 8** 122
spoon [spu:n] (Ess-)Löffel **II 2** 22
°**sports** [spɔ:ts] Sportarten, Sport **I LS** 12
sports hall ['spɔ:ts hɔ:l] Sporthalle **I B1** 30
sports star ['spɔ:ts stɑ:] Sportlerin, Sportler **V 1** 8
spray [spreɪ] Spray **VI 6** 53
spring [sprɪŋ] Frühjahr **I 8** 132
square kilometre [skweə kɪ'lɒmɪtə] Quadratkilometer **V 7** 86
square mile [skweə 'maɪl] Quadratmeile **IV 3** 35
squash [skwɒʃ] Squash **I LS** 12
stadium ['steɪdiəm] Stadion **III 5** 66
staff [stɑ:f] Personal **IV 5** 60
stall [stɔ:l] Stand **I 6** 100
stamp [stæmp] Briefmarke **III 3** 40
stand [stænd] stehen **II 2** 26; Tribüne **IV ER** 23
star [stɑ:] Star **II 5** 76
stare ['steə] starren **IV 7** 91
start [stɑ:t] starten, anfangen; Start **I 7** 118
start a fire [stɑ:t ə 'faɪə] Feuer legen **IV 3** 35
starter ['stɑ:tə] Vorspeise **II 2** 24
state [steɪt] Staat, Bundesstaat **IV 1** 12
station ['steɪʃn] Bahnhof, Busbahnhof **I 6** 102; Polizeistation **IV 5** 64; Farm **V 2** 17; Radiosender **V 6** 77
power station [paʊə 'steɪʃn] Kraftwerk **VI 6** 52
statue ['stætʃu:] Statue **III 7** 90
stay [steɪ] bleiben **II 4** 59; übernachten, wohnen **II 8** 119
stay away from [steɪ ə'weɪ frəm] die Finger von etwas lassen **V 6** 70
steak [steɪk] Steak **I LS** 12
steal [sti:l] stehlen **II 5** 72
steam [sti:m] Dampf **IV ER** 101
steel [sti:l] Stahl **IV 1** 12
steel band ['sti:l bænd] (jamaikanische) Steelband **IV 6** 76
steep [sti:p] steil **VI 5** 45
step [step] Schritt **III PR3** 122
stick [stɪk] Stock **II 5** 76
sticker ['stɪkə] Aufkleber **IV 5** 65
still [stɪl] (immer) noch **I 8** 134
stone [stəʊn] Stein **V 2** 21
Stop! [stɒp] Halt! Stopp! **I 3** 50
stop [stɒp] stoppen, anhalten **I 6** 104
store [stɔ:] Laden **IV 1** 9
department store [dɪ'pɑ:tmənt stɔ:] Kaufhaus **II 3** 40
storm [stɔ:m] Sturm **III 3** 38
°**story** ['stɔ:ri] Geschichte **I 2** 37
straight [streɪt] direkt **V 7** 89
straight on ['streɪt ɒn] geradeaus **I 6** 102
strange [streɪndʒ] seltsam, merkwürdig **III 5** 64
street [stri:t] Straße **I B5** 98
strength [strengθ] Kraft, Stärke **VI 2** 15
stressful ['stresfʊl] stressig **V 6** 71
strike [straɪk] zuschlagen, einschlagen **V 2** 20; Streik **V 3** 35
stripe [straɪp] Streifen **VI 5** 44
strong [strɒŋ] stark **II 5** 76
student (AE) ['stu:dənt] Schülerin, Schüler **V 6** 70
studio ['stju:dɪəʊ] Studio **I 5** 84
study ['stʌdi] studieren, lernen **III 6** 76
stunt [stʌnt] Stunt, Trick **VI 3** 27
style [staɪl] Stil **III 7** 88
subject ['sʌbdʒekt] Unterrichtsfach **II 1** 9
submarine ['sʌbmri:n] U-Boot **IV ER** 101
success [sək'ses] Erfolg **IV 4** 50
successful [sək'sesfəl] erfolgreich **VI 4** 33
such [sʌtʃ] solch **V 6** 72
such as [sʌtʃ æz] wie **V 1** 10
suddenly ['sʌdnli] plötzlich **I 6** 104
suffer ['sʌfə] leiden **VI 1** 9
suitcase ['su:tkeɪs] Koffer **IV 7** 88
sulk [sʌlk] schmollen **IV 7** 91
summer ['sʌmə] Sommer **I 8** 132
sun [sʌn] Sonne **II 4** 56
sunglasses ['sʌnglɑ:sɪz] Sonnenbrille **V 7** 89
sunny ['sʌni] sonnig **I B6** 116
sunset ['sʌnset] Sonnenuntergang **III 8** 102
°sunshine ['sʌnʃaɪn] Sonnenschein **III 5** 60
Sunday ['sʌndeɪ] Sonntag **I 1** 20
super ['su:pə] super, klasse **III 8** 104
superlative [su:'pɜ:lətɪv] Superlativ **III ER** 101
supermarket ['su:pəmɑ:kɪt] Supermarkt **I B5** 98
supervisor ['su:pəvaɪzə] Leiterin, Leiter **V 4** ER
supply [sə'plaɪ] Vorrat **VI 6** 51
support [sə'pɔ:t] unterstützen **VI 4** 34; Unterstützung **VI 7** 62
sure [ʃɔ:] sicher **I 7** 119
surf (the Internet) [sɜ:f θi 'ɪntənet] (im Internet) surfen **II 7** 105
surfer ['sɜ:fə] Surferin, Surfer **V 2** 18
surprise [sə'praɪz] Überraschung **V 2** 16
be surprised [bi: sə'praɪzd] überrascht/erstaunt sein **III 3** 38
surprising [sə'praɪzɪŋ] überraschend **VI 7** 64
survive [sə'vaɪv] überleben **VI 6** 51
sweatshirt ['swetʃɜ:t] Sweatshirt **I B4** 82
sweater (AE) ['swetə] Pullover **IV 1** 8
swim [swɪm] schwimmen **I 3** 51
switch [swɪtʃ] wechseln, (um-)schalten **III ER** 75
switch on/off [swɪtʃ 'ɒn 'ɒf] ein-/ausschalten **III 3** 35
sword [sɔ:d] Schwert **VI 1** 8
symbol ['sɪmbl] Symbol **VI 4** 35
symbolize ['sɪmbəlaɪz] symbolisieren **VI 5** 44
system ['sɪstəm] System **V 3** 34

T

T-shirt ['ti: ʃɜ:t] T-Shirt **I LS** 11
table ['teɪbl] Tisch **I 2** 32; Tabelle **III 5** 61
table tennis ['teɪbl tenɪs] Tischtennis **I 1** 18
taboo [tə'bu:] Tabu **VI 7** 65
take [teɪk] nehmen **I 7** 122; dauern **III 1** 9; bringen **V 2** 21
take a course [teɪk ə 'kɔ:s] eine Weiterbildung machen **V 4** ER
take action [teɪk 'ækʃən] handeln, aktiv werden **V 2** ER
take care [teɪk 'keə] aufpassen **IV 1** 10
take notes [teɪk 'nəʊts] Notizen machen **III 4** 52
take part in [teɪk 'pɑ:t ɪn] teilnehmen an **V 5** 60
take photos [teɪk 'fəʊtəʊz] fotografieren **II 2** 29
take (the dog) for a walk ['teɪk ðə 'dɒg fər ə wɔ:k] (den Hund) ausführen **I 7** 118
take up time [teɪk ʌp 'taɪm] Zeit in Anspruch nehmen **IV 1** 10
take-off ['teɪkɒf] Start **III 5** 64

talent ['tælənt] Talent **III2** 25
talk [tɔ:k] sprechen über, reden; Gespräch, Diskussion **I3** 52
talk to [tɔ:k tə] sprechen mit **II1** 8
tall [tɔ:l] groß **III1** 12
tank [tæŋk] Speicher, Wassertank **V4** 43
tap [tæp] Wasserhahn **V4** 43
tartan ['tɑ:tən] Schottenkaro, Schottenstoff **III ER** 49
taste [teɪst] schmecken **V4** 50
tattoo [tæt'u:] Tätowierung **III7** 90
tax [tæks] Steuer **IV2** 25
taxi ['tæksi] Taxi **II2** 31
tea [ti:] Tee **I7** 120
iced tea [aɪst ti:] Eistee **III1** 16
teach [ti:tʃ] unterrichten, beibringen **V2** 20
teacher ['ti:tʃə] Lehrerin, Lehrer **I B1** 30
team [ti:m] Mannschaft, Team **I1** 17
team sport [ti:m 'spɔ:t] Mannschaftssport, Mannschaftssportart **V7** 87
teaspoon ['ti:spu:n] Teelöffel **II2** 22
technical data ['teknɪkl deitə] technische Daten **VI2** 15
technology [tek'nɒlədʒi] Technik **II1** 9
teenager ['ti:neɪdʒə] Teenager **III1** 13
telephone ['telɪfəʊn] Telefon **I LS** 10
telephone box ['telɪfəʊn bɒks] Telefonzelle **I6** 104
television (TV) ['telɪvɪʒn (ti:'vi:)] Fernsehapparat **I3** 51
tell [tel] erzählen, sagen **I3** 55
temperature ['temprətʃə] Temperatur **II6** 88
temple ['templ] Tempel **IV ER** 112
ten [ten] zehn **I LS** 10
tennis ['tenɪs] Tennis **I LS** 12
tense [tents] angespannt **V6** 71
be tense [bi 'tents] angespannt sein **V6** 71
tent [tent] Zelt **II7** 108
terrible ['terəbl] schrecklich **I7** 119
terrific [tə'rɪfɪk] sagenhaft, klasse **II1** 12
test [test] Test, Klassenarbeit **II3** 47; testen **II5** 74
text message [tekst 'mesɪdʒ] SMS **VI2** 16
than [ðən] als (bei Vergleich) **II6** 86
thank [θæŋk] danken **III5** 65
Thank you. ['θæŋk ju] Danke. **I2** 36
that [ðæt] das; jene, jener, jenes **I1** 21
That's all. [ðæts 'ɔ:l] Das ist alles. **II3** 41
the [ðə] der, die, das **I1** 18
theater (AE) ['θi:ətə] Theater, Kino **III5** 64
theatre ['θɪətə] Theater **III ER** 23
their [ðeə] ihr, ihre **I6** 105
theirs [ðeəz] ihre, ihrer, ihres (pl.) **I6** 105
them [ðem] sie, ihnen **I4** 67
theme park ['θi:m pɑ:k] Freizeitpark **II6** 90
themselves [ðəm'selvz] sich, selbst **VI4** 33
then [ðen] damals **I3** 40
then [ðen] dann **I3** 51
°**therapy group** ['θerəpi gru:p] Therapiegruppe **V6** 73
there [ðeə] da, dort **I3** 51
There's something wrong with … [ðeəz 'sʌmθɪŋ rɒŋ wɪð] Mit dem/der … ist etwas nicht in Ordnung. **II2** 26
these [ði:z] diese (Pl.) **I8** 132
these days [ði:z 'deɪz] heutzutage **V4** 46
they [ðeɪ] sie (Pl.) **I1** 18
thin [θɪn] dünn **III4** 53
°**thing** [θɪŋ] Ding, Sache **I LS** 10
best thing ['best θɪŋ] Allerbeste **V5** 60
think [θɪŋk] denken **I5** 92
think about [θɪŋk ə'baʊt] halten von, (nach-)denken über **II1** 8
I don't think so. [aɪ dəʊnt θɪŋk səʊ] Ich glaube nicht. **III1** 8
think of [θɪŋk əv] denken (an) **I5** 92
third [θɜ:d] Drittel **IV2** 24; dritter, dritte, drittes **V2** 21
thirsty ['θɜ:sti] durstig **II7** 108
thirteen [θɜ:'ti:n] dreizehn **I2** 32
thirty ['θɜ:ti] dreißig **I5** 85
this [ðɪs] das; dieser, diese, dieses **I1** 16
°this is also the case [ðɪs ɪz 'ɔ:lsəʊ ðə keɪs] das ist auch der Fall **V1** 8
thousands of ['θaʊzəndz ɒv] Tausende von **V5** 60
three [θri:] drei **I LS** 10
through [θru:] durch **II6** 91
throughout [θrʊ'aʊt] während **V2** 20
throw [θrəʊ] werfen **II7** 109
throw up ['θrəʊ ʌp] sich übergeben **V6** 72
thunderstorm ['θʌndəstɔ:m] Gewitter **IV4** 51
Thursday ['θɜ:zdeɪ] Donnerstag **I1** 20
ticket ['tɪkɪt] (Eintritts-)Karte **I5** 92
tiger ['taɪgə] Tiger **IV4** 52
tights [taɪts] Strumpfhose **II5** 73
tile [taɪl] Isolierplatte **III5** 64
time [taɪm] Zeit **I B1** 30
all the time [ɔ:l ðə 'taɪm] die ganze Zeit **IV5** 60
at that time [ət ðæt taɪm] damals **V1** 10
time machine [taɪm mə'ʃi:n] Zeitmaschine **III5** 62
take up time [teɪk ʌp 'taɪm] Zeit in Anspruch nehmen **IV1** 9
times [taɪmz] mal (mathematisch) **III5** 65
timetable ['taɪmteɪbl] Stundenplan **II1** 9
tiny ['taɪni] winzig **V5** 62
°**tip** [tɪp] Tipp **II7** 112; Trinkgeld **VI3** 26
tired ['taɪəd] müde **V2** 20
°**title** ['taɪtl] Titel, Überschrift **III7** 91
to [tu:] bis **I1** 17; zu **I3** 50
toast [təʊst] Toastbrot **I LS** 12
today [tə'deɪ] heute **I1** 20
together [tə'geðə] zusammen **II1** 8
toilet ['tɔɪlət] Toilette **I4** 67
tomato, tomatoes [tə'mɑ:təʊ tə'mɑ:təʊz] Tomate, Tomaten **II2** 23
tomorrow [tə'mɒrəʊ] morgen **I8** 133
ton [tʌn] Tonne (Gewichtseinheit) **III5** 64
tonight [tə'naɪt] heute Abend **III2** 24
too [tu:] auch **I1** 17; zu **II5** 72
tool [tu:l] Werkzeug **V4** 46
top [tɒp] Spitze **IV ER** 23
on top [ɒn 'tɒp] oben **III7** 90
topic-based ['tɒpɪk beist] themenbezogen **VI2** 16
torch [tɔ:tʃ] Taschenlampe **II7** 111
touch [tʌtʃ] berühren **IV1** 12
touchdown ['tʌtʃdaʊn] Aufsetzen, Landung **III5** 65
°**tour** [tʊə] Rundfahrt, Tour **III1** 15; Tournee **VI1** 8
go on tour ['gəʊ ɒn 'tʊər] auf Tournee gehen **IV ER** 83
tour guide [tʊər gaɪd] Fremdenführerin, Fremdenführer **V3** 37
tourism ['tʊərɪzm] Tourismus **VI5** 45
°**tourist** ['tʊərɪst] Touristin, Tourist **III1** 9
tourist information centre ['tʊərɪst ɪnfə'meɪʃn 'sentə] Touristeninformation **III3** 42

tournament [tʊənəmənt] Turnier **V 1** 8
towards [tə'wɔ:dz] entgegen **II 7** 108
tower ['taʊə] Turm **III 5** 66
town [taʊn] Stadt **I 6** 102
toy [tɔɪ] Spielzeug **III 1** 13
°toy frog ['tɔɪ frɒg] Spielzeugfrosch **I 2** 37
°track [træk] Pfad, Spur **V 2** 20
tractor ['træktə] Traktor **I B6** 116
tradition [trə'dɪʃən] Tradition **V 1** 10
traditional [trə'dɪʃnl] traditionell **IV 3** 49
traffic ['træfɪk] Verkehr **III 7** 86
traffic jam ['træfɪk dʒæm] Stau **III 7** 91
traffic lights ['træfɪk laɪts] Ampel **I 6** 102
°traffic rules ['træfɪk ru:lz] Verkehrsregeln **II 4** 65
trail [treɪl] Pfad, Weg **III ER** 101
train [treɪn] Zug **II 8** 120; trainieren **IV 5** 62
trainers ['treɪnəz] Turnschuhe **II 5** 73
training ['treɪnɪŋ] Ausbildung **IV 5** 60
training camp [treɪnɪŋ kæmp] Trainingslager **III 8** 105
tranquilizer ['træŋkwɪlaɪzə] Betäubungsmittel **IV 3** 38
transport [træns'pɔ:t] Beförderung, Transport **III ER** 75
trap [træp] stauen, fangen **VI 6** 52
trapper ['træpə] Fallensteller **III ER** 101
travel ['trævl] reisen **III 4** 51
travel agency ['trævl 'eɪdʒənsi] Reisebüro **III 3** 34
°travel agent ['trævəl 'eɪdʒənt] Angestellte/Angestellter im Reisebüro **IV 7** 86
traveller ['trævlə] Reisende, Reisender **III 4** 51
treat [tri:t] behandeln **IV ER** 112
tree [tri:] Baum **I 3** 51
fir tree ['fɜ: tri:] Tanne **II 7** 113
trekking ['trekɪŋ] Trekking **III 8** 103
trendy ['trendi] modern, schick **III 5** 66
triathlon [traɪ'æθlən] Triathlon **I 8** 133
tribe [traɪb] Stamm **IV 2** 24
trick [trɪk] Trick **I 7** 122
trilogy ['trɪlədʒi] Trilogie **VI 1** 8
trip [trɪp] Ausflug, Reise **I 5** 86
tropical ['trɒpɪkl] tropisch **VI 6** 51
trouble ['trʌbl] Schwierigkeiten **IV 2** 25
troublemaker ['trʌblmeɪkə] Unruhestifterin, Unruhestifter **V 3** 34
trousers ['traʊzəz] Hose **I B4** 82
trucker ['trʌkə] Lkw-Fahrerin, Lkw-Fahrer **V 2** 17
true [tru:] wahr **III 7** 87
make … come true [meɪk … kʌm 'tru:] … wahr machen **IV 7** 95
try [traɪ] versuchen **IV 5** 64
Tuesday ['tju:zdeɪ] Dienstag **I 1** 20
°Tune in ['tju:n ɪn] Stimm (t) ein **I 1** 25
Turkish ['tɜ:kɪʃ] Türkin, Türke; türkisch **V 1** 10
turn [tɜ:n] abbiegen **I 6** 102; umdrehen, umkehren **V 4** 47
on TV [ɒn ti:'vi:] im Fernsehen **VI 1** 8
TV series [ti:'vi: 'sɪəri:z] Fernsehserie **VI 1** 8
twelve [twelv] zwölf **I LS** 10
twenty ['twenti] zwanzig **I 2** 32
twice [twaɪs] zweimal **IV 5** 61
two [tu:] zwei **I LS** 10
type (in) [taɪp 'ɪn] (ein-)tippen, eingeben **II 7** 106

U

ugly ['ʌgli] hässlich **V 6** 72
ultimate ['ʌltɪmət] ultimativ **V 5** 61
uncle ['ʌnkl] Onkel **II 8** 119
under ['ʌndə] unter **I 2** 34
underground ['ʌndəgraʊnd] U-Bahn **III 1** 12; unterirdisch **V 7** 88
understand [ʌndə'stænd] verstehen **III 1** 15
unemployed [ʌnɪm'plɔɪd] arbeitslos **V 4** 45
unhappy [ʌn'hæpi] unglücklich **II 3** 44
°unicycle ['ju:nɪsaɪkl] Einrad **II 3** 42
uniform ['ju:nɪfɔ:m] Uniform **II 1** 8
°unit ['ju:nɪt] Kapitel, Lektion **I LS** 5
unite [ju:'naɪt] sich zusammentun, vereinigen **VI 1** 8
university [ju:nɪ'vɜ:səti] Universität **V 3** 34
university entrance [ju:nɪ'vɜ:səti 'entrəns] Hochschulzulassung **VI 4** 32
unless [ən'les] es sei denn **V 6** 73
unlike [ʌn'laɪk] anders als, im Gegensatz zu **VI 1** 8
be unlucky [bi: ʌn'lʌki] kein Glück haben **II 1** 19
until [ʌn'tɪl] bis **II 5** 76
up [ʌp] hinauf **I 8** 137
°look up ['lʊk ʌp] nachschauen, nachschlagen **II 5** 72
up there [ʌp 'ðeə] da oben **III 1** 10
upstairs [ʌp'steəz] oben, die Treppe hinauf **I 4** 67
°uppers ['ʌpərz] Aufputschmittel **V 6** 70
°Urdu ['ʊədu:] Urdu (Sprache in Pakistan) **IV 6** 76
us [ʌs] uns **I 7** 118
use [ju:z] benutzen, gebrauchen **III 1** 10
°use up energy [ju:s ʌp 'enədʒi] Energie loswerden, Energie aufbrauchen **V 4** 46
used car [ju:zd 'kɑ:] Gebrauchtwagen **IV ER** 56
useful ['ju:sfəl] nützlich **IV ER** 112
useless [ju:sləs] nutzlos, unbrauchbar **V 4** 46
usual ['ju:ʒəl] gewöhnlich, sonst **V 6** 70
usually ['ju:ʒli] gewöhnlich **II 8** 120

V

No vacancies. [nəʊ 'veɪkənsi:z] Belegt/Keine Zimmer frei. **III 3** 42
vacation (AE) [və'keɪʃən] Urlaub, Ferien **V 6** 72
valley ['væli] Tal **V 2** 20
van [væn] (Umzugs-)Transporter, Lieferwagen **I B3** 64
vegetables ['vedʒtəblz] Gemüse **II 3** 42
vehicle ['vɪəkl] Fahrzeug **IV ER** 101
version ['vɜ:ʃn] Version **VI 2** 17
very ['veri] sehr **I 5** 86
vet [vet] Tierärztin, Tierarzt **I 7** 122
video ['vɪdiəʊ] Video (kassette) **I 5** 92
view [vju:] Sicht, Aussicht **III 1** 8
Viking ['vaɪkɪŋ] Wikinger **IV 2** 24
village ['vɪlɪdʒ] Dorf **I 8** 134
violence ['vaɪəlns] Gewalt **VI 5** 44
violent ['vaɪələnt] Gewalt- **V 3** 36; brutal, gewaltsam **V 6** 69
virtual ['vɜ:tʃuəl] virtuell **III ER** 23
visit ['vɪzɪt] besichtigen, besuchen **II 8** 118; Besuch **III ER** 118
visitor ['vɪsɪtə] Besucherin, Besucher **IV 3** 34
volcano [vɒl'keɪnəʊ] Vulkan **IV ER** 112
volleyball ['vɒlibɔ:l] Volleyball **I LS** 12
volunteer [vɒlən'tɪə] freiwillig, ehrenamtlich **V 4** ER
vote [vəʊt] Wahlrecht **VI 4** 32; wählen, abstimmen **VI 4** 37

W

minimum wage ['mɪnɪməm weɪdʒ] Mindestlohn **VI 4** 35
wage [weɪdʒ] Lohn **V 4** ER
wagon ['wægən] Wagen, Karre **IV ER** 101
wait [weɪt] warten **I 3** 50
waiter ['weɪtə] Kellner **II 2** 24
waitress ['weɪtrəs] Kellnerin **II 2** 32
wake up [weɪk ʌp] aufwachen **V 2** 20
walk [wɔ:k] gehen, laufen **II 1** 8; Spaziergang **II 3** 43
go for a walk [gəʊ fər ə wɔ:k] spazieren gehen **III ER** 118
walk off [wɔ:k ɒf] davonlaufen **V 2** 21
walk past [wɔ:k pa:st] vorbeigehen **IV 7** 86
°walk someone home ['wɒ:k sʌmwʌn həʊm] jemanden nach Hause begleiten **V 6** 73
take (the dog) for a walk [teɪk ðə 'dɒg fər ə wɔ:k] (den Hund) ausführen **I 7** 118
wall [wɔ:l] Wand, Mauer **III ER** 23
want [wɒnt] möchten, wollen **I 5** 88
war [wɔ:] Krieg **IV 2** 25
go to war [gəʊ tə 'wɔ:] Krieg führen **IV 2** 25
wardrobe ['wɔ:drəʊb] Kleiderschrank **I B3** 64
warehouse ['weəhaʊs] Lagerhaus **IV 5** 65
warm [wɔ:m] warm **II 4** 56
was, were [wɒz, wɜ:] war, waren **II 3** 40
wash [wɒʃ] spülen, waschen **I 7** 118
watch [wɒtʃ] anschauen, beobachten **I 3** 51; Armbanduhr **II 3** 42
watch TV [wɒtʃ ti:'vi:] fernsehen **I 3** 51
water ['wɔ:tə] Wasser **I 4** 70
watermill ['wɔtəmɪl] Wassermühle **IV ER** 101
wave [weɪv] winken **III ER** 31
wax [wæks] Wachs **III 1** 9
way [weɪ] Weg **I 3** 50
lose my way [lu:z maɪ 'weɪ] den Weg nicht finden **II 7** 110
No way. ['nəʊ 'weɪ] Absolut nicht. **II 6** 87
°way of life [weɪ əv 'laɪf] Lebensstil, Lebensart **V 1** 10
we [wi:] wir **I 1** 18
wear [weə] tragen (Kleidung) **I 5** 88
weather ['weðə] Wetter **I B6** 116
weather forecast ['weðə 'fɔ:ka:st] Wettervorhersage **IV 4** 51
web [web] Internet **V 1** 8
web designer [web dɪ'zaɪnə] Webdesignerin, Webdesigner **V 1** 8
°word web ['wɜ:d web] Wortnetz **I LS** 14
website ['websait] Webseite **II 7** 105; Internetseite **V 4** 46
website designer [websaɪt dɪ'zaɪnə] Webdesignerin, Webdesigner **V 4** 46
Wednesday ['wenzdeɪ] Mittwoch **I 1** 20
week [wi:k] Woche **I 5** 88
weekend [wi:k'end] Wochenende **I 5** 89
°weigh [weɪ] wiegen **V 2** 17
weight [weɪt] Gewicht **III 5** 64
welcome ['welkəm] willkommen **II 6** 90; begrüßen **III ER** 115
well [wel] nun … **II 5** 76; gut **III 2** 26
well-known ['welnəʊn] bekannt **V 4** 46
west [west] Westen; westlich **V 2** 20
wet [wet] nass **I 7** 122
whale [weɪl] Wal **V 7** 86
grey whale [greɪ 'weɪl] Grauwal **V 7** 89
whale watching [weɪl wɑ:tʃɪŋ] Walbeobachtung **V 7** 86
what [wɒt] was, wie; welcher, welche, welches **I LS** 9
What a … ['wɒt ə] Was für ein/eine … **I 5** 84
What a shame! [wɒt ə 'ʃeɪm] Wie schade! **III 8** 103
What about …? [wɒt ə'baʊt] Was ist/Wie sieht es aus mit …? **I 4** 68
What for? [wɒt 'fɔ:] Wofür? Wozu? **IV 3** 36
What is it in English? [wɒt 'ɪz ɪt ɪn ɪŋlɪʃ] Wie heißt es auf Englisch? **I LS** 11
What's the time, please? ['wɒts ðə taɪm pli:z] Wie viel Uhr ist es? **I 5** 85
What's your name? [wɒts jə 'neɪm] Wie heißt du? **I LS** 9
whatever [wɒt'evə] irgendeiner, irgendeine, irgendeines **V 4** 46
wheel [wi:l] Rad **V 5** 60
when [wen] wann **I 6** 108; als **I 8** 134; wenn **III 1** 9
where [weə] wo, woher **I B1** 30
Where to? [weə tə] Wohin? **II 3** 1
wherever [weə'evə] wo auch immer **IV 3** 35
which [wɪtʃ] was; welcher, welche, welches **I 8** 132
while [wɑɪl] während **IV 7** 86
whisper [wɪspə] flüstern **III ER** 118
white [waɪt] weiß **I LS** 10
Whites [waɪts] Weiße **V 3** 34
who [hu:] wer **I 1** 24
whole (of) [həʊl əv] ganz **III 1** 8
°whose [hu:z] wessen **I 4** 66
why [waɪ] warum **I 4** 66
width [wɪdθ] Breite **VI 2** 15
wife [waɪf] Ehefrau **IV 2** 25
wild [waɪld] wild **I 4** 66
wilderness ['wɪldənɪs] Wildnis **III ER** 101
wildlife ['waɪldlaɪf] Tierleben **IV 3** 36
will [wɪl] werden **I 7** 118
win [wɪn] gewinnen **II 6** 95
winner ['wɪnə] Gewinnerin, Gewinner **II 3** 45
wind [wɪnd] Wind **II 4** 56
windmill ['wɪndmɪl] Windmühle **IV ER** 101
winds [wɪndz] Windgeschwindigkeit **V 5** 61
windy ['wɪndi] windig **II 4** 56
window ['wɪndəʊ] Fenster **I 2** 32
wing [wɪŋ] Flügel **IV 4** 51
wing-span ['wɪŋ spæn] Flügelspannweite **III ER** 75
winter ['wɪntə] Winter **I 8** 132
wire [waɪə] Draht **III 6** 76
wish [wɪʃ] wünschen **V 5** 61
with [wɪð] mit **I 2** 40
within [wɪ'ðɪn] innerhalb **III 5** 64
without [wɪ'ðaʊt] ohne **VI 3** 26
wolf, wolves [wʊlf wʊlvz] Wolf, Wölfe **IV 3** 35
woman ['wʊmən] Frau **I 3** 52
women ['wɪmɪn] Frauen **I 6** 107
wonder ['wʌndə] Wunder, (sich) wundern **III 7** 87
wonderful ['wʌndəfl] wunderbar **VI 3** 27
won't (= will not) [wəʊnt] nicht werden **I 7** 119
wood [wʊd] Wald **I 8** 134; Holz **III 3** 38
word [wɜ:d] Wort **II 6** 90
°word web ['wɜ:d web] Wortnetz **I LS** 14
work [wɜ:k] arbeiten; Arbeit **I 5** 84; funktionieren **IV 7** 88
migrant worker ['maɪgrnt 'wɜ:kə] Wanderarbeiter **VI 4** 34
work long hours [wɜ:k lɒŋ aʊəz] Überstunden machen **IV 6** 78
worker ['wɜ:kə] Arbeiterin, Arbeiter **III 6** 77
worksheet [wɜ:k ʃi:t] Arbeitsblatt **III ER** 118
°workshop ['wɜ:kʃɒp] Werkstatt **I 1** 22

working conditions ['wɜ:kɪŋ kən'dɪʃnz] Arbeitsbedingungen **VI 4** 35
all over the world [ɔ:l əʊvə ðə 'wɜ:ld] auf der ganzen Welt **VI 1** 10
°**world** [wɜ:ld] Welt **III 2** 24
worldwide [wɜ:ld'waɪd] weltweit **VI 6** 50
World Cup [wɜ:ld kʌp] Weltmeisterschaft **V 3** 36
worldwide [wɜ:ld'waɪd] weltweit **VI 1** 9
worry ['wʌri] Sorge **I 3** 55; sich Sorgen machen **VI 3** 26
be worried [bɪ 'wʌrid] sich Sorgen machen **III 1** 12
Don't worry. ['dəʊnt 'wʌri] Mach dir/Machen Sie sich keine Sorgen. **I 3** 55
worse [wɜ:s] schlechter **II 6** 87
worst [wɜ:st] der/die/das Schlechteste **II 6** 87
worth [wɜ:θ] wert **V 6** 71
°**would** [wʊd] würde **II 1** 16
Would you like ...? [wʊd jə 'laɪk] Möchten Sie/möchtest du ...? **II 2** 24
wrestling ['reslɪŋ] Ringen **IV 3** 49
write [raɪt] schreiben **I 2** 36
°write down [raɪt 'daʊn] aufschreiben **I 5** 86
writer ['raɪtə] Schriftstellerin, Schriftsteller **IV 4** 52
wrong [rɒŋ] falsch **I 2** 38
get someone wrong [get 'sʌmwʌn rɒŋ] jemanden falsch verstehen **V 4** 42
There's something wrong with ... [ðeəz 'sʌmθɪŋ rɒŋ wɪð] Mit dem/der ... ist etwas nicht in Ordnung. **II 2** 26

Y

yacht ['jɒt] Jacht **VI 2** 14
year [jɪə] Jahr **II 4** 70
... years ago [jɪəz ə'gəʊ] vor ... Jahren **II 3** 46
yellow ['jeləʊ] gelb **I LS** 10
yes [jes] ja **I 1** 18
yesterday ['jestədeɪ] gestern **II 3** 44
not yet [nɒt 'jet] noch nicht **III 3** 36
you [ju:] du, ihr, Sie **I 1** 17
You're welcome. [jɔ: 'welkəm] Bitte schön. **I 5** 85
young [jʌŋ] jung **I 8** 134
your [jɔ:] dein, deine **I LS** 9
yourself [jɔ:'self] dich, selbst **V 4** 44
yours [jɔ:z] deine, deiner, deines **IV 7** 88
Yours faithfully [jɔ:z 'feiθfli] Mit freundlichen Grüßen **VI 2** 17
youth hostel ['ju:θ hɒstl] Jugendherberge **I 7** 124
°**youth league** ['ju:θ li:g] Jugendverband **V 3** 35

Z

zoo [zu:] Zoo **I 7** 122
zookeeper ['zu:ki:pə] Tierpflegerin, Tierpfleger **I 7** 122

Boys' names

Adam ['ædəm] **II 8** 122
Alexander [ælɪg'zɑ:ndər] **IV 6** 84
Anand ['ɑ:nənd] **VI 3** 26
Andrew ['ændru:] **I 1** 17
Andy ['ændi] **IV 3** 41
Ben [ben] **VI 3** 29
Bill [bɪl] **I 7** 122
Bob [bɒb] **II 3** 42
Brad [bræd] **I 5** 93
Brandon ['brændən] **III 7** 90
Brian [braɪən] **IV 3** 34
Bruce [bru:s] **V 2** 18
Calvin ['kælvɪn] **III 2** 24
Chad [tʃæd] **V 6** 70
Charlie ['tʃɑ:li] **III ER** 30
Chip [tʃɪp] **V 6** 73
Chris [krɪs] **II 5** 80
Christopher ['krɪstəfər] **IV 2** 25
Dan ['dæn] **IV 1** 12
Daniel ['dænjəl] **V 7** 88
Dave [deɪv] **IV 5** 61
David ['deɪvɪd] **I LS** 13
Don [dɒn] **III 7** 86
Edward ['edwəd] **IV 2** 29
Finn [fɪn] **VI 5** 45
Frank [fræŋk] **III 7** 90
George [dʒɔ:dʒ] **IV 1** 15
Godson ['gɒdsʌn] **V 4** ER
Harry ['hæri] **I 7** 122
Henry ['henri] **II 8** 122
James [dʒeɪmz] **VI 4** 37
Jamie ['dʒeɪmi] **IV 7** 87
Jason ['dʒeɪsn] **II 6** 92
Jeff [dʒef] **II 7** 113
Jeremy ['dʒerəmi] **IV 6** 84
Jerry ['dʒeri] **II 2** 31
Jim [dʒɪm] **III 3** 43
Jimmy ['dʒɪmi] **V 4** ER
Joel ['dʒəʊəl] **IV ER** 25
John [dʒɒn] **II 3** 49
Jon [dʒɒn] **III 2** 24
Josip ['jɔ:sɪp] **III 8** 103
Kenneth ['kenɪθ] **III 5** 75
Kevin ['kevɪn] **I 1** 16
Kyle [kaɪl] **V 6** 68
Lester ['lestə] **I 1** 16
Liam ['li:əm] **V 4** 42
Luke [lu:k] **III 7** 88
Mark [mɑ:k] **IV 3** 40
Martin ['mɑ:tɪn] **I 1** 17
Mason ['meɪsən] **IV 1** 8
Matt [mæt] **II 6** 92
Mick [mɪk] **III 3** 42
Mike [maɪk] **II 3** 46
Nadeem [nə'di:m] **V 4** ER
Nathan ['neɪθən] **III ER** 118
Neil [ni:l] **IV ER** 56
Patti ['pæti] **V 2** 17
Peter ['pi:tə] **I 3** 52
Pierre [pɪ'eə] **I 1** 16
Rashid [ræ'ʃi:d] **III 1** 8
Ravi ['ravi] **III ER** 30
Rickie ['rɪki] **IV 5** 64
Rob [rɒb] **III 2** 24
Robbie ['rɒbi] **I LS** 15
Robert ['rɒbət] **I 4** 72
Ron [rɒn] **IV 2** 27
Ryan [raɪən] **IV 6** 84
Sam [sæm] **II 7** 106
Scott [skɒt] **II 6** 92
Shahid [ʃə'hi:d] **V 4** 45
Shawn [ʃɔ:n] **V 5** 63
Simon ['saɪmən] **III 7** 94
Stephen ['sti:vən] **IV 2** 25
Steve [sti:v] **I 1** 16
Sunil [su'ni:l] **VI 3** 27
Tariq ['tɑ:rɪk] **I 8** 133
Ted [ted] **III 8** 103
Terry ['teri] **V 2** 18
Than Ha ['θɑ:n 'hɑ:] **V 2** 18
Thomas ['tɒməs] **III 6** 76
Tim [tɪm] **III 1** 17
Todd ['tɒd] **III 1** 12
Tom [tɒm] **I LS** 9
Toni ['təʊni] **V 2** 18
Trevor ['trevə] **I 8** 134
Tyler ['taɪlə] **III 5** 60
Vic [vɪk] **VI 4** 37
Wan [wɒn] **III 7** 88
Will [wɪl] **III 3** 40
Winston ['wɪnstn] **III 1** 14

Girls' names

Aisha [aɪ'i:ʃə] **V 4** 50
Alexandra [ælɪg'zɑ:ndrə] **IV 6** 84
Alice ['ælɪs] **V 4** 44
Alison ['ælɪsən] **V 4** 45
Amy ['eɪmi] **II 7** 108
Ann [æn] **I 1** 17
Anne [æn] **IV 1** 17
Anuja [ɑ:'nu:dʒɑ:] **III 8** 105

Ashley ['æʃli] **IV 8** 105
Betsy ['betsi] **V 4** ER
Brenda ['brendə] **III 7** 88
Cathy ['kæθi] **II 8** 122
Debbie ['debi] **IV 8** 122
Deborah ['debərə] **IV**
Denise [də'ni:z] **IV**
Diana [daɪ'ænə] **IV**
Donna ['dɒnə] **V 4** 42
Dorothy ['dɒrəθi] **III ER** 83
Elizabeth [ɪ'lɪzəbəθ] **IV ER** 83
Ellen ['elən] **III 3** 35
Emily ['emɪli] **III 3** 43
Gene [dʒi:n] **IV 3** 43
Hamida [hʌ'mi:dʌ] **II 1** 8
Jane [dʒeɪn] **II 2** 31
Janet ['dʒænɪt] **II 6** 90
Jenna ['dʒenə] **V 4** 45
Jennifer ['dʒenɪfər] **IV 6** 90
Jenny ['dʒeni] **II 1** 15
Jill [dʒɪl] **IV 1** 15
Joanne [dʒəʊ'æn] **V 4** ER
Julia ['dʒu:liə] **V 6** 72
Karen ['kærən] **I 5** 84
Kate [keɪt] **III ER** 30
Kendra ['kendrə] **V 6** 68
Kerry ['keri] **V 5** 60
Kim [kɪm] **VI 3** 28
Kirsty ['kɜ:sti] **V 4** 46
Klara ['klɑ:rə] **VI 5** 45
Lara ['lɑ:rə] **III ER** 118
Laura ['lɔ:rə] **III 1** 14
Laurie ['lɔ:ri] **V 6** 69
Linda ['lɪndə] **I 1** 16
Lisa ['li:sə] **I 1** 17
Lucy ['lu:si] **III 7** 88
Mandy ['mændi] **III 1** 17
Maria [mə'ri:ə] **III 5** 60
Mary ['meəri] **I 3** 52
May [meɪ] **III ER** 30
Monica ['mɒnɪkə] **IV ER** 22
Nicky ['niki] **IV 1** 8
Nina ['ni:nə] **IV 4** 53
Pam [pæm] **III 1** 19
Penny ['peni] **III 7** 87
Rachel ['reɪtʃəl] **V 6** 69
Ruth [ru:θ] **IV 3** 38
Sally ['sæli] **V 4** ER
Samira [sə'mi:rə] **V 1** 11
Sandra ['sændrə] **I 5** 91
Sarah ['seərə] **I 1** 17
Sheryl ['ʃerɪl] **V 4** 51
Sue [su:] **I 3** 52
Susan ['su:zn] **I 5** 93
Susie ['su:zi] **I LS** 9
Tina ['ti:nə] **IV 5** 60
Tracy ['treɪsi] **I 5** 91
Verena [vɜ:ri:nə] **II 5** 81
Vicky ['vɪki] **IV 5** 62

Surnames

Adams ['ædəmz] **V 4** 42
Anderson ['ændəsn] **I 4** 73
Apple ['æpl] **III 5** 69
Aravind [ɑr'vɪnd] **VI 3** 27
Ashraf ['aʃrʌf] **II 1** 8
Aston ['æstən] **IV 1** 12
Baker ['beɪkə] **III 7** 98
Banks [bæŋks] **V 4** 44
Bigfish ['bɪgfɪʃ] **IV 2** 24
Blake [bleɪk] **II 4** 61
Bridger ['brɪdʒə] **IV 3** 35
Brooks [brʊks] **II 7** 108
Carter ['kɑ:tə] **V 4** 45
Carting ['kɑ:tɪŋ] **IV 5** 64
Cole [kəʊl] **IV 6** 61
Cook [kʊk] **V 4** 44
Cooper ['ku:pə] **I 4** 77
Croft [krɒft] **III 5** 68
Dane [deɪn] **III 5** 68
Dawson ['dɔ:sən] **V 5** 62
French [frentʃ] **V 5** 60
Garry ['gæri] **IV 2** 29
Gibbs [gɪbz] **V 4** ER
Green [gri:n] **I 1** 16
Hauben ['həʊbən] **V 7** 88
Haye [heɪ] **V 4** 48
Herrick ['herɪk] **VI 4** 37
Hopkins ['hɒpkɪnz] **IV 2** 25
Jones ['dʒəʊnz] **I 5** 84
Khan [kɑ:n] **V 4** ER
Lee [li:] **III 7** 87
McArthur [me'kɑ:θə] **VI 2** 14
Marshall ['mɑ:ʃl] **III 5** 60
Matthews ['mæθju:z] **III 1** 17
McCool [mæk ku:l] **VI 5** 45
McDonald [mək'dɒnld] **III ER** 49
McGregor [mək'gregə] **III ER** 49
Miller ['mɪlə] **IV 3** 40
Mitchell ['mɪtʃəl] **IV 5** 64
Moore [mʊə] **II 7** 108
Nguyen ['nʊjən] **V 4** 18
Ogwudire [[ɒgwʊ'dɪrɪ] **V 4** ER
O'Toole [ə'tu:l] **II 7** 88
Parker ['pɑ:kə] **I 4** 72
Poulter ['pəʊltə] **I 8** 136
Rhodes [rəʊdz] **III 7** 88
Rider ['raɪdə] **II 1** 13
Robins ['rɒbɪnz] **III 3** 34
Rogers ['rɒdʒəz] **IV 5** 64
Sears [sɪəz] **V 4** 43
Simpson ['sɪmpsən] **III ER** 83
Singh [sɪŋ] **VI 3** 26
Smith [smɪθ] **III 3** 34
Spencer ['spensə] **I 2** 36
Sulter [sʌltə] **IV 5** 62
Walters ['wɒltəz] **VI 4** 37
White [waɪt] **V 4** 42
Williams ['wɪljəmz] **III 2** 27
Wilson ['wɪlsən] **VI 4** 37
Young [jʌŋ] **III 5** 64

Place names

Afghanistan [æf'gænɪstæn] **IV 6** 77
Africa ['afrɪkə] **V 1** 10
Alabama [ælə'bæmə] **VI 7** 62
Alaska [ə'læskə] **V 7** 87
Algeria [æl'dʒɪəriə] **V 3** 35
Alice Springs [ælɪs 'sprɪŋz] **V 2** 17
America [ə'merɪkə] **I 5** 84
Antarctic [æn'tɑ:ktɪk] **VI 6** 51
Arctic ['ɑ:ktɪk] **VI 6** 51
Arkansas ['ɑ:rkənsɔ:] **VI 4** 34
Asia ['eɪʒə] **V 4** 43
Atlanta [ət'læntə] **IV 1** 12
Auckland ['ɔ:klənd] **VI 2** 15
Australia [ɒ'streɪliə] **IV 4** 51
Bahamas [bə'hɑ:məz] **IV 2** 24
Bangladesh [bæŋglə'deʃ] **V 4** ER
Barbados [bɑ:'beɪdɒs] **V 1** 11
Bavaria [bə'veəriə] **IV 3** 43
Belfast [bel:fɑ:st] **VI 5** 44
Birmingham ['bɜ:mɪŋəm] **IV 5** 64
Blakewell [bleɪkwl] **VI 6** 55
Bombay [bɒm'beɪ] **VI 3** 27
Bondi ['bɒndaɪ] **V 2** 18
Botswana [bɒt'swɑ:nə] **VI 4** 35
Brighton ['braɪtn] **II 8** 118
Brisbane ['brɪzbən] **IV 4** 51
Bristol ['brɪstəl] **V 4** 46
Britain ['brɪtn] **III 4** 53
Brixton ['brɪkstən] **V 1** 11
Burma ['bɜ:mə] **IV 4** 51
Calcutta [kæl'kʌtə] **VI 3** 27
California [kælɪ'fɔ:niə] **III 5** 65
Canada ['kænədə] **V 7** 86
Central Park ['sentrl 'pɑ:k] **III 7** 84
Chattahoochee [tʃætə'hu:tʃi] **IV 1** 15
Chicago [ʃɪ'kɑ:gəʊ] **II 6** 87
China ['tʃaɪnə] **V 1** 9
Colorado [kɒlə'rɑ:dəʊ] **II 6** 89
Cork [kɔ:k] **VI 5** 45
Croatia [krəʊ'eɪʃə] **III 8** 103
Cuba ['kju:bə] **VI 4** 32
Dallas ['dæləs] **III 5** 68
Dartmoor ['dɑ:tmʊə] **II 8** 118
Dublin ['dʌblɪn] **VI 5** 44
East Coast [i:st kəʊst] **III ER** 101
England ['ɪŋglənd] **I 1** 22
Europe ['jʊərəp] **IV 6** 76
Florida ['flɒrɪdə] **II 6** 90
France [frɑ:ns] **I 1** 16
Fremantle [fri:'mæntl] **V 2** 20
Galway ['gɔ:lweɪ] **VI 5** 46
Germany ['dʒɜ:məni] **I 1** 16
Greece [gri:s] **VI 6** 51
Greenland ['gri:nlənd] **V 7** 87
Greenwich ['grenɪdʒ] **I 6** 100

Greenwich Village [ˈgrenɪdʒ ˈvɪlɪdʒ] **III 7** 86
Gulf Coast [gʌlf kəʊst] **VI 6** 51
Guyana [gaɪˈɑ:nə] **V 3** 37
Hawaii [həˈwaii:] **V 5** 61
Heathrow [ˈhi:θrəʊ] **III 1** 12
Hollywood [ˈhɒliwʊd] **II 6** 91
Hungary [hʌŋgri] **IV 6** 78
India [ˈɪndiə] **V 1** 10
Iraq [ɪˈrɑ:k] **IV 4** 51
Ireland [ˈaɪələnd] **VI 5** 44
Italy [ˈɪtəli] **V 1** 10
Jamaica [dʒəˈmeɪkə] **IV 6** 76
Japan [dʒəˈpæn] **III 8** 102
Johannesburg [ʤəʊˈhænɪzbɜ:g] **V 3** 36
Kansas City [kænzəs ˈsɪti] **V 6** 69
Kenya [ˈkenjə] **VI 4** 33
Lake District [ˈleɪk dɪstrɪkt] **IV ER** 48
Lake Ontario [leɪk ɒnˈteəriəʊ] **V 7** 88
Las Vegas [læs ˈveɪgəs] **II 6** 91
Leeds [li:dz] **III 2** 25
Liverpool [ˈlɪvəpu:l] **III 2** 25
Loch Ness [lɒk ˈnes] **II 8** 118
London [ˈlʌndən] **II 4** 62
Los Angeles [lɒs ˈændʒɪli:z] **V 7** 88
Machakos [məˈtʃɑ:kɒs] **VI 4** 37
Mackay [məˈkaɪ] **V 2** ER
Maldives [ˈmɔ:ldi:vz]
Manhattan [mænˈhætn] **II 6** 88
Massachusetts [mæsəˈtʃu:sɪts] **V 2** 26
Melbourne [ˈmelbən] **V 2** 19
Memphis [ˈmemfɪs] **VI 7** 63
Mexico City [meksɪkəʊ ˈsɪti] **V 7** 88
Miami [ˈmaɪæmi] **III 5** 60
Michigan [ˈmɪʃɪgən] **III 6** 77
Milan [mɪˈlæn] **III 6** 76
Missouri [mɪˈzʊəri] **V 6** 69
Montana [mɒnˈtænə] **IV 3** 37
Montgomery [mənt'gʌmri] **VI 7** 62
Montreal [mɒntriˈɔ:l] **V 7** 87
Mumbai [mumˈbaɪ] **VI 3** 27
Munich [ˈmju:nɪk] **III 8** 102
Nepal [nepˈɒ:l] **VI 6** 51
Netherlands [ˈneðələndz] **VI 6** 50
New Delhi [nju: ˈdelɪ] **VI 3** 26
New Jersey [nju: ˈdʒɜ:zi] **IV ER** 22
New Orleans [nju: ˈɔ:liənz] **III 5** 66
New South Wales [nju: saʊθ ˈweɪlz] **V 2** ER
New York [nju: ˈjɔ:k] **II 6** 87
New Zealand [nju: ˈzi:lənd] **VI 2** 15
North Dakota [nɔ:θ dəˈkəʊtə] **III 5** 66
Norhern Ireland [ˈnɒ:ðən ˈaɪələnd] **VI 5** 44
Norway [ˈnɒ:weɪ] **VI 7** 63
Notting Hill [nɒtɪŋ ˈhɪl] **IV 6** 76
Nunavut [ˈnu:nəvu:t] **V 7** 86
Ohio [əʊˈhaɪəʊ] **III 6** 76
Oregon [ˈɒrɪgən] **II 8** 122
Orlando [ɔ:ˈlændəʊ] **II 6** 87
Ottawa [ˈɒtəwə] **V 7** 87
Oxford Street [ˈɒksfəd stri:t] **III 1** 9
Oakland [ˈəʊklənd] **V 5** 62
Pakistan [pɑ:kɪˈstɑ:n] **IV 6** 77
Paris [ˈpærɪs] **I 1** 16
Piccadilly Circus [pɪkəˈdɪli ˈsɜ:kəs] **III 1** 12
Plymouth [ˈplɪməθ] **IV 2** 25
Portland [ˈpɔ:tlənd] **V 6** 68
Portobello Road [pɔ:təˈbeləʊ ˈrəʊd] **III 1** 9
Québec [kwɪˈbek] **V 7** 86
Queensland [ˈkwi:nzlænd] **V 2** ER
Republic of Ireland [rɪˈpʌblɪk ɒv ˈaɪələnd] **VI 5** 44
Resolute Bay [ˈrezəlu:t beɪ] **V 7** 89
San Francisco [sæn frənˈsɪskəʊ] **II 6** 90
Scotland [ˈskɒtlənd] **II 8** 118
Seattle [sɪˈætl] **II 1** 8
Shenandoah National Park [ʃenənˈdəʊə ˈnæʃənəl pɑ:k] **V 6** 69
Sherwood Forest [ˈʃɜ:wʊd ˈfɒrɪst] **II 5** 72
South Africa [saʊθ ˈæfrɪkə] **V 1** 8
Spain [speɪn] **III 8** 102
Stratford-upon-Avon [strætfədəpɒnˈeɪvn] **III ER** 117
Sydney [ˈsɪdni] **V 2** 16
Texas [ˈteksəs] **III 5** 75
Toronto [təˈrɒntəʊ] **V 7** 87
Turkey [ˈtɜ:ki] **V 1** 10
United States [ju:ˈnaɪtɪd steɪts] **III 5** 63
Upstate New York [ʌpˈsteɪt nju: ˈjɔ:k] **III 7** 86
US [ju:ˈes] **III 5** 74
USA [ju: es ˈeɪ] **II 6** 90
Vancouver [vænˈku:və] **V 7** 87
Victoria [vɪkˈtɔ:riə] **V 2** ER
Vietnam [vjetˈnæm] **V 2** 18
Virginia [vəˈdʒɪnjə] **IV 2** 25
Wales [weɪlz] **II 8** 118
Washington D.C. [wɒʃɪŋtən di: ˈsi:] **V 6** 69
Waterloo Station [ˈwɔ:təlu: ˈsteɪʃn] **III 1** 12
Watford [ˈwɒtfəd] **III ER** 117
West Indies [west ˈɪndiz] **V 1** 10
Yellowstone National Park [ˈjeləʊstəʊn næʃnl pɑ:k] **IV 3** 34
Yosemite National Park [jəʊˈsemɪti ˈnæʃnl pɑ:k] **II 7** 104

Other names

Aborigine [æbəˈrɪʤni] **V 2** 16
African National Congress [ˈæfrɪkən ˈnæʃənəl ˈkɒŋgres] **V 3** 35
Albert Facey [ælbət ˈfæsi] **V 2** 20
Amelia Earhart [əˈmi:liə eəhɑ:t] **IV 4** 51
Amy Johnson [ˈeɪmi ˈdʒɒnsən] **IV 4** 51
ANC [eɪenˈsi:] **V 3** 35
Animal Farm [ˈænɪməl fɑ:m] **II 5** 79
Arsenal [ˈɑ:snl] **II 7** 105
Arctic Ocean [ˈɑ:ktɪk ˈəʊʃən] **V 7** 87
Aston Villa [æstən ˈvɪlə] **V 4** 51
Atlanta Braves [ətˈlæntə breɪvz] **V 6** 76
Atlantic Ocean [ətˈlæntɪk ˈəʊʃən] **V 7** 87
Avril Lavigne [ˈævrɪl ləˈwi:n] **VI 1** 8
Ayers Rock [eəz ˈrɒk] **V 2** 17
BBC [bi:bi:ˈsi:] **VI 1** 9
Birmingham City [ˈbɜ:mɪŋəm ˈsɪti] **V 4** 51
Blarney Castle [ˈblɑ:ni ˈkɑ:sl] **VI 5** 45
Blarney Stone [ˈblɑ:ni stəʊn] **VI 5** 45
Bollywood [ˈbɒliwʊd] **VI 3** 27
Bonnie [ˈbɒni] **IV ER** 100
British Empire [ˈbrɪtɪʃ empaɪə] **V 1** 8
Britney Spears [ˈbrɪtni spɪəz] **III 2** 25
Bruce Springsteen [bru:s ˈsprɪŋsti:n] **V 3** 36
Buckingham Palace [ˈbʌkɪŋəm ˈpælɪs] **III 1** 8
Butter Crag [ˈbʌtə kræg] **IV ER** 49
Caribbean Sea [kærɪˈbi:ən] **V 1** 11
Cathy Freeman [kæθi ˈfri:mən] **V 2** ER
Charles Lindbergh [tʃɑ:lz ˈlɪndbɜ:g] **IV 4** 51
Chelsea [ˈtʃelsi] **II 7** 105
Chicago Bulls [ʃɪˈkɑ:gəʊ bʊlz] **II 6** 87
Chinatown [ˈtʃaɪnətaʊn] **III 7** 87
Chrysler Buliding [ˈkraɪzlə bɪldɪŋ] **III 7** 86
Columbia [kəˈlʌmbiə] **III 5** 64
Columbus [kəˈlʌmbəs] **IV 2** 24
Coniston Water [ˈkɒnɪstən ˈwɒ:tər] **IV ER** 49
Cutty Sark [kʌtɪ ˈsɑ:k] **II 7** 106
Dallas Mavericks [ˈdæləs ˈmævərɪks] **IV ER** 23
Dinnie [ˈdɪni] **V 2** 20
Disney World [ˈdɪzni wɜ:ld] **III 5** 60
Dolly [ˈdɒli] **IV ER** 100
Donald Campbell [ˈdɒnəld ˈkæmbl] **IV ER** 49
Dr Watson [dɒktə ˈwɒtsn] **II 5** 72
Eddy Grant [edi ˈgrɑ:nt] **V 3** 37
Edmund Hillary [ˈedmənd ˈhɪləri] **V 2** 21

A

abbiegen turn
abbremsen slow down
Abend evening
Abendessen dinner
Abenteuer adventure
aber but
Abfall litter
abfeuern fire
Abflug departure
Abflughalle departure lounge
(ab-)holen collect; pick up
Abmachung deal
Abreise departure
abschließen lock
Abschlusskontrolle checkout
absolut absolutely
Absolut nicht. No way.
absteigen get off
abstimmen vote
(ab-)trocknen dry
acht eight
achtzehn eighteen
achtzig eighty
Adapter adapter
Adresse address
ändern change
Äquator equator
Aerobic aerobics
Ärztin, Arzt doctor
Affe monkey
Afrikaner, Afrikanerin; afrikanisch African
Afro-Amerikanerin, Afro-Amerikaner Afro-/ African-American
AG school club
Agent agent
aggressiv aggressive
Aids AIDS
Aktion action
aktiv active
aktiv werden take action
Aktivität activity
akzeptieren accept; put up with
Alarmanlage alarm system
Album album
Alkohol alcohol
Alkoholikerin, Alkoholiker alcoholic
alle everybody; everyone
alle, alles all
allein alone
alleine on his/her own
alles everything
Allmächtiger Gott God Almighty
Alphabet alphabet
als (zeitlich) when; as
als (bei Vergleich) than
also so
alt old
Altenheim old people's home
Alter age
Alternative alternative
am on
Am Apparat. (beim Telefonieren) Speaking.
am Ende von at the end of
am Leben sein be alive
Amateur amateur
Amerikanerin, Amerikaner; amerikanisch American
Ampel traffic lights
an at
an Bord aboard
anbauen plant
anbieten offer
Andenken souvenir
anderer, andere, anderes different; other
anders als unlike
Anekdote anecdote
Anfängerglück beginner's luck
Anfang beginning
anfangen begin; start
Anführerin, Anführer leader
Angebot offer
Angelegenheit matter
angeln fish
angespannt (sein) (be) tense
Angestellte, Angestellter im Reisebüro travel agent
Angestellte, Angestellter employee
angreifen attack
Angst haben be frightened; be scared; be afraid (of)
anhaben have got on; wear
Anhänger fan
anhalten stop
Anhebung elevation
anheuern hire
anhören listen (to)
(an-)klicken click
ankommen arrive
Anlage attachment
anlegen put on
Anorak anorak
Anruf call
(an-)rufen call; phone
Anruferin, Anrufer caller
Ansage announcement
anschauen look at; watch
anschließen plug into
ansteigen increase; rise
Anstieg increase
anti- anti
Antwort answer
antworten answer
Anwaltskanzlei law firm
Anweisung instruction
Anzeige advert; advertisement
Anziehungspunkt attraction
Apartheid apartheid
Apfel apple
Apfelsine orange
April April
Arbeit job; work; employment
arbeiten work
Arbeiterin, Arbeiter worker
Arbeitgeberin, Arbeitgeber employer
Arbeitsamt job centre
Arbeitsbedingungen working conditions
Arbeitsblatt worksheet; handout
arbeitslos unemployed
(Arbeits-)Zeugnis reference
Arm arm
arm poor
Armbanduhr watch
arrangieren fix
Art kind
Artikel article
Asiatin, Asiat; asiatisch Asian
Assistentin, Assistent assistant
Atmosphäre atmosphere
Atomkraft nuclear power
Attraktion attraction
attraktiv attractive
auch also; too
auch nicht not ... either
auf in; on
auf der ganzen Welt all over the world
auf der Suche nach in search of
auf Tournee gehen go on tour
auf Wiedersehen sagen say goodbye
aufbrauchen use up
aufbrechen set off
Aufführung performance
Aufgabe job
aufgeben give up
aufgehen rise; come up
aufgeregt excited
(auf-)hängen hang (up)
aufheulen (Motor) roar
Aufkleber sticker
aufladen recharge
Aufmerksamkeit attention
Aufnahme machen make a record
aufnehmen record
aufpassen take care; look after; keep an eye on
Aufputschmittel uppers
Aufsatz essay
aufschreiben write down
Aufsetzen touchdown
aufstehen get up
aufsteigen get on; move up
aufstellen put up

(auf-)teilen divide
auftreten perform
aufwachen wake up
aufwachsen grow up
Auge eye
Augenblick moment
Augenbraue eyebrow
August August
aus out
Ausbildung apprenticeship; training
Auschecken checkout
(aus-)drucken print
auseinanderfallen fall apart
Auseinandersetzung argument; conflict
ausfindig machen locate
ausflippen flip out
Ausflug trip
ausführen take for a walk
Ausgang gate
ausgeben spend
ausgehen go off; fall out; go out
auslachen laugh at
ausländisch foreign
ausleihen (von) borrow (from)
Ausrüstung equipment
ausschalten switch off
ausschneiden cut out
aussehen wie look like
außen outside
Außenseiterin, Außenseiter outsider
außerdem besides
Aussicht view
Aussprache pronunciation
aussteigen get off
Ausstellung exhibition
Australierin, Australier; australisch Australian
(aus-)wählen choose
Auswahl choice
Auszeichnung award
Auto car
Auto-Rickscha auto-rickshaw
Autobahn highway
automatisch automatically
Automechanikerin, Automechaniker car mechanic
Autopilot autopilot
Autorennsport racing
Autowerkstatt garage
außer except for

B

Baby, Babys baby, babies
babysitten babysit
backen bake
Backofen oven
Badezimmer bathroom
Badminton badminton
Bäckerin, Bäcker baker
Bär bear
Bahnarbeiterin, Bahnarbeiter railroad worker
Bahnhof (train) station
Bahnsteig platform
bald soon
Balkon balcony
Ball ball
Ballon balloon
Banane banana
Band band
Bande gang
Bandit outlaw
Bank (Geldinstitut) bank
Bar bar
Bart beard
Baseball baseball
Basketball basketball
Batterie battery
bauen build; construct
Bauernhof farm
Baum tree
Baumarkt hardware store (AE)
Baustelle building site
beantworten answer
Bedien' dich./Bedient euch. Help yourself./Help yourselves.
beeindrucken impress
beeinflussen affect
beenden end; finish
befinden locate
Beförderung transport
befreien free
Begeisterung enthusiasm
beginnen begin
begleiten (nach Hause) walk home
beglückwünschen congratulate
begraben bury
begrüßen welcome
behalten keep
behandeln treat
behaupten claim
beherrschen rule
bei at
beibringen teach
beide both
beifügen enclose
Bein leg
beinahe almost
Beispiel example
bekannt well-known; on record
bekommen get; receive
belebt busy
belegt on record
Belegt/Keine Zimmer frei. No vacancies.
belegtes Brot sandwich
beliebt popular
bemerken notice
benutzen use
Benzin fuel; gas (AE)
beobachten watch; keep an eye on
Beobachten von Vögeln birdwatching
bequem comfortable
Beraterin, Berater adviser
bereit ready
Berg mountain
bergab downhill
Bergmann miner
Bergwerk mine
Bericht report; article
berichten report
berühmt famous
berühren touch
Beruf job
beschädigen damage
beschädigt damaged
beschäftigt busy
Beschäftigung activity; employment
besichtigen visit
besitzen have (got)
Besitzerin, Besitzer owner
besonderer, besondere, besonderes special
besonders especially
besorgen get
Besprechung meeting
besser better
Bestandteil ingredient
bestehen pass
bestellen order
Bestellformular order form
bester, beste, bestes best
bestimmt certainly
Bestseller bestseller
Besuch visit
besuchen visit; see
Besucherin, Besucher visitor
Betäubungsmittel tranquilizer
beteiligen involve
Bett bed
Beule bump
Bevölkerung population
bevor before
bewältigen manage
Bewegung move
Bewerberin, Bewerber applicant
Bewerbung application
Bewerbungsgespräch interview
Bewirtung hospitality
bezahlen pay
Bibliothek library
Bild picture; image
bilden form
Bildkarte flashcard

Bildschirm screen
Bildung education
billig cheap
Bingo bingo
Biologie Biology
bis to; until
bis an ihr Lebensende ever after
Bis später! See you.
bis zum Äußersten gehen go to the limit
bitte please
Bitte schön. Here you are./ You're welcome.
bitten um ask for
blasen blow
blau blue
bleiben stay
Bleistift pencil
Bleistiftspitzer pencil sharpener
Blitz lightning
blöd silly
blond blond; fair
bloß bare
Blume flower
Blut blood
Boden ground; bottom; soil
böse mad
Bogen bow
Bogenschießen archery
Bohrer drill
Bombe bomb
Boot boat
Bord board
Bord- onboard
Botschafter ambassador
Boutique boutique
Boxer boxer
Boykott boycott
boykottieren boycott
brauchen need
braun brown
Breite width
brennen burn
Brettspiel board game
Brief letter
Brieffreundin, Brieffreund pen friend
Briefmarke stamp
Brille glasses
bringen bring; take
Britin, Brite; britisch British
Brötchen roll
Broschüre brochure
Brot bread
Bruder brother
Brücke bridge
brutal violent
Buch book
buchen book
Buchstabe letter
buchstabieren spell
Bucht bay
Bücherregal, Bücherregale bookshelf, bookshelves
Büffel buffalo
Bürgerrechtsbewegung civil-rights movement
Büro office
Büroangestellte, Büroangestellter clerical assistant
Bulle bull
Bundesstaat state
Burg castle
Bus bus
Busbahnhof (bus) station
Busch (-land) bush
Bushaltestelle bus stop
Butter butter

C

Cafe cafe
Cafeteria cafeteria
Camcorder camcorder
Camperin, Camper camper
Campingplatz camping site
CD CD
Cent cent
Champagner champagne
Champion champion
Chance chance; opportunity
chaotisch chaotic
Charakter character
charmant charming
Chatroom chatroom
chatten chat
Checkliste checklist
Cheerleader cheerleader
Cheeseburger cheeseburger
Chefin, Chef boss
Chinesin, Chinese; chinesisch Chinese
Chips crisps
Clan clan
Clown clown
Club club
Cockpit cockpit
Cola coke
Collage collage
College college
Comicheft comic
Computer computer
Computerfreak computer freak
(Computer-)Maus mouse
Computerraum computer room
cool cool
Cornflakes cornflakes
Countdown countdown
Cousin, Cousine cousin
Cowboy cowboy
Crack (Droge) crack

D

da there
da oben up there
Dach roof
damals then; at that time
Dame lady
Dame/Herr am Empfang receptionist
Dampf steam
dankbar rewarding; grateful
Danke. Thank you.
danken thank
dann then
das this; that
Das ist alles. That's all.
Datenautobahn information highway
Datum date
dauern last; take
davonlaufen walk off
Deck deck
dein, deine your
deine, deiner, deines yours
Demokratie democracy
demokratischer Staat democracy
Demonstration demonstration
denken (an) think (of)
Depression depression
der, die, das the
deshalb so
Detail detail
Detektiv detective
deutsch; Deutsch German
Dezember December
Diät (machen) (go on a) diet
Dialog dialogue
Diamant diamond
dich (selbst) yourself
Dichter poet
Dienstag Tuesday
diese (Pl.) these
dieser, diese, dieses this
Ding thing
Dinosaurier, Dino dinosaur, dino
direkt live; straight
Diskjockey DJ
Disko disco
Diskriminierung discrimination
diskutieren discuss
Dollar dollar
Dom cathedral
Domino dominoes
Donnerstag Thursday
Donut donut
Doppel-, doppelt double
Dorf village
dort there
dort drüben over there
Drache dragon
Drachen kite

Draht wire
draußen outside
drei three
dreißig thirty
dreizehn thirteen
Drittel third
dritter, dritte, drittes third
Droge drug
Drogenhändler, Drogenhändlerin drug dealer
drücken push; press
Dschungel jungle
du you
Du Armer! Poor you!
Dudelsack bagpipes
dünn thin
dürfen be allowed to
Dürre drought
dumm silly
dunkel dark
durch through
durchdrehen go crazy
(durch-)suchen search
durstig thirsty
Dusche shower
duschen have a shower
DVD-Film DVD film

E

E-Mail e-mail
echt real
Ecke corner
Ehefrau wife
ehemalige, ehemaliger, ehemaliges former
Ehemann husband
freiwillig volunteer
Ei egg
eigener, eigene, eigenes own
Eimer bucket
ein, eine a
einchecken (am Flughafen) check in
einfach simple
Eingabetaste return key
eingängig catchy
eingeben type in
Eingeborene, Eingeborener native
eingeschaltet on
einige some; any; several
einkaufen shop
einkaufen gehen go shopping
Einkaufsliste shopping list
Einkaufszentrum shopping centre; mall (AE); shopping complex
einladen invite
Einladung invitation
einmal once
Einrad unicycle
eins one
einsam lonely
einschalten switch on
einschlafen fall asleep
einschlagen strike
einschließlich including
einschließen include
einsinken sink
einst original
einstecken plug into
einsteigen get in; get on; board
eintippen type in
Eintrittskarte ticket
Einwanderin, Einwanderer immigrant
Einzelheit detail
Eis ice
Eis (Speiseeis) ice cream
Eisbär polar bear
Eisberg iceberg
Eisenbahn railroad
Eishockey ice hockey
eisig icy
Eistee iced tea
Eiszeit ice age
Elbin, Elb elf
Elch moose, moose (pl.)
Elefant elephant
elektrisch electric
Elektrizität electricity
elf eleven
Elfin, Elf elf
Ellbogen elbow
Ellbogenschützer elbow pad
Eltern parents
Elternteil parent
empfindlich sensitive
Ende end
enden (auf) end (in)
endlich at last
Endrunde playoffs
Energie energy
Engländerin, Engländer; englisch; Englisch English
entdecken discover
Entdeckerin, Entdecker explorer
Ente duck
entführen kidnap
entgegen towards
Enthusiasmus enthusiasm
entlang along
entscheiden decide
Entscheidung decision
Entschuldigung. Excuse me.
Entschuldigung (Ausrede) excuse
Entschuldigung./Tut mir Leid. Sorry.
Entsetzen horror
entspannen relax
enttäuschen let down; disappoint
entwerfen design
entwickeln develop
Enzyklopädie encyclopedia
er he
Erde earth
Erderwärmung global warming
Erdkunde Geography
Erdreich soil
Erdteil continent
Ereignis event
Erfahrung experience
erfinden invent
Erfinderin, Erfinder inventor
Erfindung invention
Erfolg success
erfolgreich successful
Ergebnis result
erhitzen heat
erkennen realize
erklären explain; declare
Erlaubnis permit
ernennen name
Eröffnungsfeier opening ceremony
erreichen reach
erscheinen appear
ersetzen replace
erst only
erstaunlich amazing
erstaunt sein be surprised
erster, erste, erstes first
Erwachsener adult
erzählen tell
es it
Es macht mir nichts aus. I don't mind.
es schaffen make it
es sei denn unless
Es tut mir Leid. I'm sorry.
Essay essay
essen eat
Essen food
Esszimmer dining room
Ethnie race
Etui pencil case
etwa about
etwas a bit; a little; something
Euro euro
EU (Europäische Union) EU (European Union)
evangelisch protestant
exotisch exotic
Experte expert
Extra-, extra extra

F

Fabrik factory
fachmännisch professional
Fähigkeit skill

Fähre ferry
Fahne flag
fahren drive; go; ride
Fahrerin, Fahrer driver
Fahrrad bike
Fahrrad fahren cycle; ride a bike
Fahrradausrüstung cycling equipment
Fahrzeug vehicle
fair fair
Falke falcon
fallen fall
Fallensteller trapper
falsch wrong; false
falsch verstehen get wrong
Familie family
Fan fan
fangen catch; trap
Fantasie fantasy
fantastisch fantastic
Fanzeitung fanzine
Farbe colour
farbig colored (AE)
Farm farm; station
fast almost; nearly
fasziniert sein be fascinated
faule Person slob
Februar February
Federball badminton
Federmäppchen pencil case
fehlend missing
Feier celebration
feiern celebrate; have a party
Feindin, Feind enemy
Feld field
Fell fur; skin
Felsen rock
Fenster window
Ferien holidays; vacation (AE)
Ferienhaus cottage
Ferienwohnung holiday flat
Fernbedienung remote control
Fernglas binoculars
Fernsehapparat television (TV)
fernsehen watch TV
Fernsehsendung programme
Fernsehserie TV series
fertig ready
fertig machen finish; get ready
Festival festival
festnehmen arrest
feststellen realize
Fete party
Feuer fire
Feuer legen start a fire
Feuerwerk fireworks
Figur character
Film film; movie (AE)
filmen film
Filzstift felt tip
finden find
Finger finger
Firma company; firm
Fisch, Fische fish
Fischburger fishburger
fischen fish
Fischstäbchen fish fingers
Fitness fitness
flach flat
Flagge flag
Flamme flame
Flasche bottle
Fleisch meat
Fliege fly
fliegen fly
fliehen escape
Flohmarkt flea market
Floristin, Florist florist
Flosse fin
flüchten escape
Flüchtling refugee
Flügel wing
Flügelspannweite wing-span
flüstern whisper
Flug flight
Flugblatt leaflet
Flughafen airport
Flugzeug plane
Flur corridor; hallway
Fluss river
Flusspferd hippo (potamus)
förmlich formal
Försterin, Förster ranger
folgen follow
folgender, folgende, folgendes following
fordern claim
Form form
Formel 1 Formula One
Foto photo
Fotoalbum photo album
Fotoapparat camera
fotografieren take photos
Frachtraum cargo bay
Frage question
fragen ask
Französin, Franzose; französisch French
Frau, Frauen woman, women
Frau (Anrede) Mrs; Ms
Freak freak
Freeclimber free climber
frei free
Freiheit freedom
freilassen release
Freilassung release
Freitag Friday
freiwillig volunteer
Freizeit free time
Freizeitpark theme park
Freizeitzentrum activity centre
fremd foreign
Fremdenführerin, Fremdenführer tour guide
fressen eat
Freund boyfriend
Freundin girlfriend
Freundin, Freund friend
freundlich friendly
Freundschaften schließen make friends
Frieden peace
Friedensnobelpreis Nobel Peace Prize
frieren be cold
Friseurin, Friseur hairdresser
Frisur haircut
froh glad
Frosch frog
früh early
Frühjahr spring
Frühstück breakfast
frühstücken have breakfast
frustriert frustrated
fühlen feel
führen guide; lead
Führerin, Führer guide
Führerschein driver's license
Führerscheinprüfung driving test
Füller pen
fünf five
fünfzehn fifteen
fünfzig fifty
für for
füttern feed
funkeln glitter
Funkhalsband radio collar
funktionieren work
Fuß (Maßeinheit) foot
Fuß, Füße foot, feet
Fußball football; soccer (AE)
Fußboden floor
Fußgängerzone pedestrian zone
Fußstapfen footsteps

G

Gabel fork
gälisch Gaelic
Gang gang
Gang corridor
Gangschaltung rear mechanism
ganz whole (of)
Garten garden
Gast guest
Gebäude building
geben give; pass
Gebiet area; district
Landschaft district
geboren born
gebrauchen use
Gebrauchtwagen used car

Geburt birth
Geburtsort birthplace
Geburtstag birthday
gefährlich dangerous
Gefängnis prison; jail
Gefahr danger
Gefangene, Gefangener prisoner
gefroren frozen
gegen (etwas sein) (be) against
Gegenteil opposite
geheilt sein von be cured of
gehen go; walk
gehören (zu) belong (to)
Geist ghost
Geländerennen fell-racing
gelangweilt sein be bored
gelb yellow
Gelbe Liste amber list
Geld money
Geld verdienen make money
Geld wechseln change money
Geldautomat cash machine
gelegen situated
Gelegenheit chance
gemein nasty
Gemeinde community
Gemeinschaft community
Gemüse vegetables
genau exact; right
Genehmigung permit
Generalstreik national strike
Genie genius
genießen enjoy
genug enough
gepierct pierced
Geplauder chat
gerade just
geradeaus straight on
Geräusch sound
gerecht fair
Gericht (Speise) dish
gern tun enjoy
Geruch smell
Geschäft business
Geschäft/Geschäfte machen do business
Geschäftsfrau businesswoman
Geschäftsmann businessman
geschehen happen
Geschenk present; gift
Geschichte story; History
geschieden divorced
Geschirr dishes
geschockt shocked
Geschwindigkeit speed
Gesetz law
Gesetzlose, Gesetzloser outlaw
Gesicht face
Gespenst ghost
gespenstisch spooky
Gespräch talk
gestern yesterday
Gesundheitserziehung Health class
Getränk drink
Getränkeautomat soft drink machine
getrennt separate
Gewalt violence
Gewalt- violent
gewaltsam violent
Gewicht weight
Gewinn prize
gewinnen win
Gewinnerin, Gewinner winner
gewiss certainly
Gewitter thunderstorm
gewöhnlich usual; usually
Gewürz spice
Geysir geyser
Gitarre guitar
Glas glass
glauben believe
Glaubensrichtung confession
gleich same; equal
Gleichgewicht balance
Gleis platform
Gletscher glacier
glitzern glitter
Glocke bell
Glück (haben) (be) lucky
glücklich happy
glücklicher, glückliche, glückliches fortunate
Glühbirne electric light bulb
Gokart-Bahn go-cart track
Gold gold
Golf golf
Gott God
Gouverneurin, Gouverneur governor
Grammatik grammar
Gras grass
grau grey
Grauwal grey whale
Grenze border; limit
Grillfest barbecue
Grizzlybär grizzly bear
Größe height; size
groß big; large; tall
großartig great
Großbuchstaben capital letters
Großeltern grandparents
Großmutter grandmother
grün green
Grund reason
Gruppe group; band
Gruß greeting
Grußformel greeting
Guinness-Weltrekord Guinness World Record
Gummibärchen jelly baby
gut good; well; fine
gut aussehend attractive
Guten Tag. Hello.

H

Haar hair
Haarsalon salon
haben have (got)
Hähnchen chicken
Hälfte von half of
hässlich ugly
häufig frequently
Häuserblock block
Hai shark
Haken snag
halb half
halber, halbe, halbes half
Halle hall
Hallo! Hi!/ Hello.
Halt! Stop!
halten hold
halten von think about
Hamburger hamburger
Hamster hamster
Hand hand
handeln take action
Handschuhe gloves
Handwerk craft
Handy mobile phone; cell phone (AE)
hart hard; rough
Hass hate
hassen hate
Hauptgericht main course
Hauptstadt capital
Haus house
Hausarbeit housework
Hausarrest erteilen ground someone
Hausaufgaben homework
Hausaufgaben machen do homework
Hausboot barge
Haustier pet
Haustür front door
Hauswirtschaft Domestic Science
Haut skin
heben lift
heilen cure; heal
heilig sacred
Heim home
Heimat habitat
heimgehen go home
heiraten marry
heiß hot
Held hero
Heldin heroine
helfen help
hell bright; fair

Helm helmet
Hemd shirt
Henne hen
heraus out
herausfinden find out
Herausforderung challenge
Herbst autumn; fall (AE)
Herd cooker
Herde herd
Herein! Come in, please.
hereinkommen come in
Herr lord
Herr (Anrede) Mr
herumhängen hang out
herunterladen download
Herz heart
herzlichen Glückwunsch congratulations
heute today
heute Abend tonight
heutzutage these days; nowadays
hier here
Hightech- high-tech
Hilfe help; aid
Himmel sky
hinauf up
hinauswerfen kick off
hinein in; into; inside
hineinpassen fit in
hinter behind
Hinterland outback
hinüber across
hinunter down
Hinweis notice
hinzufügen add
Hit hit
Hitparade charts
Hitze heat
HIV HIV
Hobby hobby
hoch high
Hochschulzulassung university entrance
Hochwasser flood
Hockey hockey
höflich polite
Höhe height
Höhle cave
hören hear
hoffen hope
Hoffnung hope
holen get; fetch
Holz wood
Horoskop horoscope
Hose trousers
Hotdog hot dog
Hotel hotel
Hoteldirektorin, Hoteldirektor hotel manager
Hubschrauber helicopter
hübsch pretty; nice
Hügel hill
Hütte hut
Huhn chicken
Hund dog
hundert hundred
hungrig hungry
Hurra! Hurray!
Hurrikan hurricane
Hut hat

I

ich I
Ich freue mich darauf, von Ihnen zu hören. I look forward to hearing from you.
Ich glaube nicht. I don't think so.
Ich möchte/hätte gern ... I'd like ... (I would like ...)
Idealgewicht ideal weight
Idee idea
Idol idol
ihn, ihm him
ihr you
ihr, ihre her
ihr, ihre (Pl.) their
ihre, ihrer, ihres hers
ihre, ihrer, ihres (Pl.) theirs
illegal illegal
im at; in; on
im Ausland abroad
im Dunkeln in the dark
im Fernsehen on TV
im Gegensatz zu unlike
Imbiss snack
Imbissstube snack bar
immens immense
immer always
(immer) noch still
Immobilienmaklerin, Immobilienmakler estate agent
in at; into; in
in der Lage sein be able to
in der Mitte mid
in der Nähe near
in einer Hinsicht in one sense
in Ordnung OK
Inderin, Inder; indisch Indian
Indianerin, Indianer; indianisch Indian
Industriezweig industry
Infektion infection
Information (en) information
Ingenieurin, Ingenieur engineer
Inliner in-line skates
Inliner fahren skate
Innenstadt downtown
innerhalb within
Insekt insect
Insektizid DDT
Insel island
insgesamt altogether
Inspiration inspiration
Instrument instrument
interessant interesting
interessiert interested
Internat boarding school
international international
Internet Internet; web
Internetagentur Internet services company
Internetforum online forum
Internetseite website
Interview interview
interviewen interview
Interviewerin, Interviewer interviewer
investieren invest
irgendeiner, irgendeine, irgendeines whatever
irgendetwas anything
irgendjemand anybody; anyone
irgendwelche any
irgendwie somehow
irgendwo anywhere
Irin, Ire; irisch Irish
Ironman Ironman
Isolierplatte tile

J

ja yes
Jacht yacht
Jacke jacket
jagen hunt
(im Jahr) 1975 in 1975
Jahr year
Jahreszeit season
Jahrhundert century
Januar January
Jeanshose jeans
Jeansstoff denim
jeder everybody; everyone
jeder, jede, jedes every; each
jemals ever
jemand anybody; anyone; somebody; someone
jemand anderes someone else
jene, jener, jenes that
jetzt now
jetzt gerade at the moment
joggen jog
jubeln cheer
Jugendherberge youth hostel
Jugendverband youth league
Juli July
jung young
Junge boy
Jungtier cub
Juni June

K

Käfig cage
kämpfen fight
Känguru kangaroo
Käse cheese
Kaffee coffee
Kalender calendar
Kalorie calory
kalt cold
Kamera camera
Kameramann cameraman
Kampagne campaign
Kampf battle
Kanadierin, Kanadier; kanadisch Canadian
Kaninchen rabbit
kann/kannst/könnt/können nicht can't/cannot
Kannst du mir ... geben/reichen? Can you pass me ...?
Kanzlerin, Kanzler chancellor
Kapitän captain
Kapitel unit
Kappe cap
kaputt broken
kaputtgehen break (down)
Karibin, Karibe; karibisch Caribbean
Karneval carnival
Karosserie chassis
Karotte carrot
Karre wagon
Karriere career
Karte card
Kartoffel, Kartoffeln potato, potatoes
Kasino casino
Kasse counter
Kassette cassette
Kasten box
Katastrophe disaster
Kathedrale cathedral
katholisch catholic
Katze cat
kauen chew
kaufen buy
Kaufhaus department store
kaum hardly
kein, keine, keines no
kein Empfang no signal
kein Glück haben be unlucky
keiner nobody
(salziger) Keks cracker
Kellner waiter
Kellnerin waitress
kennen know
Kerl guy
Kerze candle
Ketchup ketchup
kidnappen kidnap
Kilo kilo
Kilometer kilometre
Kind child; kid
Kinder children
Kinderbetreuung childcare
Kindergärtnerin, Kindergärtner kindergarten assistant
Kindergarten kindergarten
Kinematograph kinetoscope
Kino cinema
Kirche church
Kirmes fair; fun fair
Kiwi kiwi
klar clear
klasse super; terrific
Klasse class
Klassenarbeit test
Klassenfahrt school trip
Klassenstufe grade
Klassenzimmer classroom; homeroom (AE)
klatschen clap
Klebstoff glue
Kleid dress
Kleider clothes
Kleiderschrank wardrobe
Kleidung clothes; clothing
klein little; small
Klempnerin, Klempner plumber
klettern climb
Klettern free climbing
Klima climate
Klimaanlage air-conditioning system
Klingel bell
klingen sound
Klippe cliff; crag
klopfen knock
klug clever
km/h kph (kilometres per hour)
Knall bang
Knie knee
Knieschützer knee pad
Knochen bone
Knopf button
kochen cook
Köchin, Koch cook
Köder bait
König king
Königin queen
können be able to
können; konnte (n) can, could
Körper body
köstlich delicious
Koffer suitcase
Kohle coal
Kohlendioxid carbon dioxide
Kokusnuss coconut
Kollegin, Kollege colleague
Kolonie colony
Kolonistin, Kolonist colonist
kommen come
kommentieren comment
Komm (t) schon! Come on!
kommunizieren communicate
Kompass compass
Komponistin, Komponist songwriter
Konflikt conflict
Kongress Congress
Konkurrenz competition
konnte (n), könnte (n) could
konstruieren design
Kontakt contact
Kontaktiert uns. / Setzt euch mit uns in Verbindung. Contact us.
Kontinent continent
Konto account
Kontrolle control
kontrollieren check
Konzert concert
Kopf head
Kopfhörer headphones
Kopie photocopy; copy
kopieren copy
Korallenriff coral reef
Korb basket
Korbball netball
korrekt correct
Korridor hallway
korrigieren correct
kosten cost
Kosten senken cut costs
kräftig powerful
Kraft strength
Kraftstoff fuel
Kraftwerk power station
Kran crane
krank ill; sick
krank sein be sick
Krankenhaus hospital
Krankenwagen ambulance
kreativ creative
Kreis circle
Krieg war
Krieg führen go to war
Kriminalität crime
Küche kitchen
Kühlschrank fridge
kümmern um look after
Künstlerin, Künstler artist
Kürbis pumpkin
küssen kiss
Küste coast
Kugelschreiber biro
Kuh cow
Kultur culture
Kundin, Kunde customer
Kunst Art
Kurier courier
Kurve curve
kurz short

Konfession confession

L

Label label
lachen laugh
Laden shop; store
Ladentheke counter
Lächeln smile
Länge length
Lärm noise
Läuferin, Läufer runner
läuten ring
Lage location
Lagerfeuer campfire
Lagerhaus warehouse
Land country; land
landen land
Landkarte map
Landschaft countryside
Landstraße highway
Landung touchdown
landwirtschaftlich agricultural
lang long
Langeweile haben be bored
langsam slow
langsamer fahren slow down
langweilig boring
Lasagne lasagne
lassen let
die Finger von etwas lassen stay away from
Laster lorry; road train
lateinisch; Latein Latin
laufen run; jog, walk
laut loud; noisy
Layout layout
leben live
Leben life, lives (pl.)
Lebensart way of life
lebenslänglich for life
Lebensmittelgeschäft grocery store
Lebensmittelhändlerin, Lebensmittelhändler grocer
Lebensraum habitat
Lebensstil way of life
Leber liver
Leder leather
leer empty
legen put
Legende legend
Lehre apprenticeship
Lehrerin, Lehrer teacher
Lehrgang course
Leiche body
leicht easy
leichter, leichte, leichtes light
Leid tun feel sorry
leiden suffer
leise quiet
Leiterin, Leiter supervisor
Lektion unit
lernen learn; study
lesen read
letzter, letzte, letztes last
Leute people; guys
Licht light
liebe Grüße love
Liebe/Lieber ... (Anrede im Brief) Dear ...
lieben love
Liebende lovers
Liebespaar lovers
lieber tun prefer
Lieblings- favourite
Lied song
Lieferwagen van
liegen lie
Liga league
Limonade lemonade
Lineal ruler
Link link
links left
Lippe lip
Liste list
Liter liter (AE)
live live
LKW lorry; road train
Lkw-Fahrerin, Lkw-Fahrer trucker
Loch hole
locker cool
Löffel spoon
löschen delete
Löwe lion
Lohn wage
lokal local
Lokomotive locomotive
Lord lord
Lüge lie
lügen lie
Luft air
lustig funny

M

Mach dir/Machen Sie sich keine Sorgen. Don't worry.
machen do; make
Macht power
Mädchen girl
männlich male
März March
Magersucht anorexia
Magie magic
magisch magical
Magnet magnet
magnetisch magnetic
Mahlzeit meal
Mai May
mailen mail
Mais corn (AE)
mal (mathematisch) times
malen paint
Mama mum; mom (AE)
Manager agent
manchmal sometimes
Mann, Männer man, men
Mannschaft team
Mannschaftssport team sport
Mannschaftssportart team sport
Markel label
Marketing marketing
Marketingassistentin, Marketingassistent marketing assistant
Markt market
Marmelade jam
marschieren march
Maschine instrument
Maschine machine
Mast mast
Mathe (matik) Maths
Mauer wall
Maus mouse, mice (pl.)
Mechanikerin, Mechaniker mechanic
Medaille medal
Medikamente medication
Meer sea
Meeresspiegel sea level
Meerschweinchen guinea pig
mehr more
mehrere several
Mehrheit majority
Mehrzahl plural
Meile mile
mein, meine my
meine, meiner, meines mine
meinen mean
Meinung opinion
Meisterin, Meister champion
Menge crowd
merkwürdig strange
messen measure
Messer knife, knives (pl.)
Meter metre; meter (AE)
Metzger, Metzgerin butcher
mich me
mich (selbst) myself
mieten hire
Milch milk
Milchshake milkshake
militärisch military
Million million
Millionärin, Millionär millionaire
mindestens least
Mindestlohn minimum wage
Mineralien minerals
Minute minute
mir me

mit with; by
Mit freundlichen Grüßen Yours faithfully
mitbringen bring along
miteinander each other
Mitfahrgelegenheit lift
Mitglied member
mitnehmen (im Auto) give a lift
Mittag essen have lunch
Mittagessen lunch
Mittagszeit lunchtime
Mitte middle
Mittwoch Wednesday
Mobiltelefon mobile phone; cell phone (AE)
Mode fashion
Modedesign fashion
Model model
Modell model
Modellauto model car
Moderator game show host
modern modern; trendy
modernisieren modernize
möchten want
Möchten Sie/möchtest du ...? Would you like ...?
mögen like
möglich possible
Möglichkeit possibility; opportunity
Mörderin, Mörder killer
Moment moment
Monat month
Mond moon
Monopoly Monopoly
Monster monster
Montag Monday
Montageband assembly line
Mord murder
Morgen morning
morgen tomorrow
morgens in the morning
Moschee mosque
Moslemin, Moslem; moslemisch Muslim
Motor engine
Motorhaube hood (AE)
Motorrad motor bike
motzen moan
Mountainbike mountain bike
müde (sein) (be) tired
Müll rubbish
Müllsammler scrap-picker
Müllverkäufer scrap-picker
Münze coin
Müsli muesli
müssen have to; must
muffig smelly
Museum museum
Musical musical
Musik music
Musikerin, Musiker musician
Musikfirma music company
ein Muss a must see
Mut courage
mutig brave
Mutter mother
Mutti mum; mom (AE)

N

nach after
(nach-)denken über think about
Nachbarin, Nachbar neighbour
Nachbarschaft neighbourhood
Nachbau reproduction
nachdem after
nachgeben give in
Nachmittag afternoon
Nachname family name
Nachos nachos
Nachricht message
Nachrichten news
nachschauen look up
nachschlagen look up
die ganze Nacht all night
Nacht night
Nachtisch dessert
nachts at night
Nadel needle
Nadelbaum fir tree
nächster, nächste, nächstes next
Nagel nail
nah close
Nahrungskette food chain
Name name
Namensschild name card
Nase nose
nass wet
nass werden get wet
Nationalfeiertag national holiday
Nationalität nationality
Nationalpark national park
natürlich of course; natural
Natur nature
Nebel fog
neben next to
nebenan next door
neblig foggy
Negerin, Neger negro
nehmen have; take
nein no
nennen call; name
auf die Nerven gehen annoy someone
nervös nervous
Nest nest
nett nice; pretty; cute
neu new
Neuigkeiten news
Neujahr New Year's Day
neulich the other day
neun nine
neunzehn nineteen
neunzig ninety
nicht not
nicht dürfen mustn't
nicht einmal not even
nicht gehorchen disobey
nicht müssen needn't
nicht werden won't (= will not)
nichts nothing
niedlich cute
niemals never
niemand nobody
Nigger nigger
Nilpferd hippo (potamus)
noch ein (e) another
Noch etwas? Anything else?
noch nicht not yet
(noch) warten hang on
non-stop non-stop
Norden; nördlich north
normal normal
Note grade (AE)
Notizbuch notebook
Notizen notes
Notizen machen take notes
Notrufzentrale verständigen dial 999
November November
nützlich useful; practical
null (bei Telefonnummern) oh
Nummer number
nun ... well
nur only; just
nutzlos useless

O

obdachlos homeless
oben (die Treppe hinauf) upstairs
oben on top
oberhalb above
Oberhaupt chief
Obst fruit
obwohl although
oder or
öffnen open
Öl oil
ölen oil
örtlich local
Ofen oven
offen open
offiziell official
oft often
ohne without
ohnmächtig werden faint
Ohr ear
okay OK
Oktober October

Olympische Spiele Olympic Games
Oma grandmother; grandma
Onkel uncle
Onlinebanking online banking
Opa grandpa
Oper opera
Opposition opposition
Optimistin, Optimist optimist
Orange orange
Ordner folder; file
Organisation organisation
organisieren organise
original original
Orkan hurricane
Ort place
orten locate
Osten east
Osteuropa eastern Europe
Ozean ocean

P

Paar pair
paar a few; some
packen pack
Packung packet
Paket package
Pakistanerin, Pakistaner; pakistanisch Pakistani
Palast palace
Panther panther
Papagei parrot
Papier paper
Paradies paradise
Park park
parken park
Parkplatz car park
Parlament parliament
Partnerin, Partner partner
Partnerschule partner school
Party party
passen zu go with
passieren happen
Pause break
Pech bad luck
peinlich embarrassing
Pelz fur
Pence (britisches Geld. 100 pence = £1) pence; penny
perfekt perfect
persönlich personal
Person person
Personal staff
Personalchefin, Personalchef personnel manager
Pessimistin, Pessimist pessimist
Pfad trail; track
Pfadfinderin Girl Guide
Pfeil arrow
Pferd horse
Pferdestärke (PS) horsepower
Pflanze plant
pflanzen plant
pflücken pick
Pfund (Gewichtseinheit) pound
Pfund (britische Währung) pound
Phonograph (Tonaufnahmegerät) phonograph
Picknick picnic
Piercing piercing
Pilot pilot
Pinguin penguin
Pipeline pipeline
Pizza pizza
Pizza essen gehen go for a pizza
Pizzaservice pizza service
Plakat poster
Plan plan
planen plan
Planet planet
Plastik plastic
Platschen splash
Plattenvertrag recording contract
Platz place
plötzlich suddenly
Plural plural
Pokal cup
Politik politics
politisch political
Polizei police
Polizeistation station
Polizist policeman
Polizistin policewoman
Polizistin, Polizist copper
Pony pony
Popcorn popcorn
Porträt portrait
Postamt post office
Poster poster
Postkarte postcard
Präposition preposition
Prärie prairie
Präsentation presentation
präsentieren present
Präsident president
praktisch practical
Preis price; prize; award
Priester priest
(Privat-)Zimmer mit Frühstück bed and breakfast
pro ... per ...
pro Tag a day
Probe rehearsal
Problem problem
Produktion production
Produzentin, Produzent producer
produzieren produce
professionell professional
Programm programme
Projekt project
Propeller propeller
Protest protest
protestantisch protestant
Protestierender, Protestierende protestor
prüfen check
Publikum audience
Pullover pullover; sweater (AE)
Pumpe pump
pumpen pump
putzen clean
Puzzle puzzle; jigsaw puzzle

Q

Quadratkilometer km2 (square kilometre)
Quadratmeile square mile
qualifiziert qualified
Quizsendung quiz show

R

Rache revenge
Rad wheel
Radar radar
Radfahrerin, Radfahrer cyclist
Radiergummi rubber
Radio radio
Radiosender station
Rätsel puzzle
rätselhaft mysterious
Räuberin, Räuber robber
Rafting rafting
Rahmen frame
Rap rap
rappen rap
rasen race
Rasse race
Rassen- racial
Rassentrennung segregation
Rassentrennung aufheben desegregate
rasten rest
raten guess
Ratschlag advice
Ratte rat
Rau rough
Rauch smoke
rauchen smoke
Raum space
Raumfähre space shuttle
Raumschiff spaceship
Recht right
Recht haben be right
rechts right
Rechtsanwältin, Rechtsanwalt lawyer
rechtzeitig just in time
Recyclingpapier recycled paper

Rede speech
reden talk
Regal, Regale shelf, shelves
Regatta race
Regel rule
regelmäßig regular
regeln fix
Regen rain
Regenwald rain forest
Reggae reggae
regieren rule
Regierung government
regnen rain
regnerisch rainy
reich rich
Reihenfolge order
Reim rhyme
reinigen clean
Reise trip; journey
Reisebüro travel agency
reisen travel
Reisende, Reisender traveller
Reisepass passport
Reisnudeln rice noodles
reiten ride
Reiten horse riding
Reiterin, Reiter rider
reißen rip
Reklame machen advertise
Rekord record
Rektorin, Rektor headmaster
religiös religious
Religion religion
Religionsunterricht R.E. (Religious Education)
Rennboot racing boat
rennen run; race
Rennen race
reparieren repair; fix
Reporter reporter
Reproduktion reproduction
Reservat reservation
respektiert respected
Rest rest
Restaurant restaurant
retten save
richtig right; correct; properly
riechen smell
riesig huge
Riesin, Riese giant
Rinder cattle
Ring ring
Ring als Clip clip-on ring
Ringen wrestling
Roboter robot
Rock skirt
rocken rock
Rocker rocker
Rockmusik rock (music)
Rockstar rock star
Rodeo rodeo
rollen roll
Rollen tauschen change parts
Rose rose
rot red
Rothirsch, Rothirsche elk, elk
Rucksack rucksack; backpack (AE)
rudern row
Rückseite back
Rugby rugby
Ruhm fame
rund round
Runde round
Rundfahrt tour

S

Saal hall
Sache thing
Sängerin, Sänger singer
Säulendiagramm bar chart
sagen say; tell; comment
sagenhaft terrific
Salat salad
Salz salt
sammeln collect; raise
Sammlung collection
Samstag Saturday
Sand sand
Sandsturm sandstorm
Sandwich sandwich
Satellitentelefon satellite phone
Sattel saddle
Satz sentence; phrase
sauber clean
sauber machen clean up
saurer Regen acid rain
Schachtel box
Schaden damage
Schälchen bowl
Schaf, Schafe sheep
schaffen manage
scharf hot
Schatten shadow
(schau-)spielen act
schauen look
Schaufenster shop window
Schauspielerin, Schauspieler actress, actor
Scheibe disk
schick trendy
schicken send
Schicksal fortune
schieben push
Schiene rail
schießen shoot; fire
Schild sign
Schinkenspeck bacon
Schlacht battle
Schläger bat; racket
schlafen sleep
Schlafzimmer bedroom
schlagen hit
Schlange queue; snake
Schlankheitsmittel diet pills
schlecht bad
schlecht bezahlt low-paid
schließen close
Schließfach locker
schließlich finally; in the end
schließlich after all
schlimm bad
Schloss castle
Schlüssel key
Schlüsselwort key word
Schlussverkauf sale
schmecken taste
schmelzen melt
Schminke make-up
schmollen sulk
Schmuck jewelry
schmücken decorate
schmutzig dirty
Schnappschuss snapshot
Schnee snow
Schneemann snowman
Schneemobil snowmobile
Schneeschuh laufen snowshoeing
schneiden cut
schneien snow
schnell fast; quick
schnell fahren speed
Schnellimbiss fast food
Schock shock
schockierend shocking
schön beautiful; fine
Schön dich zu treffen. Nice to meet you.
Schokolade chocolate
Schokoladenpudding chocolate pudding
schon already
schon einmal ever
Schott bulkhead
Schottenkaro tartan
schottisch Scottish
Schrank cupboard
Schraube screw
Schreck shock
Schrecken horror
schrecklich terrible
schreiben write; mail
Schreibtisch desk
schreien shout; cry
Schriftstellerin, Schriftsteller writer
Schritt step
Schülerin, Schüler pupil; student (AE)
Schüssel bowl
schütteln shake
schützen protect

Schuh shoes
Schulausflug school trip
Schule school
Schulhof playground
Schulleiterin, Schulleiter headmaster
Schultasche school bag
Schulter shoulder
Schuluniform school uniform
Schulverein school club
Schutzgebiet sanctuary
schwanger pregnant
schwarz black
Schwarze Blacks
schwarzes Brett notice board
Schwein pig
Schweiß perspiration
schwer heavy
Schwert sword
Schwester sister
schwierig difficult; hard
Schwierigkeiten trouble
(Schwimm-)Becken pool
Schwimmbad swimming pool
schwimmen swim
Science Fiction science fiction
sechs six
sechzehn sixteen
sechzig sixty
See lake
Seehund seal
Seemann sailor
Segel sail
segeln sail
Seglerin, Segler sailor
sehen see; look
Sehenswürdigkeit sight
sehr very
Sehr geehrte Damen und Herren Dear Sir or Madam
Seife soap
Seifenoper soap
Seil rope
sein be
sein, seine his
sein, seine its
seit ever since
seit einer Ewigkeit for ages
seit since (Zeitpunkt); for (Zeitraum)
seitdem ever since
Seite side
Sekretärin, Sekretär secretary
Sekunde second
selbst themselves
selbstsicher confident
selbstverständlich of course
seltsam strange; funny
Senatorin, Senator senator
senden send
Sendung program (AE)
September September
setzen put
Sex sex
sich themselves
sich kratzen scratch
sich an den Händen fassen join hands
sich anhören sound
sich anmelden für sign up for
sich ausdenken imagine
sich auswirken auf affect
sich befassen mit deal with
sich benehmen wie act like
sich beschweren complain
sich beteiligen engage
sich bewerben um apply for
sich (einen Arm, ...) brechen break (an arm, ...)
sich erinnern remember
sich erkundigen inquire
sich freuen auf look forward to
sich hinlegen lie down
sich hinsetzen sit down
sich konzentrieren concentrate
sich kümmern um care for
sich leisten afford
sich scheiden lassen get divorced
sich selbst himself
sich Sorgen machen be worried
sich Sorgen machen worry
sich umsehen look around
sich verantwortlich fühlen feel responsible
sich verlaufen be lost
sich verletzen hurt
sich verlieben fall in love
sich verstecken hide
sich weigern refuse
sich wundern wonder
sich zusammentun unite
sich zwingen force oneself
sich übergeben be sick; throw up
sicher safe; sure
Sicherheitsüberprüfung safety check
sichern save
Sicht view
Sie you
sie she
sie, ihnen them
sie (Pl.) they
sieben seven
siebzehn seventeen
siebzig seventy
Siedlung plantation
Signal signal
Silvester New Year's Eve
singen sing
Single single
Sippe clan
Sippschaft clan
Situation situation
Sitz seat
sitzen sit
Sitzung meeting
Skateboard skateboard
Skater skater
Ski ski
Ski fahren gehen go skiing
Ski laufen ski
Skilanglauf cross country skiing
Sklave slave
Sklavenhalter slaveowner
SMS text message
Snack snack
so (dass) so
so ... wie as ... as
Socken socks
Sofa sofa
sofort immediately
Software software
sogar even
Sohn son
solch such
Soldatin, Soldat soldier
sollen, sollten should
Solo-, solo solo
Sommer summer
Sonderangebot special offer
Sonne sun
Sonnenbrille sunglasses
Sonnenenergie solar power
Sonnenschein sunshine
Sonnenuntergang sunset
sonnig sunny
Sonntag Sunday
sonst noch else
Sorge worry
Sorte sort
Soße sauce
Souvenir souvenir
spät late
Spaghetti spaghetti
Spanierin, Spanier; spanisch Spanish
spannend exciting
sparen save
sparsam economical
Spaß fun
spazieren gehen go for a walk
Spaziergang walk
Spaß machen make fun
Speed speed
Speicher tank
speichern save
Speise dish
Speisekarte menu
spektakulär spectacular
Spiegel mirror
Spiel game; match
spielen play; perform
Spielerin, Spieler player

Spielzeug toy
Spielzeugfrosch toy frog
Spitze top
Sport sports
Sportarten sports
Sporthalle sports hall
Sportlerin, Sportler athlete; sports star
Sportunterricht P.E. (Physical Education)
Sprache language
Spray spray
sprechen speak
sprechen mit talk to
sprechen über talk about
springen jump
Sprinterin, Sprinter runner
Spülbecken sink
Spüle sink
spülen wash
Spur track
Squash squash
Staat state
Staatsangehörigkeit nationality
Stadion stadium
Stadt city; town
Stadtplan map
Stärke power; strength
Stahl steel
Stamm tribe
Stand stall
Star star
stark strong; powerful
starren stare
Start start; take-off; lift-off
starten start
stattdessen instead
Statue statue
Stau traffic jam
stauen trap
Steak steak
Steckdose socket
Stecker plug
stehen stand
stehlen steal
steigen increase
steil steep
Stein stone
stellen put
stellvertretende Premierministerin, stellvertretender Premierminister deputy prime minister
sterben die
Steuer tax
Stiefel boots
Stier bull
Stil style
still quiet
Stimm (t) ein Tune in
Stock stick
stöhnen moan
stören disturb
Stoff cloth
stolpern über fall over
stolz proud
Stopp! Stop!
stoppen stop
Sträfling convict
Sträflingsschiff convict ship
Strand beach
Straße road; street
Streiche spielen play tricks
streichen paint
Streifen stripe
Streik strike
Streit (haben) (have an) argument
stressing stressful
Strom electricity
Strumpfhose tights
studieren study
Studio studio
Stück piece
Stuhl chair
Stunde hour
Stundenplan timetable
Stunt stunt
Sturm storm
suchen nach look for
Suchmaschine search engine
Sucht addiction
süchtig (werden) (get) addicted
Süden; südlich south
Südwesten; südwestlich south-west
süß cute
super super
Superlativ superlative
Supermarkt supermarket
Suppe soup
surfen surf
Surferin, Surfer surfer
Sweatshirt sweatshirt
Symbol symbol
symbolisieren symbolize
System system
Szene scene

T

T-Shirt T-shirt
Tabelle table
Tablette pill
Tabu taboo
täglich daily
Tänzerin, Tänzer dancer
Tätowierung tattoo
Tafel board
Tafel (Schokolade) bar
den ganzen Tag all day
Tag day
Tagebuch diary
eines Tages one day
Tageslicht daylight
tagsüber in the daytime
Tal valley
Talent talent
Tanne fir tree
Tante aunt
Tanz dance
tanzen dance
Tanzschritt move
Tanzveranstaltung dance
tapfer brave
Tasche bag
Taschenführer pocket guide
Taschengeld pocket money; allowance (AE)
Taschenlampe torch
Tasse cup
Tastatur keyboard
Taste key
Tatsache fact
tatsächlich in fact
Taucher diver
Tausende von thousands of
Taxi taxi; cab (AE)
Team team
Technik technology
technische Daten technical data
Tee tea
Teelöffel teaspoon
Teenager teenager
Teich pond
Teil part; piece
teilen share
teilnehmen an take part in
Teilzeitbeschäftigung part-time job
Telefon telephone; phone
Telefonzelle telephone box
Teller plate
Tempel temple
Temperatur temperature
Tennis tennis
Test test
testen test
teuer expensive
Texterin, Texter songwriter
Theater theatre; theater (AE)
Theaterstück play
themenbezogen topic-based
Therapiegruppe therapy group
tief deep
tiefgekühlt frozen
Tier animal
Tierärztin, Tierarzt vet
Tierheim animal home
Tierleben wildlife
Tierpflegerin, Tierpfleger zookeeper
Tiger tiger

Tintenpatrone cartridge
Tipp tip
tippen type
Tisch table
den Tisch decken lay the table
Tischtennis table tennis
Titel title
Toastbrot toast
toben go wild
Tochter daughter
Todesfall death
Todesopfer death
töten kill
Toilette toilet
toll amazing
Tomate, Tomaten tomato, tomatoes
Tonne (Gewichtseinheit) ton
tot dead
total absolutely
Tour tour
Tourismus tourism
Touristeninformation tourist information centre
Touristin, Tourist tourist
Tournee tour
Tradition tradition
traditionell traditional
träumen dream
tragen carry; wear
Trainer coach
trainieren train
Trainingslager training camp
Traktor tractor
Transport transport
Transporter van
Traumberuf dream job
traurig sad
treffen meet; hit
Treffen meeting
treiben drive
Treibhausgas greenhouse gas
Trekking trekking
trennen separate
Trennwand bulkhead
Triathlon triathlon
Tribüne stand
Trick trick; stunt
Trilogie trilogy
trinken drink
Trinkgeld tip
trocken dry
Trockenheit drought
Trommel drum
tropisch tropical
trotzdem nonetheless
Tschüs Bye
Tür door
Türkin, Türke; türkisch Turkish
Türklingel doorbell
Tüte bag
tun do; make
Turm tower
Turnhalle gym
Turnier tournament
Turnschuhe trainers
Typ guy

U

U-Bahn underground
U-Boot submarine
üben practise
über about; over; across; above
überall everywhere
überhaupt at all
überleben survive
übernachten stay
überqueren cross
überraschend surprising
überrascht sein be surprised
Überraschung surprise
Überschrift title; heading
überschwemmen flood
Überschwemmung flood
Überstunden machen work long hours
(Übungs-)Heft exercise book
... Uhr ... o'clock
Uhr clock
ultimativ ultimate
um ... herum around
umdrehen turn
Umhang cloak
umkehren return; turn
umknicken fold over
Umlaufbahn orbit
umschalten switch
Umschalttaste shift key
umsiedeln migrate
umsteigen change trains
Umwelt environment
Umwelt-, die Umwelt betreffend environmental
Umweltverschmutzung pollution
umziehen move
unabhängig independent
Unabhängigkeit independence
unaufgeklärte Verbrechen crimes unsolved
unbrauchbar useless
und and
Unfall accident
Ungarin, Ungar; ungarisch Hungarian
Ungeheuer monster
Ungerechtigkeit injustice
unglücklich unhappy
unheimlich spooky
Uniform uniform
Universität college; university
Unruhestifterin, Unruhestifter troublemaker
uns us
unser, unsere our
unsere, unserer, unseres ours
unten (die Treppe hinunter) downstairs
unter under
Unterhaltung entertainment
unterirdisch underground
unterrichten teach
(Unterrichts-)Stunde lesson
Unterrichtsfach subject
unterschiedlich different
unterschreiben sign
Unterschrift signature
Unterseite bottom
unterstützen support
Unterstützung support
unterwegs out
Urdu (Sprache in Pakistan) Urdu
Urlaub vacation (AE)
ursprünglich original

V

Vater father; dad
Vati dad
Verabredung date
verabschieden pass
Veränderung change
verärgert sein be angry
Veranstaltung event
verantwortlich responsible
Verantwortung responsibility
Verband bandage
Verbindung connection; link
Verbrechen crime
verbrennen burn
verbringen spend
verdammt damn
verdienen earn
Verehrerin, Verehrer admirer
Verein club
vereinigen unite
vergangen past
Vergangenheit past
vergessen forget
Vergleich comparison
vergleichen compare
vergraben bury
Verhaltensregeln in der freien Natur country code
Verkäuferin, Verkäufer shop assistant
verkaufen sell
Verkehr traffic
Verkehrsmittel means of transport
Verkehrsregeln traffic rules

verlässlich reliable
verlassen leave
verlegen embarrassed
verletzt injured
verlieren lose
vermeiden avoid
vermieten rent out
vermissen miss
Vermittlung operator
verpassen miss out on
verrückt (nach) crazy (about)
verschieden different
verschwinden disappear
Version version
verspätet delayed
versprechen promise
verstehen understand
versuchen try
Vertrag contract
verursachen cause
vervollständigen complete
verwirrt confused
Video (kassette) video
Videokamera video camera
Viehzüchterin, Viehzüchter farmer
viel, viele a lot; lots of; many; much; plenty
vielleicht perhaps; maybe
vielleicht may
vier four
Viersitzer four-seater
vierte, vierter, viertes fourth
vierzehn fourteen
vierzig forty
virtuell virtual
Visagistin, Visagist make-up artist
Vizepräsident deputy president
völlig completely
Vogel bird
voll full; busy
voller Energie energetic
Volleyball volleyball
vollständig complete
Vollzeitbeschäftigung full-time job
vom Stapel lassen launch
von from; of
vor (örtlich) in front of
vor allem above all
vor kurzem recently
vor (zeitlich) before
vor ... Jahren ... years ago
vorbeigehen walk past
vorbereiten prepare
Vorbild idol
Vorgesetzte, Vorgesetzer boss
Vormittag morning
Vorrat supply
vorsichtig careful
Vorspeise starter
vorstellen introduce someone
Vorteil und Nachteil pro and con
Vortrag presentation
vorwärts forward
vorziehen prefer
Vulkan volcano

W

Waage scale
Wachs wax
wachsen grow
wählen elect; vote; (Tel.) dial
während during; while; throughout
Wärterin, Wärter guard
Waffe gun
Wagen wagon
Wahl choice; election
Wahlrecht vote
wahr true
Wahrsagerin, Wahrsager fortune teller
wahrscheinlich probably
Wal whale
Walbeobachtung whale watching
Wald forest; wood
Wand wall
Wanderarbeiter migrant worker
wandern hike
Wanderung hike
wann when
warm warm
warten wait
warum why
was what; which
Was für ein/eine ... What a ...
Was ist/Wie sieht es aus mit ...? What about ...?
Was kostet das?/Was macht das? How much is it?
Was möchtest du...?/Was hättest du/hätten Sie gern...? What would you like ...?
waschen wash
Wasser water
Wasserhahn tap
Wassermühle watermill
Wassertank tank
Webdesignerin, Webdesigner web designer; website designer
Webseite website
wechseln switch
weg away
Weg route; way; trail
wegbleiben keep away
wegziehen migrate
weh tun hurt
weiblich female
weiblicher Cowboy cowgirl
Weihnachten Christmas
weil because
weinen cry
weiß white
Weiße Whites
weit far
weiter (weg) further
Weiterbildung course
weiterer, weitere, weiteres another
weitergehen go on
weitermachen go on
welcher, welche, welches what; which
Welt world
Weltall space
Weltmeisterschaft World Cup
weltweit worldwide
Wendung phrase
ein wenig a bit
wenig little
wenig, wenige few
weniger less
wenigstens at least
wenn if
wer who
Werbeplakat advertising poster
Werbung marketing
werden become
werfen throw
Werkstatt workshop
Werkzeug tool
wert worth
wessen whose
Westen; westlich west
Wettbewerb contest; competition
Wetter weather
Wettervorhersage weather forecast
wichtig important
wie how; what; like; such as
wie dem auch sei however
Wie geht es dir/Ihnen? How are you?
Wie heißt du? What's your name?
Wie heißt es auf Englisch? What is it in English?
Wie schade! What a shame!
Wie viel Uhr ist es? What's the time, please?
wieder again
wieder aufladbar rechargeable
Wiederholung revision
wiegen weigh
Wikinger Viking
wild wild
Wildhüterin, Wildhüter ranger; park ranger
Wildnis wilderness
willkommen welcome
Wind wind

Windgeschwindigkeit winds
windig windy
Windmühle windmill
winken wave
Winter winter
winzig tiny
wir we
wirklich really
Wirtschaft economy
wissen know
Wissenschaft science
Wissenschaftler scientist
Witze machen joke
wo where
wo auch immer wherever
Woche week
Wochenende weekend
Wörterbuch dictionary
Wofür? What for?
Wohin? Where to?
Wohlfahrtsorganization charity
wohnen live; stay
Wohnmobil motorhome
Wohnung flat; apartment (AE)
Wohnzimmer living room
Wolf, Wölfe wolf, wolves
Wolke cloud
Wolkenkratzer skyscraper
wolkig cloudy
wollen want
Wort word
Wortnetz word web
Wozu? What for?
wünschen wish
würde would
Würfel dice
Wüste desert
wütend mad
wütend sein be furious
Wunder wonder
wunderbar wonderful
Wurzel root

Z

Zähne putzen brush one's teeth
Zahl number
Zauberei magic
Zaun fence
zehn ten
Zeichen sign
Zeichentrickfilm cartoon
zeichnen draw
zeigen show
Zeile line
Zeit time
die ganze Zeit all the time
Zeit in Anspruch nehmen take up time
Zeitmaschine time machine
Zeitschrift magazine
Zeitung newspaper
Zeitungsanzeige newspaper advert
Zelle cell
Zelt tent
zelten camp
zelten gehen go camping
Zeltlager camp
Zeltplatz camping site
Zentimeter centimetre
Zentralverriegelung central locking system
Zentrum center (AE)
zerbrechen break
zerbrochen broken
zerstören destroy
Zerstörung devastation
Zeugnis report card (AE)
ziehen pull
ziemlich quite
Zigarette cigarette
Zimmer room
Zirkus circus
Zoo zoo
Zoohandlung pet shop
zu to; too
zu dem Ergebnis kommen find that
zu Hause at home
(zu-)hören listen (to)
(zu-)künftig future
zündend catchy
zuerst at first
Zug train
Zuhause home
Zukunft future
zum Frühstück for breakfast
zuordnen match
zur Welt bringen give birth
zurück back
zurückkehren return
zurücklassen leave
zusammen together
(zusammen-)brechen break (down)
zusammenstoßen run into
zuschlagen strike
zuständig responsible
zustellen deliver
zuversichtlich confident
zwanzig twenty
zwei two
zweimal twice
zweite, zweiter, zweites second
Zwiebel onion
zwischen between
zwölf twelve

Check the answers

Exam practice 1

1 Global understanding
1. When Ellen was at school she was able to buy/bought a boat.
2. Ellen wrote about 2,500 letters.
3. When Ellen went to Brest in France, she only had a one-way ticket.
4. Kingfisher offered Ellen 2 million pounds to sponsor her in the Vendée Globe.
5. Ellen trained to sleep 15 minutes at a time.
6. Ellen loves racing through the water.

2 Questions on Ellen

a) 1. She saved her money and put it into her "yacht box".
2. Because she was looking for sponsors.
3. Because she wanted to save money.
4. Because she wanted to learn to sleep for 15 minutes at a time.
5. After her success in a transatlantic race she found a sponsor for the Vendée Globe.

b) Individuelle Antworten

3 An open-ended story
Individuelle Texte

4 The Kingfisher story
1. began
2. was, started
3. had been designed, wanted to make
4. was launched, fell, climbed, showered, 've waited, won't forget

5 Ellen's blog

Kate Hillborne: Hast du oft Langeweile?

Ellen: Ich muss sagen, dass es in den letzten zwei Monaten nicht eine Sekunde gegeben hat, in der ich mich gelangweilt habe. Man verbringt die ganze Zeit damit, das Wetter zu beobachten und dafür zu sorgen, dass das Boot so schnell segelt, wie es nur geht. Das ist ganz schön viel Arbeit.

Andrew John: Kannst du wirklich schlafen, ohne dir darüber Gedanken zu machen, was draußen passiert?

Ellen: Nein, eigentlich nicht. Wenn du schläfst, ist es eine Art von Halbschlaf. Ich habe ein Computerprogramm, das genau überwacht, was mit dem Boot passiert. Normalerweise wache ich gleich auf, wenn sich der Wind verändert.

Raymond Zaloof: Du bist seit dem 9. November von zu Hause fort. Wenn es etwas gäbe, was du jetzt haben könntest, was wäre das?

Ellen: Etwas, das ich mir sehr wünsche, wäre, dass alle Wettbewerbsteilnehmer sicher zurückkommen.

6 Yacht races
1. exciting 2. bored 3. scary 4. tiring 5. interested

7 Difficult days
1. feel, does not help
2. is going, 'm putting
3. are coming, 're getting
4. hurts, 'm losing
5. look, is changing
6. don't work/aren't working, is getting

8 Opposites
1. spend 2. sell 3. smallest 4. right 5. uncle 6. hate

9 Listen and say

[ɑː] dark, glasses
[æ] back, understand
[ɒ] yacht
[ɔː] water
[eɪ] came, female

10 Just in time
Individuelle Texte

11 At the airport

a) 1 – 4 – 6 – 5 – 3 – 2

b) arrival hall, baggage reclaim, boarding card, check-in desk, departure lounge, security check, passport control

Exam practice 2

1 Global understanding
1. true 2. false 3. false 4. true 5. false

2 Questions about Whoopi
1. She started taking drugs.
2. She had some acting jobs and worked as a bricklayer and a funeral parlor make-up artist.
3. Her mother told her that nobody would respect a name like that.
4. She took it on tour to Europe and won the Grammy.
5. He gave her the main part in The Color Purple which won her an Oscar nomination.
6. She was the chaotic fortune teller in the film Ghost.
7. She works in campaigns to stop AIDS and drug addiction and she helps the homeless.

3 Sister Act
Filmkritik: Sister Act
Endlich ein Film, in dem Whoopi Goldberg ihr wahres komödiantisches Talent zeigen

kann. Whoopi spielt eine fantastische Dolores Van Cartier, eine Sängerin im Casino ihres Freundes. Aber ihr Freund ist ein Gangster und eines Tages sieht sie, wie er seinen Fahrer umbringt. Von da an ist Dolores Leben in Gefahr. Sie läuft zur Polizei und um sie zu schützen, stecken sie sie in ein Kloster. Zuerst ist D. nicht sehr glücklich darüber, im Kloster zu leben, aber sie beginnt die Schwestern mit ihren modernen Ideen zu beeinflussen. Sie ist für den Chor verantwortlich und bringt den Schwestern alles über Jazz bei. Die Mutter Oberin hält es nicht für eine gute Idee D. im Kloster zu haben, aber die Schwestern fangen an, D. sehr zu mögen. Sie bringt Abenteuer und Abwechslung in ihr langweiliges Leben. Die komischen Schauspieler und die verrückten Situationen werden Sie zum Lachen bringen. Der Gesang ist so gut, dass Sie mitsingen werden wollen. Jeder wird diesen Film genießen, besonders die Fans von Whoopi Goldberg.

4 Open-ended story
Individuelle Texte

5 Reported speech
1. She said she had really liked W.G.'s last film because she had played a strong character.
2. She explained that W. had had a hard life as a black American child.
3. She said that W. had worked hard and had been very successful in Hollywood.
4. Sue told Kyle that she thought that W. was a great actress and that she loved her films.
5. Sue also said that W. would always be a special woman for her.
6. Sue explained that W. had given young black American girls like her hope for the future.
7. Sue also said that she didn't want to be a film star, but that she wanted a good career for herself.
8. She added that when she looked at W., she knew that if she worked hard she would have a good career, too.

6 Opposites
1. cry 2. appear 3. dirty 4. more 5. lose 6. die 7. cheap 8. dry 9. destroy 10. switch off 11. friend 12. warmer

7 Listen and say: [dʒ] **and** [tʃ]
[dʒ]: jungle, jeans, geography, dangerous, garage
[tʃ]: children, adventure, teacher, chance, charity

8 The house of Ruth
is, started, supports, has helped, offers, had become, were able, showed, gave

9 Johnny Depp in his own words
b) 1 **a**, 2 **b**, 3 **b**, 4 **a**
c) 1. Johnny's parents moved from Kentucky to Florida when he was very young.
2. He wasn't the most popular kid in school.
3. At 12 his mom bought him an electric guitar.
4. At 16 he dropped out of high school.
5. He wanted to be a musician.
6. In Los Angeles he was introduced to Nicolas Cage.
7. His latest movies are Chocolat, Charlie and the Chocolate Factory and the Pirates of the Caribean series.

Exam practice 3

1 Questions on Greenpeace
1. Greenpeace's enemies are governments and big companies because Greenpeace has fought and won many battles to protect the environment and it has strong and widespread international connections.
2. Because they were scared that the bomb might cause an earthquake and because there are lots of birds, otters and other animals that live on the island.
3. In 1971 they got a lot of public interest and in 1972 another nuclear bomb testing on the island was stopped.
4. It is fighting against loggers who are cutting down trees illegally.
5. Because 50% of the world's animals which live on land need the Amazon rain forest to survive.
6. Because in another 30 years it may be too late to save our planet.

2 Vocabulary
1. banners 2. non-governmental 3. island 4. illegally 5. protect 6. huge 7. test 8. survive

3 Three Greenpeace campaigns
Individuelle Texte

4 Additional work
Individuelle Antworten

5 Save the planet
Spare Wasser!
– Lasse keinen Wasserhahn laufen, wenn du kein Wasser brauchst.
– Dusche statt zu baden.
– Schalte Geschirrspüler oder Waschmaschine erst ein, wenn sie voll sind.

Spare Energie!
– Lasse die Lichter im Haus nicht an, wenn du sie nicht brauchst.
– Verwende Energiesparlampen. Sie mögen teurer sein, aber sie halten acht Mal länger als normale, verbrauchen ein Viertel der Energie und sind genauso hell.

- Wenn du die Heizung zuhause um einen Grad Celsius zurückstellst, wirst du nicht nur Energie sondern auch Geld sparen.
- Stelle kein heißes Essen in den Kühlschrank und lasse die Tür nicht längere Zeit offen stehen.

Hilf der Erde!
- Pflanze Bäume in deinem Garten oder in der Schule. Sie verbrauchen Kohlendioxid und helfen die Luft zu reinigen.
- Fahre nicht mit dem Auto, wenn du nicht musst. Zu Fuß gehen oder Fahrrad fahren ist sowieso besser für dich.
- Warum gründest du nicht deine eigene Umweltorganisation in der Schule mit einigen Freunden und Lehrern?

6 Solar Power

a) Musterbrief:

Absender

3rd March 20..

Clean Power Ltd.
11 Rait Street
London
UK

Dear Sir or Madam,

I saw your ad and I am very interested in getting solar power in my home. Could you please tell me what benefits I'll get from using solar power? Is it expensive? How much do I have to pay for delivery and installation?

I would also like to know if it works in winter, too. Could you please send me some brochures of your products?

Thank you in advance for helping me.

Yours sincerely

b) Individuelle Texte

7 Passive
1. Global warming is caused by greenhouse gases.
2. Many protests to save the environment have been planned by Greenpeace.
3. In the future, diseases will be spread by global warming.
4. Forests all over the world are being destroyed by acid rain.
5. Nuclear bomb testing on Amchitka was stopped by Greenpeace.

8 Reported speech
1. He said that Greenpeace had started with protests against nuclear bomb testing.
2. He explained that for almost 40 years Greenpeace had fought many battles to protect the environment.
3. He added that they were a non-violent organisation. They wanted to make our planet a better place to live on.
4. He told me that in the future they would try to do more for the rain forests.
5. Finally he said that Greenpeace would never give up its fight to save our planet because in 30 years it might be too late.

9 If-clauses

If you turn down the heating, you will save energy. If they had planted more trees, the air would have been cleaner. If you rode your bike more often, you would be fitter. If more people had protested, they wouldn't have built the new road. If you choose solar power power, you will get clean power.

10 Listen and say: 'ea'

[iː] disease, mean, increase, heat
[e] bread, already, weather, spread
[ɜː] rehearsal, earth, earn, search
[ɪə] idea, appear, hear, realise

Questionnaire

Unit 2

Auswertung des Fragebogens

1. a **2** b **1** c **0**
2. a **1** b **2** c **0**
3. a **0** b **1** c **2**
4. a **1** b **0** c **2**
5. a **1** b **0** c **2**
6. a **1** b **0** c **2**

0-4 points: You feel good where you are. If you moved to another country, you would probably feel lost. You need your home, your family and your friends.
5-8 points: You could be happy in another country, but you prefer your home. You enjoy going on holidays to different countries, but you probably wouldn't like to live there for a long time.
9-12 points: You are interested in new people and places, and you would probably feel at home quickly in another country. You make new friends easily, so you wouldn't feel lost.

Unit 4

Auswertung des Fragebogens

1 **a**, 2 **b**, 3 **a**, 4 **a**, 5 **c**, 6 **b**, 7 **c**, 8 **b**, 9 **a**, 10 **b**, 11 **b**, 12 **c**

How many of your answers were right?
0-4: Not bad. If you want to find out more about this topic you can check the internet.
5-8: Well done! You know a lot about teenagers' rights in Britain.
9-12: That was fantastic! You know almost everything about British teenagers' rights.

Unit 6

Auswertung des Fragebogens

1 **d**, 2 **e**, 3 **f**, 4 **a**, 5 **c**, 6 **b**

Bildquellen

Umschlag 1 iStockphoto (Aldo Murillo), Calgary, Alberta; Umschlag 2 Mauritius (Photo Researchers), Mittenwald; 4.1 Cinetext, Frankfurt; 4.2 Getty Images (UK/ALLSPORT), München; 4.3 Getty Images (SASCHA BAUMANN/AFP), München; 5.1 CSI, New Delhi; 5.2 Fotosearch RF, Waukesha, WI; 6.1 shutterstock (Nola Rin), New York, NY; 6.2 Corel Corporation, Unterschleissheim; 6.3 shutterstock (Joe Gough), New York, NY; 7.1 Corbis (Bettmann), Düsseldorf; 7.2 Picture-Alliance (akg-images), Frankfurt; 8.1 Getty Images (SASCHA BAUMANN/AFP), München; 8.2 Cinetext, Frankfurt; 9.1 Corbis (Stephen Hird/Reute), Düsseldorf; 9.2 Getty Images (ROBERT SULLIVAN), München; 14.1 Getty Images (UK/ALLSPORT), München; 15.1 Action Press (REX FEATURES LTD), Hamburg; 22.1 Picture-Alliance (epa), Frankfurt; 25.1 MEV, Augsburg; 26.1 CSI, New Delhi; 27.1 Corbis (Catherine Karnow), Düsseldorf; 28.1 CSI, New Delhi; 30.1 terre des hommes Deutschland e.V., Osnabrück; 32.1 Picture-Alliance, Frankfurt; 32.2 Corbis, Düsseldorf; 33.1 Corbis (David Stoecklein), Düsseldorf; 33.2 Corbis (Joe McDonald), Düsseldorf; 34.1 The Independent 22/5/95, Illustration: Peter Schrank; 34.2 Corbis (Rick Friedman), Düsseldorf; 35.1 Fotosearch RF, Waukesha, WI; 35.2 Corbis (Lewis Wickes Hine), Düsseldorf; 37.1 Getty Images PhotoDisc, Hamburg; 40.1 Picture-Alliance (Jerzy Dabrowski), Frankfurt; 41.1 ullstein bild (KPA Archival Collection), Berlin; 43.1 laif (UPI Photo/Jim Ruymen), Köln; 44.1 iStockphoto (RF), Calgary, Alberta; 44.2 shutterstock (Nola Rin), New York, NY; 45.1 shutterstock (Joe Gough), New York, NY; 45.2 Corbis (Michael St. Maur Sheil), Düsseldorf; 48.1 Avenue Images GmbH (Corbis RF), Hamburg; 50.1 Helga Lade (P. Thompson), Frankfurt; 50.2 Helga Lade (P. Thompson), Frankfurt; 51.1 Corel Corporation, Unterschleissheim; 55.1 MEV, Augsburg; 58.1 ullstein bild (ddp), Berlin; 59.1 MEV, Augsburg; 60.1 Getty Images PhotoDisc, Hamburg; 62.1 Corbis (Bettmann), Düsseldorf; 63.1 Picture-Alliance (akg-images), Frankfurt; 66.1 Corbis (Bettmann), Düsseldorf; 68.1 shutterstock (Galina Barskaya), New York, NY; 68.2 shutterstock (Aga & Miko (arsat)), New York, NY; 68.3 Getty Images (Digital Vision), München; 68.4 Corbis (Ted Levine/zefa), Düsseldorf; 69.1 iStockphoto (Izabela Habur), Calgary, Alberta; 69.2 Getty Images, München; 69.3 Keystone (Mario Di Rosa), Hamburg; 69.4 iStockphoto (ron sumners), Calgary, Alberta; 74.1 MEV, Augsburg; 75.1 Mauritius (Rosenfeld), Mittenwald; 77.1 Corbis (Emely/zefa), Düsseldorf

Textquellen

S. 47: *Peace on Earth*, Text: Hewson, Paul David/Evans, Dave/Mullen, Larry/Clayton, Adam, © Polygram International Music Publ., Universal Music Publ. GmbH, Berlin; S. 52: *The Rape of the World*, Text: Chapman, Tracy, © SBK APRIL MUSIC INC./PURPLE RABBIT MUSIC, EMI Songs Musikverlag GmbH, Hamburg; S. 72/73: *Sierra Wave* from Good Rockin' Tonight, A Collection of Short Stories by William Hauptman, © 1988 by William Hauptman. Used by permission of Bantam Books, a division of Random House, Inc.; S. 74: *The man who invented football*, reprinted from GREAT SNAKES by Kit Wright (Viking, 1994), © Kit Wright 1994; *For Word*, reprinted from FUNKY CHICKENS by Benjamin Zephaniah (Viking, 1996), © Benjamin Zephaniah 1996; S. 75: *The Want-Want Twins*, reprinted from THREE HAS GONE by Jackie Kay (Blackie, 1994), © Jackie Kay 1994